全人教育英语专业本科教材系列

总顾问　刘润清

总主编　文　旭

文体学

编著　宋成方

参编　张冬冰

中国人民大学出版社

·北京·

图书在版编目（CIP）数据

文体学：英文 / 宋成方编著. --北京：中国人民大学出版社，2025. 4. --（全人教育英语专业本科教材系列）. -- ISBN 978-7-300-33594-0

Ⅰ. H052

中国国家版本馆 CIP 数据核字第 2025TQ3903 号

全人教育英语专业本科教材系列

总顾问　刘润清

总主编　文　旭

文体学

编　著　宋成方

参　编　张冬冰

Wentixue

出版发行	中国人民大学出版社		
社　　址	北京中关村大街 31 号	**邮政编码**	100080
电　　话	010–62511242（总编室）		010–62511770（质管部）
	010–82501766（邮购部）		010–62514148（门市部）
	010–62511173（发行公司）		010–62515275（盗版举报）
网　　址	http:// www. crup. com. cn		
经　　销	新华书店		
印　　刷	北京密兴印刷有限公司		
开　　本	889 mm × 1194 mm　1/16	**版　　次**	2025 年 4 月第 1 版
印　　张	13.25	**印　　次**	2025 年 4 月第 1 次印刷
字　　数	326 000	**定　　价**	58.00 元

序

熟悉我本人简历和科研成果的师生和亲友，都会注意到我为国内学者写了 **150** 多份序言。我曾坦率地做过解释，任何一位高校的中青年教师在完成繁重教学任务的同时，能（编）写出一部专著或教材，很不容易，值得鼓励。因此我很少将邀请我写序的中青年作者拒之门外。

除上述原因外，我接受写序更主要的是为了自己，那就是作者给我提供了一个学习机会，让我可以掌握国内外一些学科或专业的最新进展，引导我跟上时代的步伐。毕竟我这个年龄去学校的图书馆或外国语学院的阅览室很不方便；在家使用电脑在网络上查找资料也总会碰到这样或那样的操作困难。我得经常求助于年轻教师和研究生来家帮助我解决这样或那样的问题。这次，对外经济贸易大学的宋成方教授邀请我为《文体学》(*Stylistics*）这部教材写序，通读电子版后，我对国内外文体学教学和科研有了不少新的认识，再次证实了我的上述观点。因此，我在这里对宋成方教授出版新著既表示祝贺，也表示感谢。

那么，本教材中哪些方面使我如此激动呢？早在 **1981** 年我从澳大利悉尼大学语言学系进修回国后，便面临一个现实问题。我在悉尼大学进修的是语言学，而北大英语系的传统是文学。为了解决这个矛盾，我当时便想到文体学，这是一门英语专业的文学方向和语言学方向的本科生都能接受的课程。不过，我当时的讲稿比较简单，只是将系统功能语言学理论指导下的“话语分析”和“篇章语言学”这两门课程的部分内容，拼拼凑凑，成为最初的文体学讲稿。如今看了宋成方教授的这本教材，才感到他的教材又全面又深入。尽管他在教材中也以系统功能语言学理论为主线，但他添补了20世纪80年代后该理论的最新发展和内容。我这里特别要提到的是本教材贯穿了韩礼德的“适用语言学”(appliable linguistics）的思想。搞学术研究不是拉一派、打一派，而是按照韩礼德的教导，探讨各个理论的“适用”之处，并将其融入自己的讲稿或论著。宋成方教授在本书中便介绍了其他语言学理论适用于文体分析的内容，如乔姆斯基的转换生成语法、莱考夫的认知语言学，以及传统的结构主义语言学。我还注意到，宋成方教授也吸收了一些国内外语言学最新研究的动向，将其应用于研究和分析文体的某些方面，如认知隐喻学和多模态学。这说明宋成方教授能以自己的实际行动在教学科研中贯彻韩礼德的学术思想，这也说明宋的许多观点来自对各种语言学理论的理性融合。

宋成方教授为何能取得上述丰硕成果？这便要谈谈他与众不同、得天独厚、令人无比羡慕的成长过程。在中国海洋大学攻读硕士研究生阶段，宋的导师便是响当当的现为同济大学博士生导师的张德禄教授。他是较早在悉尼大学进修语言学的学者之一。这就是说，张德禄教授为宋打好了系统功能语言学和文体学的基础。2004 年宋考入北京大学外国语学院英语系攻读博士学位。其导师姜望琪教授是我国改革开放后第一位在英国拿到硕士学位的进修教师，并且是北大英语系第一位为研究生开设语言学课程的老师。但更主要的是宋入学后，2007 年北京大学和悉尼大学达成了联合培养博士生的合作协议，经悉尼大学审核通过后，宋成为北大—悉尼大学联合培养的第一个博士生［Ph.D（cotutelle）］，开始在姜望琪和马丁（J.R. Martin）二位教授的共同指导下学习并且写作博士论文，最后在两个学校分别获得各自颁发的博士学位。在此期间，除马丁外，宋还结识了麦蒂森（Christian M.I.M. Matthiessen）、范·鲁文（Theo van Leeuwen）等多位教授。回国后，2010 至 2012 年，宋在清华大学“外国语言文学博士后科研流动站”工作，与刘世生教授合作，从事评价理论和文体学领域的研究工作。众所周知，刘世生是我在北大培养的博士生，主攻文体学。申丹教授筹建“中国修辞学会文体学研究会”（现为中国逻辑学会文体学专业委员会）时，我推荐刘为秘书长。刘后来又接替申丹教授为第二任会长。从本教材的篇章中可以看到宋成方教授多次引用了申丹教授和刘世生教授的论著，特别是宋和刘世生的合著。今天看来，宋成方教授在文体学教学科研上的成就，是他对国内外各位导师的最有价值、最有意义、最有感情的汇报，特别是对已故刘世生教授的汇报。

最后，我觉得有必要提一下，宋成方教授不仅在教学科研上取得重大成就，作为共产党员，他还积极从事教学管理工作，担任对外经济贸易大学英语学院的副院长。同时，他又能接受党和政府的安排，于 2023 年 8 月以中组部第十一批援疆干部身份赴石河子大学外国语学院挂职副院长。

通过本书的出版，愿我国高校出现更多的宋成方教授！

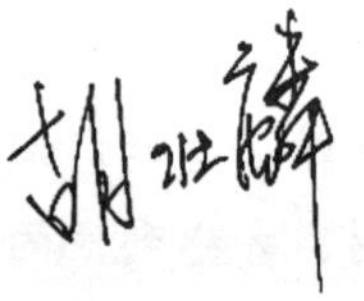

北京大学外国语学院

2024 年 8 月 20 日

前 言

英语单词stylistic就构词而言，既是名词style的形容词形式，也是名词stylistics的形容词形式。对应地，英语 stylistic analysis 也有两个意思：the analysis of style 和 the analysis from a specific stylistic approach；用汉语表述，前者是文体分析，后者是文体学分析。虽然文体分析预设着文体学分析，文体学分析也必然是文体分析，但是两者侧重点不同。

本科生文体学教材编写有两种取向。一种是结果取向，偏重于介绍不同文体以及分析不同文体得出的结论，即不同文体的语言形式特征（和功能解读）；该取向教材，在某种程度上是文体分析教程。另一种是过程取向，主要介绍文体学理论和文体学分析方法，展示文体学分析过程；该取向教材是文体学分析教程。

第一种取向的教材系统介绍不同文体的形式特征，有利于学生掌握不同文体，能够为学生完成的语言产出提供是否得体的检验清单。第二种取向的教材目的在于教会学生如何从某个理论视角进行文体学分析，更有助于提升学生的分析能力和鉴赏能力；能够像解剖课一样展示高质量文本的各种特征，能够像从幕后视角揭秘魔术一样揭去经典文本的神秘面纱，从而更好地服务学生语言产出能力的培养。

目前呈现给大家的这本书坚持“授之以渔”的原则，采用过程取向，力求为国内高校本科文体学教学提供一本实践性强、趣味性浓，同时又与时俱进的文体学教材。

实践性强有两层含义。第一，本教材“十年磨一剑”“点滴渗入”的编写原则经过了十余轮的教学实践检验，主要内容来源于十余载的教学积累。基于本教材的文体学教学效果优秀，学生评价说：这是一门每位学习英语的学生都应该必修的课程。第二，文体学本质上是一门应用型学科，以文体分析实践为导向。本书除第一章之外的每个章节都提供了大量文体学分析样本。多轮教学实践表明，充足的文体学分析示例让学生养成了探究语言表达释解意义机制的习惯。

趣味性也有两个方面的意思。趣味性、知识性和思想性一般被认为是教学的三种境界。在本书中，趣味性首先来自选择分析有趣的文本，而有趣既指单纯的好笑和好玩，也指精神层面的愉悦：谐趣横生的文字游戏、令人忍俊不禁的幽默、广为传唱的流行歌曲、蕴藉隽永的诗歌、引人入胜的小说、赏心悦目的散文都被包含在教材之中。其次，本书注重发掘妙趣横生文本自身的知识性和思想性，或者说本书用一种有趣的方式讲授知识、发掘思想。比如，在中外多种语境下出现的披萨切多少块的幽默梗（见第4章第4小节），实际上能够喻设不同语言对外部世界的不同释解，能够解释很多跨语言沟通过程中产生的误解。

与时俱进指本教材以党的二十大精神为指导，积极探索如何融入课程思政元素，做到育人和育才相结合。首先，本教材结合教学实践和语言学的发展进行理论创新和教材编写创新：一、为方便学生理解文体学的框架，区分文体学概念（stylistics concepts）和文体学分析时使用的概念（stylistic concepts），前者指定义文体学的理论概念，后者指文体学分析过程中从语言学等学科中借用的概念；二、结合多模态研究的成果，把语音和书写看作意义生成的资源，给予它们与语言的语篇层和词汇语法层同等的地位，分章节单独论述；三、将文体学最新发展，如语料库文体学、认知文体学、多模态文体学，融入教材之中，并理清它们在文体学分析中的关系。

其次，本教材对分析文本的选择以是否符合社会主义核心价值观为准绳。一般而言，人文学科"育人"有两个渠道：让学生阅读经典文学作品和感悟经典作品的经典解读。本教材选择的经典文本虽然来自不同的文化，但是毫无例外都积极向上；其中的中文文本［如毛泽东主席的《七绝·为女民兵题照》（见第3章）、王震将军的一首无题诗（见第6章）］更是彰显了革命豪情，传承了红色基因。基于语言分析的解读能够让学生在欣赏文字之美的同时得到精神上的熏陶。

最后，比较是文体学分析的核心，前景化就是与背景相比较而来的概念，本教材有意识地设置了各种比较。比较本身，实际上，在人类的认知过程中扮演着重要角色，"以史为鉴""见贤思齐""比物假事"都强调了比较的意义和价值。单就"新"而言，本教材比较了新发展的语言学理论与经典语言学理论（见第2章），比较了同一文本用新发展的理论和经典理论进行分析时的不同［如从描写语法和功能语法两个视角对 *The Inheritors* 的分析（见第5章第4节）］，还对同一文本用同一理论新的发展进行了重新分析（如5章第4节对 *The Inheritors* 用功能语言学最新发展的分析）。除此之外，本教材的比较还包括英汉两种语言之间的比较［如对英汉两种语言对一天的划分的比较（见第4章第4节）］、同一诗歌文本不同韵律选择的比较（见第3章第4节）、同一故事不同视角呈现的比较（见第6章练习3）、同一文本不同模态的比较（见第6章练习题6）、中文文本与英语译文之间的比较以及不同译文之间的比较［如《七绝·为女民兵题照》与三个不同英文译文之间的比较（见第3章）］、同一文本不同部分在同一理论视角下的比较（见第5章练习题6）。这些贯彻全书的比较能有效培养学生的辩证思维、系统思维和批判思维能力。

本教材共有7章，理想的进度是前2章每章用2个课时完成；后面5章每章用6个课时完成，其中4个课时可用来讲解，2个课时可用来做学生展示和教师点评。全书可满足16~18周的教学需求。为方便使用，本教材的教师用书每个章节都配有中文提要、练习题及参考答案。

正如前文所述，本教材"十年磨一剑"，自2012年至今，已经以自编讲义形式使用了十多年。本教材能够正式出版，我首先感谢使用过本教材的学生。他们或积极肯定本教材的内容，激励我做得更好；或毫不留情地指出某些方面的不足，促使我积极改进。在我把自编讲义改写成书的过程中，几位同事和学生给我提供了各种帮助。对外经济贸易大学的张冬冰副教授和李靓教授，两位在语言学和文学领域颇有建树、在教学方面成绩斐然的老师，逐章通读了全书，提出了非常好的完善意见。

对外经济贸易大学的李若姗博士在本科生阶段使用过本教材的讲义；她从清华大学获得博士学位入职贸大后，在文体学课上也使用过本教材的最初版本，并提供了部分课后练习题的答案。在伦敦大学学院深造的王佳葭在本科生阶段也使用过本教材的讲义，她通读了本书书稿，提出了多处修改意见，并且帮助我完成了很多编辑工作。此外，我还要感谢教育部“新文科背景下商务外语专业建设探索与实践”（项目号：2021050011）项目的支持，以及对外经济贸易大学教务处给予的立项支持，感谢中国人民大学出版社编辑的耐心和细心工作。最后，我还要感谢石河子大学，在石河子大学的援疆工作给我提供了开阔视野的机会，使我有幸接触到更多有意义和价值的文本，从而丰富了本教材的内涵。

虽然时间和精力投入很多，但是由于自己能力有限，教材中难免出现疏漏，恳请教材使用者多多批评指正。

宋成方

2025 年 4 月 16 日

CONTENTS 目　录

List of Tables

List of Figures

Chapter 1

Introduction

1.1 What stylistics is

In stylistics literature, two main views about stylistics exist. One group of stylisticians perceive stylistics as a sub-discipline of linguistics, focusing on the systematic analysis of various language styles. On the other hand, another group views stylistics as an interdisciplinary field with its unique standing, primarily informed by insights from linguistics and literary studies, potentially borrowing ideas from disciplines such as visual arts and cognitive science. Regardless of the divergent perspectives on the disciplinary categorization of stylistics, both viewpoints align on three critical points.

Firstly, both perspectives place texts at the core of stylistics. The sub-disciplinary view emphasizes the formal aspects of a text, influenced by factors such as genre, context, historical period, and authorship. On the other hand, the interdisciplinary view puts greater emphasis on literary works, as it cites literary studies as one of its contributory disciplines.

Secondly, both perspectives underscore the crucial role of linguistics in stylistic analysis. In the sub-disciplinary perspective, style typically refers to the formal features of a text at various language levels (e.g. sounds, words, grammar, textual structure), and linguistics enters the picture by providing analytical tools and insight into the functional significance of these formal features for the interpretation of the text. In the interdisciplinary perspective, linguistic description is considered foundational to stylistic analysis, with the junction of linguistic description and literary interpretation constituting the sphere of stylistics.

Thirdly, stylistics' evolution from a sub-discipline to an independent interdiscipline demonstrates its eclecticism. As a sub-discipline, stylistics effectively utilizes concepts from other linguistic sub-disciplines like phonology, lexicology, syntax, semantics, and pragmatics in its analyses. As an interdiscipline, stylistics embraces new language study approaches, emerging literary theories, and theories from other disciplines, provided they illuminate the analysis of texts. Disciplines that have integrated into stylistic analyses of literature include, but are not limited to, visual arts, philosophy, cultural theory, sociology, history, and psychology. The eclecticism has been praised as one of stylistics' advantages due to its potential for inspiration.

The interdisciplinary definition encapsulates the latest conceptions of stylistics from practitioners in the field, yet it does not encompass all stylistic efforts or practices. Highlighting literary studies as one of its foundational disciplines relates to the fact that most stylistic focus has been dedicated to literary texts to date. Nevertheless, stylisticians are now involved with a far broader spectrum of discourses, including non-fictional forms such as advertising, academic writing, news reports, as well as non-printed forms such as TV and pictorial advertising, film, multimodal publications, and more.

A much more inclusive and detailed definition of stylistics compared to the two mentioned above has been proposed in Nørgaard, Montoro and Busse (2010: 1–2).

> Stylistics is the study of the ways in which meaning is created through language in literature as well as in other types of text. To this end, stylisticians use linguistic models, theories and frameworks as their analytical tools in order to describe and explain how and why a text works as it does, and how we come from the words on the page to its meaning. The analysis typically focuses qualitatively or quantitatively on the phonological, lexical, grammatical, semantic, pragmatic or discoursal features of texts, on the cognitive aspects involved in the processing of those features by the reader as well as on various combinations of these. While some stylistic approaches primarily show an interest in the producer of the text, investigating, for instance, the style of a particular author, other stylisticians focus more on the text itself (broadly understood to encompass all types of discourse), and still others devote their attention to the reader and the role readers play in meaning construction. New developments in stylistics emphasize that the production of meaning needs to be accounted for as a double exercise encompassing as much text-informed inferences as the mental processes that allow text comprehension.

1.2 What stylistics does

The last definition introduced above makes it clear that stylistics aims to explore how meaning is created in a text. But meaning is both ontogenetically and logogenetically complicated. Example 1.1 is a nursery rhyme.

Example 1.1

Simple Simon met a pieman

Going to the fair;
Says Simple Simon to the pieman,
"Let me taste your ware."

Says the pieman to Simple Simon,
"Show me first your penny."
Says Simple Simon to the pieman,
"Indeed I have not any."

Simple Simon went a fishing
For to catch a whale:
All the water he had got
Was in his mother's pail.

From an ontogenetic perspective, Hasan (1989: 26–28) differentiates between appreciation and appraisal in order to illustrate the meanings created in a text and the purpose of stylistics. According to her, appreciation has varying degrees and can range from the evident delight and engagement of a nine-month-old listening to *Simple Simon met a pieman*, to the added referential meanings derived from words and clause structures when that child becomes four or five years old. As the reader transitions from childhood through adolescence and then adulthood, their appreciation of the rhyme evolves towards a deeper "engagement" with the text, that is, appraisal. Furthermore, appreciation is a personal experience. For a young child, appreciation revolves around simply "receiving with pleasure" without the need to justify or explicitly demonstrate the basis for that enjoyment or preference (i.e., the central task of appraisal). Hasan (1989: 26–28) contends that this dynamic shifts significantly as the child progresses through the educational system, and stylistics becomes necessary when that change occurs.

> There comes a stage when the child must change her perspective. She may be called upon to explicitly state her "response" to a poem, she may be asked to evaluate it in comparison with some other piece of work; or the exercise might demand a comparison of themes, or styles, and so on. At this stage then, it is no longer simply a question of receiving with pleasure, of understanding and enjoying the meanings of the text; it is more a question of being able to state clearly the nature of one's response, and to examine explicitly the bases for it. At this stage, then, appreciation must give way to appraisal; the private must be made public; the internalised must be overtly externalisable—it should be possible to talk coherently about the bases of one's preference and evaluation.

Logogenetically speaking, stylistics works to relate linguistic facts (linguistic description) to meaning (interpretation) in as explicit a way as possible. Example 1.2 is a line from a classic drama.

Example 1.2

Come, we burn daylight, ho! (William Shakespeare, *Romeo and Juliet*, I, iv, 43)

As far as linguistic description is concerned, a normal paradigm for the verb *burn* should be constructed in comparison with the metaphorical construction:

Normal paradigm	**Abnormal paradigm**
We burn paper	We burn daylight
We burn wood	
We burn coal	
We burn oil	
We burn fuel	
Etc.	

The comparison leads us to an interpretation of the line. The object of *burn* must be a tangible, burnable material or a generic term for such substances. To burn something implies its destruction or consumption. A potential interpretation of this unique construction could be "we are using up daylight". It remains a metaphor, albeit a fairly common one in English; we cannot literally consume daylight. However, daylight serves as a medium we utilize for numerous activities, and if we do not use it properly then we may run out of time to do what needs to be done. Therefore, the interpretation could be that we can waste time (Short, 2013: 4–8).

Stylistics actually means more than relating interpretation to linguistic description. Stylisticians suggest that linguistic description and its relationship with interpretation should also be discussed as explicitly, as systematically, and in as detailed a way as possible (Short, 2013: 5). The requirements of explicitness, systematicality, and detailedness are summarized as three basic principles, mnemonically as three "Rs" in Simpson (2014: 4).

- ❑ stylistic analysis should be rigorous
- ❑ stylistic analysis should be retrievable
- ❑ stylistic analysis should be replicable

The three "Rs" are explained as follows (Simpson, 2014: 4):

To argue that the stylistic method be *rigorous* means that it should be based on an explicit framework of analysis. Stylistic analysis is not the end-product of a disorganised sequence of *ad hoc* and impressionistic comments, but is instead underpinned by structure models of language and discourse that explain how we process and understand various patterns in language.

To argue that stylistic method be *retrievable* means that the analysis is organised through explicit terms and criteria, the meanings of which are agreed upon by other stylisticians. Although precise definitions for some aspects of language have proved difficult to pin down exactly, there is a consensus about what most terms in stylistics mean [...]. That consensus enables other stylisticians to follow the pathway adopted in an analysis, to test the categories used and to see how the analysis reached its conclusions; to retrieve, in other words, the stylistic method.

To say that a stylistic analysis seeks to be *replicable* does not mean that we should all try to copy each other's work. It simply means that the methods should be sufficiently transparent so as to allow other stylisticians to verify them, either by testing them on the same text or by applying them beyond that text. The conclusions reached are principled if the pathway followed by the analysis is accessible and replicable. To this extent, it has become an important axiom of stylistics that it seeks to distance itself from work that proceeds *solely* from untested or untestable intuition.

1.3 The purposes of teaching stylistics

Stylistics has been taught both as part of English courses for its pedagogical value and as an independent course. In both contexts, there are three tiers of purpose as categorized in Burke (2010):

The teaching of stylistics in the modern day university classroom is a useful and worthy endeavour. Knowledge gained in such courses assists our undergraduate and graduate students in understanding how language, grammar and rhetoric function in texts. The knowledge they acquire leads them first to comprehend the basic grammatical and rhetorical concepts. This is followed by a second level of "practical" knowledge, whereby students are able to analyse texts with the tools they have acquired at the first stage. The third stage is when students go into a mode of synthesizing all they have learned, which, in turn, allows them to move on to the production stage. Such a process is valuable, for example, in the contemporary university creative writing classroom.

The three tiers of purpose, established and widely recognized, are embraced by many. Pedagogical stylisticians, in fact, suggest that the third tier does not represent the ultimate goal of stylistics education. They believe that it has the potential to accomplish more than merely developing language-related skills during the production stage, and argue that it can also build and improve students' transferable skills and cultivate their aesthetic taste:

It (stylistics, editors' note) engages my students with interesting and enjoyable texts and, at the same time, improves their analytical skills and increases their ability to come to terms with, and enjoy, other, more challenging, texts. It improves their ability to analyse language and understand its complexity

> and sophistication. It builds and improves a considerable range of *transferable skills* (editors' emphasis), ranging from practical and language-analytical skills to the interpersonal and more abstract thinking and argument skills so important in the modern world. And, to my mind most important of all, it can open up a world of careful and rational examination of issues and the reflective pleasures of detailed and careful aesthetic response. (Short, 2011: 47)

By indicating that stylistics engages students with a variety of text types, the quote accentuates an additional function of stylistics. From the perspective of sociology of education, the cultivation of ideal personalities and adoption of ideological stances are products of both an immersion in highly-valued texts and in-depth studies of esteemed literary works (Maton, 2014: 189–190). Given that the texts analyzed in stylistics classrooms are often masterpieces, stylistics holds a unique place in whole-person education, where ethics, moral values, and aesthetic tastes are emphasized.

The purposes of teaching stylistics discussed above can be illustrated in Figure 1.1. On the one hand, it familiarizes students with linguistic knowledge, helps students develop stylistic competence, that is, the ability to interpret texts based on the textual analysis within a linguistic framework, and finally empowers students with advanced literacies, namely skills and competencies that enable communication in increasingly diverse ways and promote the understanding and use of text for a variety of purposes. On the other hand, students are expected to apply the analytical skills in other contexts, and to develop more abstract abilities. The ultimate aim is to educate students to be a rational person with fine aesthetic taste and high moral values.

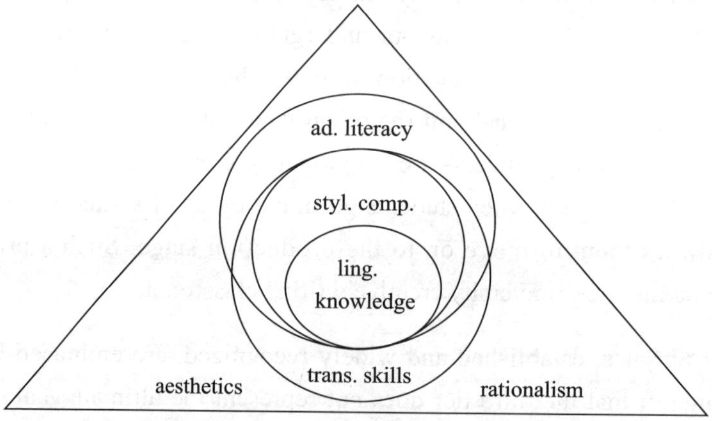

Figure 1.1 The purposes of teaching stylistics

1.4 The organization of this book

The main contents of this book are selected with careful consideration of both the main topics discussed in Sections 1.1–1.3 and the academic background of the target students. To start with, the two major informing disciplines are both rich in contents: linguistics has many branches and numerous approaches, and literary studies have contributed plenty of criticisms of literary works from various theoretical perspectives. However, although linguistic knowledge serves as the foundation of the architecture of stylistics, it is essential only in the sense that it supplies the tools. Much like one doesn't need to master all knives to be a proficient butcher, a student need not learn every branch and school of linguistics to excel as a stylistician. Some students in a stylistics class may lack prior linguistics coursework, and those who have attended might only possess a basic understanding of linguistic concepts. The linguistic notions introduced in this book are primarily from structural and functional linguistics, which are reader-friendly and most commonly employed in stylistic analysis. Nevertheless, other approaches are also presented for the sake of comparison.

Additionally, renowned literary works with their established interpretations serve as excellent teaching materials. However, most of our students will likely engage with more non-literary than literary texts throughout the remainder of their college years and into their future professions. Therefore, this book examines both practical texts and literary masterpieces. When we make use of literary works, we tend to favor poems and excerpts from well-known drama and novels. Poems, being the focus of early stylistics, are ideal for this purpose due to their manageable size. Well-known drama and novels preclude the necessity for additional student reading.

Linguistic systems each have unique means of making meaning. The literary and non-literary texts we analyze in this book are primarily English. To illustrate more clearly how a text makes meaning through its linguistic choices, we also examine Chinese texts. This cross-linguistic comparison helps clarify the process of meaning-making.

Following this introductory chapter, Chapter 2 is dedicated to providing an overview of key concepts in stylistics. These include the poetic function proposed by Roman Jakobson, the notion of foregrounding, various language levels and corresponding linguistic branches, as well as the Systemic-functional Linguistic models (SFL for short). The introduction of the poetic function is considered to mark the beginning of modern stylistics, and the theory of foregrounding forms the basis of nearly all stylistic analyses. The different language levels, their respective linguistic branches, and the SFL models offer a catalogue of the analytical "tools". These concepts will be examined more thoroughly in the subsequent four chapters.

Chapters 3 to 6 "drip-feed linguistic information throughout the course" rather than "teach it up-front before proceeding to apply linguistic techniques of analysis to real texts" (McIntyre, 2011: 15), a strategy highly recommended by Short and Breen (1988). And these theories and concepts are mainly developed on the basis of analyses of verbal language(s) and are mainly employed as analytical tools in stylistic analyses of verbal texts. Chapter 7 turns to theories and concepts proposed in multimodal studies, which take into account phonic and graphic substances as well as different semiotic modes and their integration in multimodal texts.

Exercises:

1. How to define stylistics?
2. What makes up a qualified stylistic analysis?
3. What are the principles that stylistic analyses are expected to follow?
4. What is a linguistic model? How many linguistic models do you know?
5. What separate roles do linguistics and literary studies play in a stylistic analysis?

Chapter 2

Stylistics and Stylistic Concepts

2.1 Concepts defining stylistics and used in stylistic analysis

Stylistics, as a distinct field of study, traces its growth from a narrow focus on poetry in the early days to an encompassing study of all literary genres and ultimately, both literary and non-literary texts. This evolution showcases a myriad of concepts employed in stylistics, which can be categorized into two types. The first category consists of stylistics concepts, which define stylistics. The second category includes those concepts that are applied in the process of stylistic analysis, which can be referred to as stylistic concepts.

According to Leech (2013: 4), stylistics is very much an applied and practical discipline, which means that stylistics has a limited number of stylistics concepts. However, it benefits from a variety of concepts sourced from informing disciplines. Sections 2.2 and 2.3 introduce two groups of stylistics concepts, and Sections 2.4 and 2.5 introduce some stylistic concepts borrowed from linguistic theories, that is, linguistic terms.

2.2 The poetic function

Language operates within two dimensions, aptly referred to as the horizontal and vertical dimensions. The understanding of the two terms can be simplified by visualizing Examples 2.1–2.3 by adopting the sinistrodextral writing system, which means writing from left to right, while putting the candidate items vertically:

Example 2.1

鸟宿池边树，僧________月下门。（贾岛《题李凝幽居》）
（敲、推）

Example 2.1'

推
鸟宿池边树，僧 敲 月下门。

Example 2.2

春风又________江南岸，明月何时照我还？（王安石《泊船瓜洲》）
（到、过、绿、入、满）

Example 2.2'

到
过
春风又 绿 江南岸，明月何时照我还？
入
满

Example 2.3

He ________ in the dead of winter. (W. H. Auden, *In Memory of W. B. Yeats*)
(died, perished, disappeared, passed on, passed away, kicked the bucket)

Example 2.3'

died
perished
He disappeared in the dead of winter.
passed on
passed away
kicked the bucket

The vertical dimension organizes linguistic items into a system, while the horizontal dimension organizes linguistic items into a structure. The relation among the items in a system is that of selection, and the relation among the items in a structure is that of combination. In the first example, the two Chinese verbs are in the relation of "either … or …", and each of them can combine with the nominal phrase 月下门 to form a structure. The relationships of selection and of combination are technically referred to as paradigmatic and syntagmatic relationships in linguistics.

Jakobson (1960) proposes a model of language which comprises six key functions: "conative", "phatic", "referential", "emotive", "poetic" and "metalingual". The poetic function projects the principle of equivalence from the axis of selection into the axis of combination (Jakobson, 1960: 358). It appeals to stylisticians because it allows stylisticians to base their appraisals on a comparison of one linguistic actual with other possibles. In Example 2.2, 绿 is the poet's choice and its innovative collocation with 春风 and 江南岸 achieves a unique rhetorical effect (which arguably makes the expression an impressive line in a poem) that other possible collocations cannot. If you are familiar with economics, you can easily understand this poetic function in terms of opportunity cost, that is, the loss of potential gain from other alternatives when one alternative is chosen. In Example 2.2, if 到 is chosen, the "opportunity cost" will be the loss of linguistic innovativeness of the line and the failure to provide a vivid description of early spring.

In Examples 2.1 and 2.2, the potential words are straightforward lexical items. However, Example 2.3 illustrates a more diverse range of forms and styles, with the final choice taking multiple factors into account. Simpson (2014: 54–55) outlines three such considerations. Firstly, *passed away* is a euphemistic cliché, and *kicked the bucket* is an informal style. Both of them are inappropriate in the context of a poetic elegy. Secondly, words such as *died* and *disappeared* are favored due to their phonetic associations with other words within the line—these connections make them preferable over *perished* and *passed on*. For instance, the initial consonant /d/ in *died* and *disappeared* alliterates with the same consonant in *dead*. The word *disappeared* has an additional phonetic advantage as its ending consonant forms a consonance with the ending consonant of *dead*, and its third, stressed syllable contains a diphthong whose first element is the vowel /ɪ/ – similar to the vowel found in *He*.

Lastly, semantic considerations play a crucial role in finalizing the choice of words. The season "winter" symbolizes death, creating new significations when combined with the words *dead* and *disappeared* within the same grammatical context. This structural combination triggers a conceptual metaphor, where the concept of death is represented in terms of a journey. We often make use of this LIFE IS A JOURNEY metaphor in everyday conversation when talking of the "dearly departed", or when someone is said to be "passing away" or "going to a final resting place". Choosing *disappeared* in the line forms another linguistic realization of the metaphor, subtly suggesting the idea of being lost or straying from a journey. This is subtly accomplished through the inferred connection between the process of disappearing and the allusions to death and seasons within the same line. The way W.H. Auden uses language provides a good illustration of Jakobson's poetic function at work: the particular language patterns he develops work to establish connections (a principle of equivalence) between the words he chooses from the pool of possible words (the axis of selection) and the words that are combined across the poetic line (the axis of combination).

2.3 Foregrounding

The concept of foregrounding originates from art criticism, where art critics typically differentiate between the foreground and background of a painting. For instance, consider Leonardo da Vinci's renowned masterpiece, *Mona Lisa*. In this painting, Mona Lisa serves as the foreground, positioned centrally and towards the bottom of the canvas. Appearing larger than other objects in the scene, she constitutes the primary focus of the artwork. As stylistic analysis consists of both linguistic description and interpretation, the notion of foregrounding is crucial in stylistics from both descriptive and interpretative perspectives. Douthwaite (2000) opts to define foregrounding in terms of description while acknowledging its interpretative significance as follows:

> [C]ognitive psychology has demonstrated that habituation in perception and comprehension is a normal phenomenon in human life. Habituation routinises life, it dulls the senses and the critical faculties. One way of combating habituation is to experience an entity in a novel fashion so that our attention is arrested, and our automatic mode of processing together with the standard response we produce to the familiar stimulus are impeded, slowed down, surprised even. This obliges us to examine the entity more closely and from a new perspective. As a result we are challenged to place a new interpretation on reality.
>
> Impeding normal processing by showing the world in an unusual, unexpected or abnormal manner is termed defamiliarization. Thus defamiliarization may be achieved by subverting the rules governing perception and behaviour. The linguistic technique employed in subverting the world in this manner is termed foregrounding.

Short (2013) chooses first to discuss linguistic patterns that attract readers' (and hearers') attention, and then define foregrounding as the psychological effect of those techniques. This book puts the two together, and defines it as a form of textual patterning which is motivated specifically for literary-aesthetic purposes, following Simpson (2014: 52).

2.3.1 Deviation

The first way to achieve foregrounding is through deviation, which means breaking the norms of language. Example 2.2 provides a good illustration, because 绿 in Chinese is normally used to modify a noun as in 绿苹果 (green apples) or used after a verb to describe a resultative state as in 变绿 (to become green). And although we also do sometimes use it as a transitive verb, for example in 绿了芭蕉 (to have greened plantain), we seldom use it as a transitive verb followed by a place noun.

Traditionally, norms or rules of language are considered an aspect of linguistic competence among native speakers, while deviation tends to be seen as a matter of subjective judgment. However, advancements in corpus linguistics have made it possible to objectively "calculate" language norms and deviations. This calculation process consists of three steps.

Firstly, a reference corpus must be constructed or chosen. The advancements in computer power since the 1980s have significantly improved the compilation of large-scale language corpora. Large and textually diverse corpora, such as the *British National Corpus* (BNC)—comprising approximately 100 million running words and over 4,000 texts—offer a broadly representative and balanced cross-section of the use of the English language as a whole. Additionally, small-scale corpora have been developed for various purposes. All of them can serve as reference corpora.

Secondly, the text under study (Ts) is compared with a reference corpus (Tr) statistically in terms of frequency of observed features, that is, any linguistic phenomenon in a text that can be reliably identified and counted.

Thirdly, linguistic items of different sizes listed in order of keyness are obtained. Keyness means "distinctiveness value", in the sense that the linguistic items most "over-represented" in Ts (when compared with Tr) will be at the top of the list—with a high positive value—whereas any linguistic items equally common in both the text under study and the reference corpus will appear in the middle of the list (with a value of zero), and the linguistic items "under-represented" in Ts—and therefore most "over-represented" in Tr—will appear at the bottom of the list with a high negative value. The use of "over-represent" and "under-represent" here, by the way, is devoid of any value judgment: these terms simply refer to the relative frequency of a linguistic item in Ts versus Tr. The keyness list can be easily obtained by using softwares like Wordsmith Tools and Wmatrix.

Consequently, in practical terms, deviation can be quantified as a positive significant score on the scale of keyness. This implies that the feature above the score is significantly more frequent in Ts than in Tr. Table 2.1 offers an illustration of this. In this instance, "The Mark on the Wall" is the text being examined (Ts), and the "General Fiction" section of the Lanc-32 corpus serves as the reference corpus (Tr), providing a baseline for typical fiction writing of that era. The top 12 words shown in the table are ranked by keyness, which is derived by comparing "The Mark on the Wall" with the selected reference corpus using Wmatrix. The fact that the word *mark* tops the list demonstrates its frequency diverges significantly from the norm identified in fictions from the same period.

Table 2.1 Keywords: Words of abnormally high frequency in "The Mark on the Wall" (adopted from Leech, 2013: 169)

Most "over-represented" keywords in "The Mark on the Wall" compared with 1931 general fiction (with numbers of occurrences in the text in brackets)

1. mark	(15)	7. of	(130)
2. is	(44)	8. nail	(4)
3. wall	(14)	9. reality	(4)
4. thoughts	(9)	10. tablecloths	(4)
5. Whitaker	(6)	11. worshipping	(4)
6. one	(31)	12. tree	(6)

2.3.2 Parallelism

Repetition, or over-regularity, is another means to achieve foregrounding. In Example 2.3, the repetition of the consonant /d/ helps to highlight the two words "disappeared" and "dead" and their relation.

Simple repetition is, however, a relatively restricted method of producing foregrounding. A much more interesting method is that of **parallelism,** where some features are held constant (usually structural features) while others (usually lexical items, *e.g.* words, idioms) are varied:

Example 2.4

We are the hollow men
We are the stuffed men
[8 lines omitted]
Shape without form, shade without colour,
Paralysed force, gesture without motion;
[26 lines omitted]
This is the dead land
This is the cactus land ...

(T. S. Eliot, *The Hollow Men*)

In Example 2.4, there are three groups of parallelism. To start with, the structure and most of the words in the first line are repeated in the second, giving us a parallel structure which is a "repetition" of "We are the X men". Secondly, the next two lines mainly consist of repetitions of "A without B". And the last two lines contribute a third parallel structure "This is the Y land". What is interesting about parallel structures, in addition to their perceptual prominence, is that they invite the reader to search for meaning connections between the parallel structures, in particular in terms of the parts which are varied. In the first parallel structure, *hallow* and *stuffed* are a pair of antonyms. And this semantic relation is arguably shared by *dead* and *cactus* in the third parallel structure. In the second parallel structure, the three As (*shape, shade, gesture*) and *force* probably name constituents of body in a very broad sense.

2.3.3 External and internal foregrounding

The Rubin's Vase Ambiguous Figure, alternately known as Rubin's Face or Figure-Ground Vase (see Figure 2.1), was first introduced by Edgar John Rubin (1886–1951), a philosopher and psychologist from Denmark. Rubin first presented this optical illusion in his 1915 doctoral thesis titled *Synsoplevede figurer*. This illusion allows us to see either a vase, when focusing on the white part, while the faces blend into the background, or two opposing faces in profile when concentrating on the black area, making the vase inconspicuous. In essence, the foreground and background can often be interchangeable, a principle that also applies to the concept of foregrounding.

Figure 2.1 The Rubin's Vase Ambiguous Figure

For illustration, consider the appendix excerpt from Ernest Hemingway's (1952) novella *The Old Man and the Sea* (see Appendix 2.1) analyzed in Simpson (2014: 53). If we zero in on the smallest nominal groups—nouns and their immediate modifiers—we can notice an overused or repetitive pattern: "the + noun". Of the 20 highlighted linguistic items, 12 (indexed with bare numbers) fit this pattern. This repetition, characterized by a lack of adjectives, significantly diverges from what we would typically expect from prose fiction of the twentieth century. An additional five numbered items (indexed with numbers in circles) also follow this prominent "no-adjective" pattern. For instance, *one* in the fourth item acts as a numeral, while *left* in the first and second, *back* in the fifth, and *gaff* in the third nominal group function to categorize nouns rather than describe them. Comparing to a more complex nominal group structure as the norm, this simple pattern becomes foregrounded. It epitomizes Hemingway's characteristic writing style, often described as "flat", "dry", "restrained", "journalistic", or even "tough guy".

> He knelt down and found [1]the tuna under [2]the stern with [3]the gaff and drew it toward him keeping it clear of (1)the coiled lines. Holding [4]the line with ① his left shoulder again, and bracing on ② his left hand and arm, he took [5]the tuna off ③ the gaff hook and put [6]the gaff back in place. He put ④ one knee on [7]the fish and cut strips of (2)dark red meat longitudinally from [8]the back of [9]the head to [10]the tail. They were (3)wedge-shaped strips and he cut them from next to ⑤ the back bone down to [11]the edge of [12]the belly.

But this foregrounding itself becomes the norm when we focus on the other three nominal groups identified with numbers in brackets: *the coiled lines*, *dark red meat*, *wedge-shaped strips*. It means that nominal groups with some adjectival modifications change their status from background to foreground and "no-adjective" nominal groups work the other way around. To make clear the differences between the two types of foregrounding, the type like "the + noun" achieved with reference to the notional external stylistic backdrop is referred to as external foregrounding, and the type like "the + modifier + noun", working inside the text as a kind of deviation within a deviation, is termed as "internal foregrounding" (Simpson, 2014: 53).

2.4 Levels of language, linguistic branches, and foregrounding

Chapter 1 and the previous sections in this chapter have already introduced some metalingual terms, that is, linguistic terms used to discuss language itself. Given stylistics' focus on texts as its primary research objects, these terms are indispensable. These terms belong to two categories—a set that denotes language facts and another containing linguistic concepts, established to describe, analyze, or theorize these facts. The two categories can be illustrated by terms italicized in the left column and concepts in the right column (Simpson, 2014: 5) (see Table 2.2).

Table 2.2 Level of language and branch of language study

Level of language	Branch of language study
The *sound* of spoken language; the way words are pronounced.	phonology; phonetics
The patterns of *written* language; the shape of language on the page.	graphology
The way *words* are constructed; words and their *constituent structures*.	morphology
The way words combine with other words to form *phrases* and *sentences*.	syntax; grammar
The words we use; the *vocabulary* of a language.	lexical analysis; lexicology
The *meaning* of words and sentences.	semantics
The way words and sentences are used in everyday situations; the meaning of language in *context*.	pragmatics; discourse analysis

The demarcation of language into different levels and the proposal of corresponding linguistic branches help to make the analysis of texts itself more organized and principled, more in keeping with the rigorous, retrievable, and replicable principles introduced in Chapter 1. For example, they can be employed to make a systematic account of foregrounding introduced in the above subsection. Each level of language, and the concepts developed from various perspectives for conducting analysis at each level, will be more thoroughly explored in future chapters. The following illustrations of foregrounding at each level of language are made very briefly.

Foregrounding at the level of sound

Example 2.5

A voice so thrilling ne'er was heard
In spring-time from the cuckoo-bird,
Breaking the silence of the seas
Among the farthest Hebrides.

(Wordsworth, *The Solitary Reaper*)

Example 2.6

A good cook could cook as much cookies as a good cook who could cook cookies.

Example 2.5 is a case of foregrounding out of deviation at the level of sound. In the first line, *ne'er* pronounced as [neə] should be *never* with the pronunciation of ['nevə(r)]. With *ne'er*, the line consists of 8 syllables, making an iambic tetrameter (a line consisting of four metrical feet where an unstressed syllable is followed by a stressed syllable). If the line uses *never* instead, the rhythmic pattern will be broken.

Example 2.6 is an illustration of foregrounding achieved by means of over-regularity at the same level. In this tongue twist, the consonants of /k/ and /g/ are repeated over and over again.

Foregrounding at the graphological level

Example 2.7

If it happens
SHOULD SOME MADMAN
PRESS THE BUTTON AND THE
DREADFUL SIRENS SOUND, I SHALL
LIKE MANY OTHERS SEEK A REFUGE
UNDERGROUND, BUT NOT IN ANY BUNKER
OR SUBTERRANEAN TOMB—I'LL PASS MY FINAL
HOURS BEFORE INEVITABLE DOOM IN MY
COMFORTABLE CELLAR STOCKED WITH
MEMORABLE WINE—THERE IN ROMAN
FASHION
I'LL
LANGUOROUSLY
RECLINE,
DRINK
THE DIONYSIAC SPRINGS
COMPLETELY DRY, THEN QUIETLY DIE.

(Philip A. Nicholson, *If It Happens*)

The poem by Nicholson achieves foregrounding through deviation by arranging its words into the shape of mushroom, echoing the subject matter of the poem.

Foregrounding at the level of word

Example 2.8

Their distant husbands lean across mahogany
And delicately manipulate the market,
While safe at home, the tender and the gentle
Are killing tiny mice, dead snap by the neck,

Asphyxiating flies, evicting spiders,
Scrubbing, scouring aloud, disturbing cupboards,
Committing things to dustbins, twisting, wringing,
Wrists red and knuckles white and fingers puckered,

(Elma Mitchell, *Thoughts after Ruskin*)

By examining the verbs in Example 2.8, we can discern a contrast between verbs in the present tense (such as *do* or *does*) and those employing progressive participles (like *doing*). The progressive participles achieve foregrounding in terms of over-regularity, vividly delineating the intense, and occasionally harsh activity tied to women's domestic responsibilities.

If we consider the usage of progressive participles as the norm, then verbs such as *lean* and *manipulate* become foregrounded because they deviate from this established pattern. As such, the narrative contrasts the flurry of activity associated with housewives to the more leisurely, measured and controlling existence of their male counterparts.

Foregrounding at the level of sentence

Example 2.9

Fat people eat accumulates.

Foregrounding at the level of sentence has already been illustrated by Example 2.4, whose first two lines repeat the same sentence structure. Example 2.9, often termed as garden path sentence, gives us another illustration of syntactic foregrounding. The preliminary reading may make you feel puzzled: Fat people eat what? And what accumulates? And it may seem like nonsense if you allow the sentence to take you by the hand and lead you down the garden path, to a dead end. In fact, this sentence means that fat that is eaten by people tends to accumulate. Although there is no deviation in the usual sense, it does have the effect of slowing down the reading and challenging you to have a different reading.

Foregrounding at the level of meaning

春风又绿江南岸 (see Example 2.2) provides an illustration of semantic foregrounding through the means of deviation. Among the five candidate items, 到 is a more accepted collocate of 江南岸; however, 绿 is chosen to form a more eye-catching structure.

Foregrounding at the level of discourse

Figure 2.2 presents a minimalistic line drawing inspired by a popular photo featuring Dr. Zhang Jinshuo, a prominent zoologist. The image's humor originates from the use of an expression in brackets. The title *Dr.* and the subject's name clarify that the image is meant to introduce an individual, while the monkey present in the photo merely represents Dr. Zhang's field of expertise.

Figure 2.2 Dr. Zhang Jinshuo (first from the left), National Zoological Museum of China[①]

Although humans and monkeys are categorically distinct, the phrase *first from the left* seemingly places them within the same category. The interplay between expectation and deviation results in a humorous effect, stemming from the deviant usage of the descriptive phrase.

2.5 Systemic-functional linguistic models of language

2.5.1 Halliday's framework of levels for linguistic description

Language is too complicated for all its features to be described by any one method, within any one scheme of categories (Halliday, McIntosh, and Strevens, 1964: 17–18). The practice of splitting a language up into "levels" in order to talk about it is long established and well founded. The levels of language and branches of linguistics introduced above are familiar to students who have attended some introductory linguistics courses and are widely adopted in stylistics courses. But they are just one way to talk about language, and they, although friendly to beginners in the fields of linguistics and stylistics, are not so powerful.

This section introduces a model developed from a functional perspective, which, in fact, has been popularly used in today's stylistic analysis. The model is shown in tabular form in Halliday, McIntosh and Strevens (1964: 18) (see Table 2.3).

① Many thanks to Mr. Mi Guannan (米冠南) for this hand-drawn illustration based on the photo.

Table 2.3 Levels of language and linguistic analysis

Subject concerned:		**Linguistics**			
	Phonetics				
Level (*general*):	SUBSTANCE (phonic or graphic)	relation of form and substance	FORM	CONTEXT (relation of form and situation)	Situation (non-linguistic phenomenon)
Level (*specific*):	PHONETICS	PHONOLOGY	GRAMMAR & LEXIS (vocabulary)	SEMANTICS	
	SCRIPT	"GRAPHOLOGY" (writing system)			

This model is more powerful than the one described in Section 2.4 in that the parallel levels are re-organized into an organic whole, with their differences and inter-relations clearly stated.

The distinction between language facts and linguistic concepts are recast as the distinction between language properties and linguistic analysis, which are represented separately at different rows in the model. It can be seen that the eight levels introduced in Section 2.4 are now classified into four categories. The first two levels of language in Section 2.4 are firstly grouped together to emphasize their similarities as media of language and then finely divided to stress the differences between phonic or graphic substance and relation of form and substance. The last two levels of language in Section 2.4 are summarized as context. All the middle levels are included in the category of form. As for the linguistic concepts introduced in Section 2.4, phonetics, phonology, and graphology are re-organized with reference to the corresponding language levels. And all the branches of linguistics dealing with linguistic units ranging from lexis to sentence are referred to as grammar & lexis. Lastly, semantics and pragmatics in Section 2.4 are largely studied under the heading of semantics.

This model shows the different aspects of linguistic patterning that have to be accounted for. Halliday, McIntosh and Strevens (1964: 19–20) provide a detailed explanation of the model.

> [...]; when we call them "different aspects of linguistic patterning", "linguistic" here means "of language". But, since they are properties of language events, they will also be reflected in the description of language; so that "linguistic" also implies "of linguistics". There is, however, a difference. Language does display the different types of pattern—primarily, as we have seen, those of form and those of substance; but it displays them, not in clear contradistinction to each other, but in interaction in one and the same event and with no sharp boundaries between them. Like the patterns associated with many other forms of social activity, the patterns of language are superimposed on one another: they do not follow each other in time. A handshake, for example, could be described in substance: as a physical and physiological activity. Precisely the same event can be described from the

point of view of its form (its place in the total framework of meaningful gestures and actions—both what it might have been but was not, say a salute or a kiss, and what went before and after it) and of its context (who were the participants, what was their relation to each other, under what conditions did they meet?). Both form and context are aspects of the meaning of the activity. So with language. The same event has substance and also form and context; both the substance (the medium of the activity) and the form and context (its internal and external meaning) have their patterns.

With substance, form and context it is clear, on the whole, which patterns belong to which; the problem is to find suitable theories to account for, and state, these patterns, and then to describe them accurately and consistently. With the total set of levels, however, there arises the further problem of drawing the boundaries. Phonic and graphic substance are clearly differentiated: this is a matter of the medium—speech or writing. The distinction here is not between different kinds of pattern in the same event but between different kinds of event. But two events differing in the nature of their substance, one spoken and the other written, can be alike in meaning (form and context), so that even here there is a problem—where do they meet, and how alike can they be? The least obvious distinction perhaps is that between grammar and lexis, since these are two aspects of linguistic form; yet we gain by separating them, because they represent two different ways in which language is organized, internally, into meaningful patterns, and there are different things to be said about each.

As mentioned in Section 1.2, a linguistic description of the text under study is the first step in stylistic analysis. This explanation makes clearer a text, as a linguistic product, can be described at a certain linguistic level or at several, even all, linguistic levels. And the linguistic description at the chosen level(s) can be done from different theoretical approaches.

2.5.2 Sydney School's framework for discourse analysis

The model represented in Table 2.3 is primarily for purposes of language teaching, the levels of form and grammar & lexis occupy the central position. But stylistics studies texts. The later development of the model, conveniently referred to as Sydney School's framework for discourse analysis, offers a more powerful toolkit.

The language model represented in Figure 2.3 and its later development from the functional perspective has been described as "extravagant"; their extravagance has evolved to manage the complexity of the phenomenon it describes (Martin and Rose, 2007: 3). But despite the complexity of language in social contexts, the basic principles from a functional perspective for managing it are relatively simple. Two theoretical dimensions have been devised to explore the phenomena of discourse:

- [relevant] levels of language: as grammar, as discourse, and as social context (known as the strata of language)

● three general functions of language in social contexts: to enact our relationships, to represent our experience, and to organize discourse as meaningful text (known as metafunctions).

Strata: grammar, discourse and social context

The object of stylistic analysis is texts. In linguistic models, texts are located at the stratum of discourse. In Sydney School's framework for discourse analysis as outlined in Martin and Rose (2007: 4), discourse analysis interfaces with the analysis of grammar and the analysis of social activity, somewhere between the work of grammarians on the one hand and social theorists on the other. Figure 2.3 symbolizes grammar, discourse and social activity as a series of circles, in which discourse nestles within social activity and grammar nestles within discourse, suggesting three complementary perspectives on a single complex phenomenon. This symbolization suggests two important points. Firstly, the three strata differ in size; texts are bigger than a clause but smaller than a culture. Grammarians usually focus on clause types and their components, but texts generally extend beyond single clauses, leading the discourse analysts to have a broader scope of concerns (expanded horizons). Similarly, cultures express themselves through a multitude of texts. Social theorists are more interested in the relationships of social contexts, rather than their internal organization as texts (global horizons). Secondly, discourse analysis employs the tools of grammarians to identify the roles of wordings in text passages, and employs the tools of social theorists to explain why they make the meanings they do.

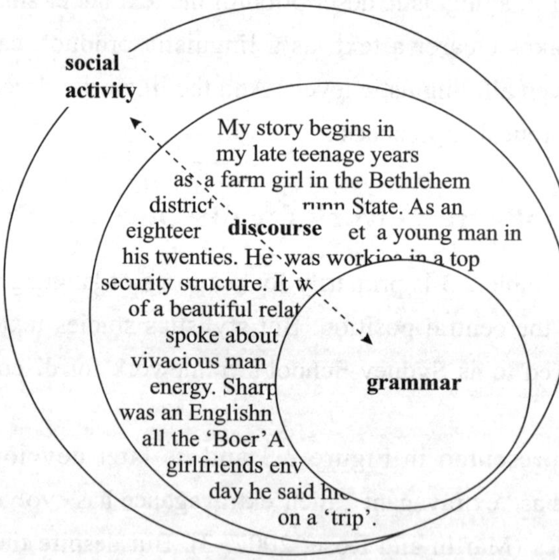

Figure 2.3 Points of view on discourse: from social activity and from grammar (Martin and Rose, 2007: 5)

Realization: culture, meaning and wording

The theoretical dimension of language stratification works in tandem with the concept of realization. Symbolically positioned at different strata, social activity, discourse and grammar are different kinds of phenomena, operating at different levels of abstraction: a culture is more abstract than a text, and the meanings that make up a text are in turn more abstract than the wordings that express them. This suggests that the relation between grammar, discourse and social context is not structural; cultures are neither a combination of text, nor are texts a combination of clauses. The relation between them is that of realization; social contexts are realized as texts which are realized as sequences of clauses (Martin and Rose, 2007: 4).

The concept of realization can be metaphorically likened to re-coding, similar to how hardware is mapped through software to produce the images and words we observe on our computer screens. Another way of thinking about this is symbolization, which can be illustrated by the national flag of the People's Republic of China. The national flag is a red rectangle emblazoned with five yellow five-pointed stars. Among the five stars, one of them is bigger than the other four and is placed in the left. The other four are smaller, encircling the big star on its right in the shape of an arch.

Xinhua News Agency's reply to readers published by *People's Daily* on November 15, 1949 provides an explanation of the symbolic meaning of the flag's design①. The English version of the explanation reads as follows:

> The red color of the flag symbolizes revolution; the stars take on the yellow color in order to bring out their brightness on the red ground. The larger star represents the CPC, while the four smaller ones, the Chinese people. The relationship between the stars means the great unity of the Chinese people under the leadership of the CPC.②

So the colors, the stars, and the design all realize or symbolize some meaning. Just as the meaning of our national flag is more than the sum of its colors, depicted items and their arrangement, discourse is more than the sum of its wordings, and culture more than the sum of its texts. The realizational relation between them carries the meanings of "symbolizing", "encoding", "expressing", "manifesting" and so on (Martin and Rose, 2007: 6).

Metafunctions: interpersonal, ideational and textual

The model of language in social context recognizes three general social functions that we use language for: (i) to enact our social relationships; (ii) to represent our experience to each other; and (iii) to organize our enactments and representations as meaningful text (Martin and Rose, 2007: 7). These are known as the metafunctions of language in social activity:

- the interpersonal metafunction to enact relationships
- the ideational metafunction to represent experience
- the textual metafunction to organize text.

① http://www.cflac.org.cn/zt/60years/guoqi.htm?eqid=e03726b6000b24f500000004643d6389.

② http://gh.china-embassy.gov.cn/eng/gyzg/gjgk/.

As social discourse progresses, these three functions intertwine, enabling us to simultaneously accomplish all three social functions. This means that we can examine any piece of discourse from any of these three perspectives, and identify different functions realized by distinct patterns of meaning. (Martin and Rose, 2007: 7)

Functional models of language perceive language as a meaning-making potential, and their roomy theoretical framework presents unique benefits in stylistic analysis. Firstly, the realization relationship between different language strata offers a bridge between wordings and meaning, as well as between meaning and thematic interpretation of the analyzed text (Hasan, 1989: 99). Secondly, the multi-metafunctional approach can facilitate the analysis of different strands of meaning of the text being studied.

Exercises:

1. Choose the word that is best to finish the following sentences, and defend your choice with reference to the concept of poetic function:

 1) A frosty winter night—my love,
 Chill wind ________ (murmurs, mutters, breathes, whispers) sweet adoration.
 Binds my body with the finest wool,
 The darkest of sweet sensations.

 (John Anderson, *Night, My Lover*)

 2) This living hand, now warm and capable
 Of earnest grasping, would, if it were cold
 And in the ________ (piercing, utter, icy, bitter) silence of the tomb,
 So haunt thy days and chill thy dreaming nights
 That thou wouldst wish thine own heart dry of blood
 So in my veins red life might stream again.
 And thou be conscience-calmed—see here it is—
 I hold it towards you.

 (John Keats, *The Living Hand*)

2. In the following three passages, is there any foregrounding? If yes, analyze it in terms of the level of language and briefly state its stylistic effect in each passage.

 1) I have known the inexorable sadness of pencils. (Theodore Roethke, *Dolor*)

2) The smaller fish is now in an air bubble
spinning
and turning
and making its way upward
(Tomlin, 1994)

3) This topic is all about how and why writers ***FOREGROUND*** parts of their texts and what meanings and effects are associated with these foregroundings. The theory of ***FOREGROUNDING*** is probably the most important theory within Stylistic Analysis, and foregrounding analysis is arguably the most important part of the stylistic analysis of any text.

3. The Chinese song《我终于失去了你》was released in the 1980s and is still quite popular. Please identify the foregrounding in the lyrics with the help of CCL corpus built by Peking University (http://ccl.pku.edu.cn:8080/ccl_corpus/).

4. What are the similarities and differences among the three models of language mentioned in this chapter?

5. Try to analyze the poem *The Rose Family* by Robert Frost by using the concepts introduced in this chapter and interpret its theme based on your analysis.

The rose is a rose,
And was always a rose.
But the theory now goes
That the apple's a rose,
And the pear is, and so's
The plum, I suppose.
The dear only knows
What will next prove a rose.
You, of course, are a rose—
But were always a rose.

Chapter 3

Sounds and Metrical Patterns in Poems

3.1 Sounds (and written forms) in poems

七绝·为女民兵题照

毛泽东

一九六一年二月

飒爽英姿五尺枪，
曙光初照演兵场。
中华儿女多奇志，
不爱红装爱武装。

Militia Women

Inscription on a Photo

February 1961

(Translated by Xu Yuanchong)

So bright and brave, with rifles five feet long,
At early dawn they shine on drilling place.
Most Chinese daughters have a desire so strong,
To face the powder, not powder the face.

MILITIA WOMEN
Inscription on a Photograph
February 1961
(Translated by Hua-ling Nieh Engle and Paul Engle)

Fresh, brave looks—five foot rifles.
First rays of morning light on the drilling ground.
China's girls, alive with highest hope,
they like uniforms, not dresses.

MILITIA WOMEN
(Translated by Willis Barnstone)

Early rays of sun illumine the parade grounds
and these handsome girls heroic in the wind,
with rifles five feet long.
Daughters of China with a marvelous will,
you prefer hardy uniforms to colorful silk.

MILITIA WOMEN
Inscription on a Photograph
—a chueh chu
February 1961
(Foreign Languages Press, 1976)

How bright and brave they look, shouldering five-foot rifles
On the parade ground lit up by the first gleams of day.
China's daughters have high-aspiring minds,
They love their battle array, not silks and satins.

The above-cited poem by Mao Zedong was initially composed in 1960 and underwent revisions in 1961. Several translators have provided English-language translations, with the four presented directly following the original being widely recognized. As Robert Frost once reportedly stated, "poetry is what gets lost in translation". So, what is lost in the translation of this poem from Chinese to English, as demonstrated above? Before diving into a linguistic analysis, this question may also be addressed by invoking the conduit metaphor of language. Herein, ideas or meanings are viewed as objects, while the linguistic expressions act as their containers. Are the core ideas or contents of the poem lost in translation? It appears not. Despite differing in syntactic structure and word choice, the four English translations maintain a high degree of fidelity to the original, effectively portraying the bravery and heroism of Chinese women in the militia. The loss in translation, then, pertains to the linguistic expressions themselves. These expressions can take either spoken or written forms. Focusing on the spoken aspect, it's readily evident that when read aloud, the English translations lack the original's catchy rhythm and melodic cadence.

As native Chinese speakers with an educational background, we understand what sets apart a "chueb chu" (绝句) in Chinese poetry. This form of poetry consists of four lines, each containing either five or seven characters. There is an interplay of tonality between the concluding characters in the third and fourth lines, while the closing characters in the first, second, and fourth lines are typically of the "Pyng" (Even) tone. With reference to the quoted poem, lines 1, 2, and 4 follow a rhyme scheme that aligns with the /ɑŋ/ sound.

Chinese is a mono-syllabic language, with each character having a mono-syllabic equivalent in the sound system. Thus, the requirement for a specific number of characters in the original poem corresponds to a set number of syllables, which is not met in the English translations. Additionally, the tonal patterns and rhyme schemes of the original poem described earlier are lost in the four English translations.

Taking into account Robert Frost's observation, these lost elements are essential in defining poetry. The difficulty in translating these features, at least from Chinese to English, likely stems from the differences in the sound systems of the two languages. This makes it challenging to preserve the original poem's unique tonal patterns, rhyme schemes, and syllable structures while rendering the translation in English.

As depicted in Table 2.3 within Chapter 2, sounds are the spoken medium of language, while scripts are the written medium of language. Figure 3.1 shows Mao Zedong's original handwritten version of the poem. This chapter concentrates on exploring the formal aspects of the spoken English language and its contribution to the poetic function. The examination of the material aspects of both spoken and written language media will be reserved for Chapter 7.

Figure 3.1 Militia Women (A chueh chu with 7 characters) (The handwriting by Mao Zedong)①

① http://www.gov.cn/test/2009-11/11/content_1461821.htm.

3.2 Segmental sounds and suprasegmental features

Phonetics and phonology are two branches of linguistics involved in the study of sounds. As Bussmann (2000) has stated, phonetics examines the concrete articulatory, acoustic, and auditory characteristics of all possible sounds present in various languages. Meanwhile, phonology focuses on semantically relevant speech sounds (i.e., phoneme) and analyzes their pertinent characteristics, relations, and systems, both synchronically and diachronically.

In order to thoroughly analyze the sound features that define English poetry to a particular extent, we must familiarize ourselves with the phonetic analysis of English segmental sounds and the phonological descriptions of English syllables, tone groups, and stress patterns in words and sentences.

3.2.1 English speech sounds

The phonetic analysis of speech sounds primarily involves classification tasks. Firstly, a basic distinction is made between vowels and consonants based on the presence or absence of constriction in the airstream during the articulation process. Consonants are sounds produced with a specific manner of constriction at a certain point in the vocal tract, whereas vowels are sounds articulated without any constriction in the airstream.

3.2.1.1 English consonants

The above-mentioned defining feature of consonants reveals that consonants are distinguishable based on both their manner and place of constriction of airstream, which are technically known as the manner of articulation and the place of articulation. The places of articulation are the places where the vocal organs come close to constrict airstream. The vocal organs involved in the production of consonants are illustrated and mostly annotated in Figure 3.2. The manners of articulation mean how airstream is constricted when air flows through vocal organs which come close during the production of consonants. Bussmann (2000: 97) presents a comprehensive consonant chart that describes English consonants in detail, classifying them according to their place and manner of articulation (Refer to Table 3.1).

Rows 1–4 summarize the places of articulation, listing the vocal organ(s) which work to narrow down the passage of the airstream. Column *a* outlines the manners of articulation. The two interdependent factors give rise to the classification of consonants diagrammed along Rows 5–6 and Columns *b–d.* Column *e* adds a further distinction between voiceless and voiced sounds. Voiceless sounds are the ones produced with no vibration of vocal folds when the air from the lungs passes between them, and voiced sounds are the one produced with vibration. Rows 7–15 and Columns *f–n* comprehensively list all English consonants.

With the aid of such a chart, every English consonant can be meticulously detailed and differentiated from the others. For instance, /f/ is a voiceless labiodental fricative, which is brought about by loosely approaching the upper teeth and the lower lip, nearly obstructing the airstream, and subsequently allowing the air to escape through the narrow gap.

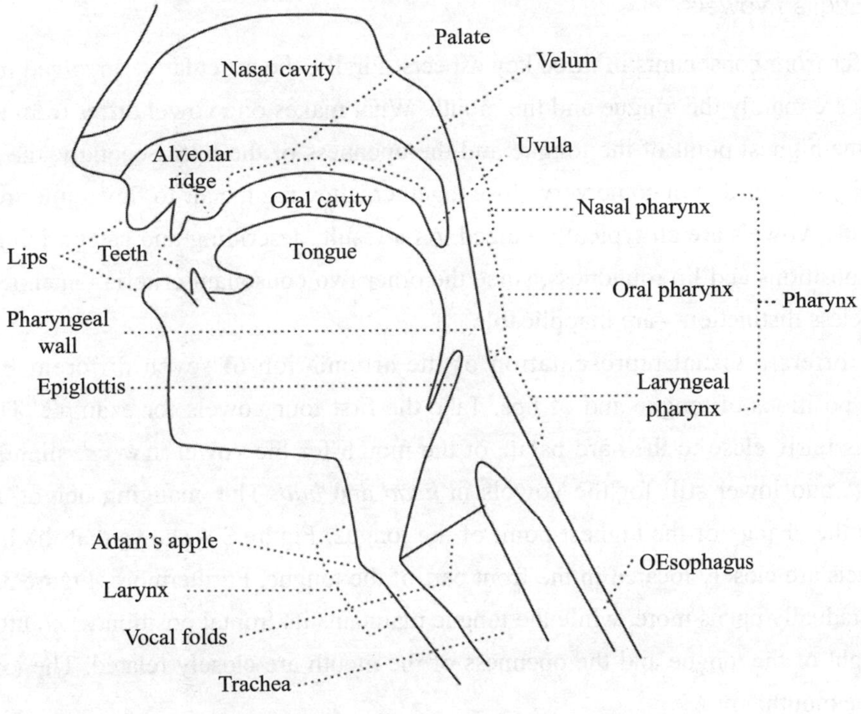

Figure 3.2 The vocal tract (Rogers, 2013: 5)

Table 3.1 Consonant chart (adopted from Bussmann, 2000: 97)

a	b	c	d	e	f	g	h	i	j	k	l	m	n	
	points of articulation	places of articulation			upper lip	teeth		alveolar ridge	hard palate		soft palate	uvula	larynx	1
					(labium)	(dentes)		(alveolus)	(palatum)		(velum)	(uvula)	(larynx)	2
		articulatory organs			lower lip		tongue							3
							tip of the tongue (apex)		blade of the tongue (corona)	root of the tongue (dorsum)		)		4
manner of articulation	classification of consonants				labials		dentals		palatals		velars	uvulas	laryngeals	5
					bilabials	labiodentals	interdentals	apico-alveolars	palate-alveolars	palato-dorsals	velars-dorsals			6
constriction	obstruents	fricatives		voiceless (fortis)		f	θ	s	ʃ				h	7
				voiced (lenis)		v	ð	z	ʒ					8
formation of stop · with a following oral release		plosives		voiceless (fortis)	p			t			k			9
				voiced (lenis)	b			d			g			10
· with release and a following constriction		affricatives		voiceless (fortis)					tʃ					11
				voiced (lenis)					dʒ					12
· with a lowered palate	sonorants	nasals			m			n		ŋ				13
· with lateral constriction		liquids	laterals						l					14
			approximants						r	j	w			15

3.2.1.2 English vowels

Vowels differ from consonants in three key aspects. Firstly, the articulators involved in the production of vowel sounds are mainly the tongue and the mouth. What makes one vowel differ from another includes the position of the highest point of the tongue and the openness of the lips. Secondly, the articulators that function to specify vowels do not come very close together, allowing the air to flow quite freely through the vocal tract. Thirdly, vowels are all typically voiced. As a result, describing and categorizing vowels hinges on the tongue's positions and lip roundness, since the other two consonant criteria—manner of articulation and voiced/voiceless distinction—are inapplicable.

Figure 3.3 offers a visual representation of the articulation of seven different English vowels, highlighting the positions of tongue and of lips. Take the first four vowels for example. The figure shows that the tongue is fairly close to the hard palate of the mouth for the vowel in *heed*, slightly less close for the vowel in *hid*, and lower still for the vowels in *head* and *had*. The changing height of the tongue is accompanied by the change of the highest point of the tongue. Figure 3.4 shows that the highest positions for the four vowels are closely located in the front part of the tongue. Furthermore, Figure 3.3 demonstrates that the mouth gradually opens more, while the tongue maintains its frontal position when uttering these four vowels. The height of the tongue and the openness of the mouth are closely related. The lower the tongue, the more open the mouth.

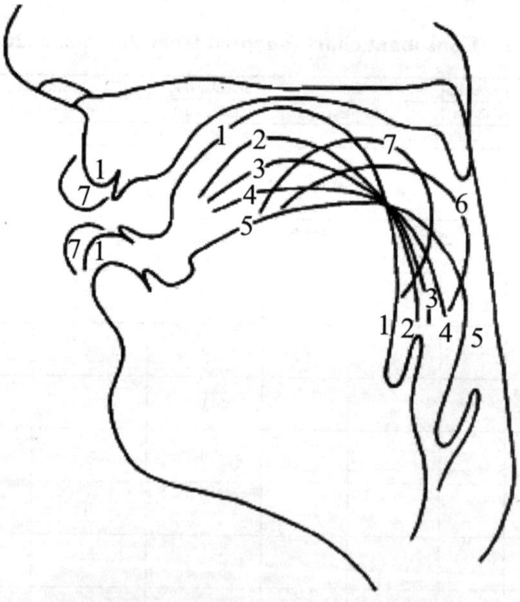

Figure 3.3 The positions of vocal organs for the vowels in the words 1 *heed*, 2 *hid*, 3 *head*, 4 *had*, 5 *father*, 6 *good*, 7 *food*[①] (Ladefoged, 1993: 12)

① The lip positions for vowels 2, 3, and 4 are in between those shown for 1 and 5. The lip position for vowel 6 is between those shown for 1 and 7.

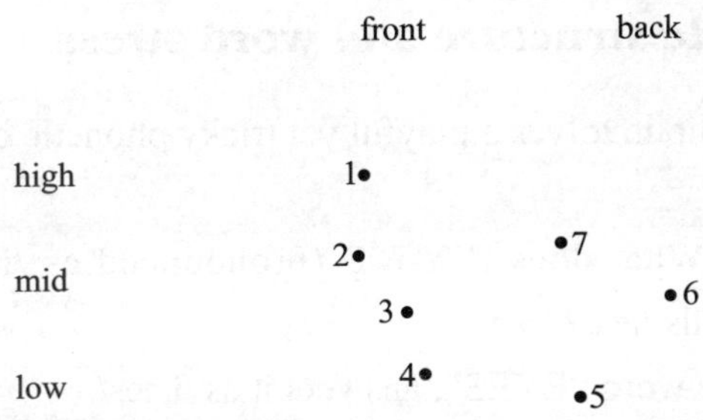

Figure 3.4 The relative positions of the highest positions for the tongue in the vowels in 1 *heed*, 2 *hid*, 3 *head*, 4 *had*, 5 *father*, 6 *good*, 7 *food* (Ladefoged, 1993: 13)

The description of the English vowels is more difficult than the description of consonants. The primary reason is that the accents of English differ more in their use of vowels than in their use of consonants. Figure 3.5 provides a chart which helps classify the vowel sounds in BBC English (termed *Received Pronunciation* in linguistics). According to the chart, the vowel sound in *heed* can be described as a "close, front" vowel; the vowel sound in *hid* can be loosely classified into the same category, but it is pronounced with the mouth opening a little bit wider and with the tongue being a little bit lower.

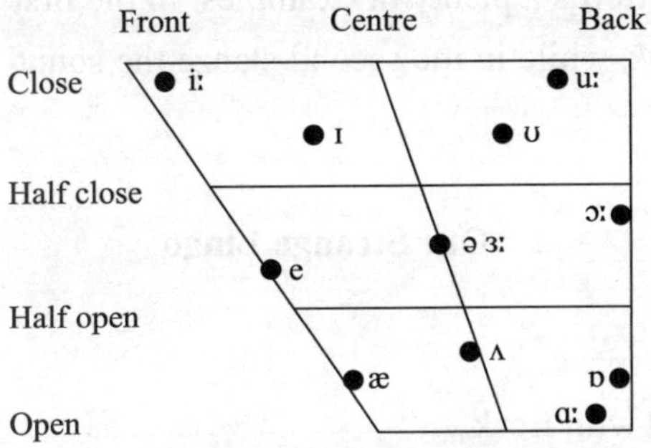

Figure 3.5 A chart of English pure vowels (Jones, 1999: 5)

In addition to pure or single vowels, English also has diphthongs, which consist of a combination of two vowel sounds. Figure 3.6 provides an illustration of how diphthongs in BBC English are produced. The arrow indicates direction. When a diphthong is pronounced, our vocal organs move from the base vocalic position to the end vocalic position. For example, the sound /eɪ/, as in *hate*, is produced when our vocal organs move from /e/ to /ɪ/.

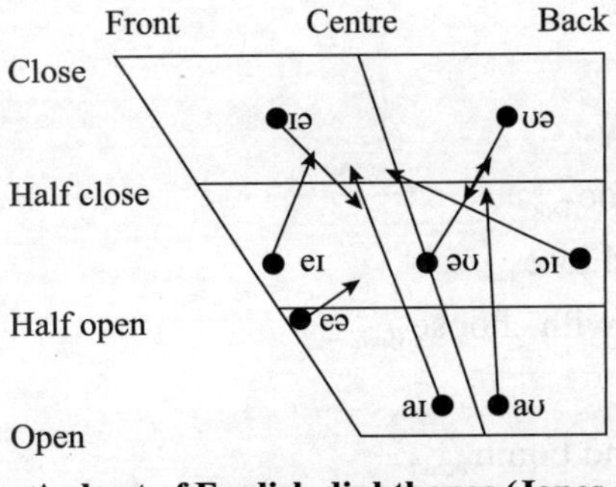

Figure 3.6 A chart of English diphthongs (Jones, 1999: 5–6)

3.2.2 English syllable structure and word stress

There is an amusing video clip involves a playful yet tricky phonetic question. Here's how the scenario unfolds:

Person 1 asks Person 2, "What does E-Y-E-S (pronounced as /i:/-/waɪ/-/i:/-/es/) spell if Y-E-S (pronounced as /waɪ/-/i:/-/es/) spells /jes/?"

Person 2, misinterpreting the word "EYES", answers it as /i:jes/.

Person 1 then bursts into laughter, because the answer is not /i:jes/ but /aɪz/, which is the correct pronunciation of the English word "EYES".

The video became quite popular because of the humorous miscommunication and the unexpected reaction from the person answering the question. There are valuable insights to be drawn from this amusing video clip. The first is that English letters and sounds do not always match. For example, the letter *y* is pronounced as /j/ in the word *yes*. Second, the same letter may stand for different sounds. For instance, when the respondent pronounced *e-y-e-s* as /i:jes/, the first *e* made the /i:/ sound, and the second *e* made the /e/ sound. In fact, it has been widely accepted that the match between English spelling and pronunciation is a nightmare. *Our Strange Lingo* affords a plenty of examples. In the first stanza, *ea* is pronounced as /eɪ/ in *break* and as /i:/ in *speak* and *freak*, while in the second stanza the sound /ɜ:/ is written as *er* in *verse*, *or* in *worse*, and *ear* in *heard*.

Our Strange Lingo

When the English tongue we speak$_{\text{/spi:k/}}$,
Why is break$_{\text{/breɪk/}}$ not rhymed with freak$_{\text{/fri:k/}}$?
Will you tell me why it's true
We say sew$_{\text{/səʊ/}}$ but likewise few$_{\text{/fju:/}}$?

And the maker of the verse$_{\text{/vɜ:s/}}$,
Cannot rhyme his horse$_{\text{/hɔ:s/}}$ with worse$_{\text{/wɜ:s/}}$?
Beard$_{\text{/bɪəd/}}$ is not the same as heard$_{\text{/hɜ:d/}}$
Cord$_{\text{/kɔ:d/}}$ is different from word$_{\text{/wɜ:d/}}$.

Cow$_{\text{/kaʊ/}}$ is cow but low$_{\text{/ləʊ/}}$ is low
Shoe$_{\text{/ʃu:/}}$ is never rhymed with foe$_{\text{/fəʊ/}}$.
Think of hose$_{\text{/həʊz/}}$, dose$_{\text{/dəʊs/}}$, and lose$_{\text{/lu:z/}}$
And think of goose$_{\text{/gu:s/}}$ and yet with choose$_{\text{/tʃu:z/}}$

Think of comb$_{\text{/kəʊm/}}$, tomb$_{\text{/tu:m/}}$ and bomb$_{\text{/bɒm/}}$,

Doll$_{\text{/dɒl/}}$ and roll$_{\text{/rəʊl/}}$ or home$_{\text{/həʊm/}}$ and some$_{\text{/sʌm/}}$.
Since pay$_{\text{/peɪ/}}$ is rhymed with say$_{\text{/seɪ/}}$
Why not paid$_{\text{/peɪd/}}$ with said$_{\text{/sed/}}$ I pray$_{\text{/preɪ/}}$?

Think of blood$_{\text{/blʌd/}}$, food$_{\text{/fuːd/}}$ and good$_{\text{/gʊd/}}$.
Mould$_{\text{/məʊld/}}$ is not pronounced like could$_{\text{/kʊd/}}$.
Wherefore done$_{\text{/dʌn/}}$, but gone$_{\text{/gɒn/}}$ and lone$_{\text{/ləʊn/}}$.
Is there any reason known$_{\text{/nəʊn/}}$?

To sum up all, it seems to me
Sound and letters don't agree.

Thirdly, when we speak English we don't speak the language letter by letter but syllable by syllable. In a certain sense, a syllable is the smallest possible unit of speech. There are two types of theories attempting to define syllables. One of them tries to define syllables in terms of properties of sounds, such as sonority (acoustic energy) or prominence (some combination of sonority, length, stress, and pitch). The other holds that a syllable is a unit in the organization and planning of the sounds of an utterance. For descriptive purposes, a syllable is divided into onset and rhyme, and the rhyme is further divided into the nucleus, which is the vocalic element, and the coda, which consists of any ending consonants (See Figure 3.7). Among the three elements, only the nucleus is obligatory, and the other two are optional. For example, the word *I* consists of a single syllable that has only a rhyme, which only has a nucleus. Syllables with a coda are referred to as closed syllable, and syllables without a coda are termed open syllables.

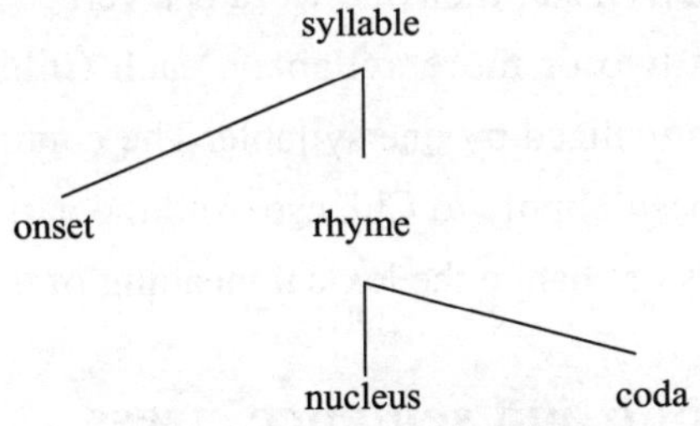

Figure 3.7 Syllable structure

Languages differ considerably in the syllable structures they permit. The differences become clear when one language is transliterated into another. The following are two English words and their Chinese transliterations:

Example 3.1

umbrella 俺妈不来啦
landlord 懒得劳动

The first English word has 3 syllables, but the Chinese transliteration has 5 syllables; the second English word has 2 syllables, while the Chinese transliteration has 4 syllables. The differences are due to the fact that English and Chinese syllables differ in their structure.

Firstly, the possible consonants used at the end of a syllable are different in the two languages. In Chinese, only two consonants can occur at the end of syllables, that is, /n/ and /ŋ/; whereas, almost all consonants can occur at the end of syllables in English. It means that English syllables ending with a consonant other than /n/ and /ŋ/ are likely to be transliterated into two Chinese syllables by adding an extra rhyme to the ending consonant (see Figure 3.8). For example, the first syllable /ʌm/ in *umbrella* is transliterated into 俺妈, and the first syllable /lænd/ and the second syllable /lɔːd/ in *landlord* are separately transliterated into 懒得 and 劳动.

Secondly, English syllables allow consonant clusters both at the beginning and at the end of their syllables, while Chinese syllables don't. For example, the second syllable /bre/ in *umbrella* has two consonants as its onset. When transliterated into Chinese, a vowel sound has to be inserted between them, hence 不来 in Chinese.

There is a third difference between English and Chinese syllables. If an English word has more than one syllable, the syllables are pronounced with different amounts of energy in the flow of speech. The ones pronounced with a greater amount of energy are termed stressed syllable, and the ones with a lesser amount are termed unstressed syllables. For example, the first word puts stress on the second syllable and is pronounced /ʌm'brelə/, and the second word puts stress on the first syllable and is pronounced /'lændlɔːd/. Most English words having two or more syllables put stress on one and only one fixed syllable. Some words like *record* can have variable word stresses, but the variation is meaningful. If the word stress is put on the first syllable, it is pronounced /'rekɔːd/; in this case, the word is a noun. If the word stress is put on the second syllable, it is pronounced /rɪ'kɔːd/; then, the word is a verb.

While the English words has two or more syllables, each Chinese character, which, most of the times, stands for a Chinese word, is realized by one syllable. The contrast between stressed and unstressed syllables within an English word doesn't apply to Chinese. And the variation of the amount of energy when pronouncing a Chinese syllable doesn't change the lexical meaning of the word it stands for.

3.2.3 English tone group and sentence stress

Segmental or individual sounds combine with each other to form syllables. The largest unit in spoken language is tone group. The physical reason for this unit is that we need to breathe. In fact, there is also a cognitive basis to the tone group. While we are speaking in a tone group, we are planning the next one; so, one tone group carries one idea at a time. Linguistically speaking, this one-idea-at-a-time basis means that a tone group corresponds to a grammatical unit, whether it is a clause-complex, a clause, or a phrase. Because of the multiple motivations, tone groups are also termed tone units, intonation groups, or sense groups.

As there are different ways to break a sentence into its grammatical units, a sentence can be divided into different tone groups and thus has different meanings. The following is an example:

Example 3.2

The prince said the princess had been unfaithful.

A. / The prince said / the princess had been unfaithful./
Meaning: The prince said (that) the princess had been unfaithful.

B. / The prince / said the princess / had been unfaithful./
Meaning: "The prince," said the princess, "had been unfaithful."

(https://englishonline.tki.org.nz/English-Online/Planning-for-my-students-needs/Exploring-language/Intonation/Tone-Groups)

As shown in Figure 2.3 in Chapter 2, a sentence not only makes meaning at the syntactic level, it also construes meaning at the stratum of discourse. To fully understand how it conveys discourse information, we need to step back for a while to discuss the feature of stress of a tone group. Although tone groups in a sentence can have different pitches, the different pitches have no meaning-changing effect on the stress feature of tone groups. Additionally, a lot of sentences have only one tone group. Therefore, the feature of stress of a tone group is generally discussed as sentence stress. But for the convenience of discussion, we use tone groups as the basic unit.

Descriptively speaking, a tone group consists of a series of syllables. As mentioned in Section 3.2.2, a poly-syllabic word doesn't spend equal amount of energy when pronouncing its syllables, neither does the tone group. The general principle is that a tone group puts stress on content words, including nouns, notional verbs, adjectives, adverbs, numerals, demonstrative and reflective pronouns, interrogative words, and interjections. The other words like articles, prepositions (especially the monosyllabic ones), auxiliaries, conjunctions, determiners, and personal, possessive, and relative pronouns are usually unstressed. If a content word has only one syllable, the word is stressed; if a content word has more than one syllable, the stress is on the syllable which receives the word stress. As this type of stress is notionally determined, it is known as notional stress.

But this stress distribution according to word classes face challenges under various contexts. For example, the stress of the sentence *I ran quickly to the desk* can be on any of the six words to make different points[①]. And this type of sentence stress is termed as logical stress.

- ***I*** ran quickly to the desk. (emphasizes who is doing the running)
- I ***ran*** quickly to the desk. (emphasizes what action is being done)
- I ran ***quickly*** to the desk. (emphasizes the way in which you ran, but does not fundamentally change the meaning of the sentence)
- I ran quickly ***to*** the desk. (inappropriate notional stress, but emphasizes the direction in which you ran)

① https://magoosh.com/english-speaking/sentence-stress-in-english/.

- I ran quickly to ***the*** desk. (inappropriate notional stress, but emphasizes that it was a specific desk)
- I ran quickly to the ***desk***. (emphasizes the object or location to which you ran)

This stress variation sometimes has dramatic effect. When Paapa Essiedu, a British actor, performed the opening line of *Hamlet*'s "To be or not to be" soliloquy, he got advice from Tim Minchin, Benedict Cumberbatch, Dame Harriet Walter, David Tennant, Rory Kinnear, Sir Ian McKellen, Dame Judi Dench, and King Charles Ⅲ (Prince Charles at that time). They all performed it in a different way by stressing a different word:

Tim Minchin:
To be ***or*** not to be, that's the question.
Benedict Cumberbatch:
To be or ***not*** to be, that's the question.
Dame Judi Dench:
To be or not ***to*** be, that is the question.
Dame Harriet Walter:
To be or not to ***be***, that's the question.
David Tennant:
To be or not to be, ***that*** is the question.
Rory Kinnear:
To be or not to be, that ***is*** the question.
Sir Ian McKellen:
To be or not to be, that is ***the*** question.
Prince Charles:
To be or not to be, that is the ***question***.

3.3 Sound and metrical patterning

Figure 3.8 above uses "rhyme" to refer to a segment of a syllable, which comprises a vowel sound and potentially some consonants. Furthermore, "rhyme" is used more broadly to describe different types of sound patterns. In fact, poems are frequently characterized by such rhymes, which contribute to their inherent musicality. An exemplary illustration of this can be found in the Chinese poem mentioned at the start of this chapter.

3.3.1 Syllable structure and sound patterning

The phonetic and phonological concepts discussed in the previous section equip us with the analytical tools needed to examine and understand the rhyme and rhythm found in poetry. Until now, a variety of rhyme terminology has been suggested to explain different sound patterns. Table 3.2 compares these terms as they are used in four influential works. It is crucial, during any stylistic analysis, to adhere to a single set of terms to prevent any potential confusion.

Table 3.2 Rhyme and related terms

Brooks and Warren (2004: 523–525)		Short (2013: 107–114)	Jeffries and McIntyre (2010: 36–40)	Thornborrow and Wareing (2000: 30–32)
		Eye rhyme		
Rhyme		Rhyme	Rhyme	Rhyme
Front rhyme	Alliteration	Alliteration	Consonance/Alliteration	Alliteration
Slant rhyme	Consonance			Consonance
Interior rhyme	Assonance	Assonance	Assonance	Assonance
				Reverse rhyme
				Pararhyme
				Repetition

Eye rhyme is only mentioned in Short (2013). It refers to groups of words where there is no phonetic rhyme but where there is graphological parallelism involving more than one letter in each sequence, for example *bough*/*cough* (Short, 2013: 108).

Rhyme, however, is predominantly considered a sound-based phenomenon. In its broadest definition, rhyme refers to the matching of sounds in the accented syllables of at least two words (Brooks and Warren, 2004: 523), encompassing various types of sound patterns. In a narrower interpretation, a rhyme is identified when two or more words share the same final vowel and consonant sounds, such as in *dig* and *fig*.

Narrowly defined rhyme can be categorized based on the stress level of the matched syllables, the number of matched syllables, and the position of the rhyming words. When the shared final vowel and consonant sounds are stressed, it is called a masculine rhyme (e.g., *lean* and *green, reuse* and *abuse*). In contrast, if these shared sounds occur in an unstressed syllable, it is deemed a feminine rhyme (e.g., *measure* and *leisure*). The masculine rhyme examples involve single-syllable matches, while the feminine rhyme example showcases a two-syllable match, resulting in a fuller rhyme. Rhyming words positioned at the end of different lines create an end rhyme, while those within the same line establish an internal rhyme.

Example 3.3

Come live with me and be my love
And we will all the pleasures prove

In the two lines from Marlowe's poem, *The Passionate Shepherd*, the rhyme between *me* /miː/– *be* /biː/ constitutes an internal rhyme. Thornborrow and Wareing (2000: 30–32) hold that both *love* and *prove* would likely have been pronounced with the same vowel sound by Marlowe, similar to our modern pronunciation of *prove* rather than *love*. They suggest that these words form what could be interpreted as an end rhyme.

Alliteration, also referenced as front rhyme in Brooks and Warren (2004: 523–525), refers to the sound pattern that identifies initial consonants, such as in *me* and *my*. Consonance (also referred to as slant rhyme) in Brooks and Warren (2004: 523–525) and in Thornborrow and Wareing (2000: 30–32), describes the sound pattern that depends on identical ending consonants, like *will* and *all*. Short (2013: 107–114) employs the term alliteration as an umbrella term to describe these two sound patterns. Conversely, Jeffries and McIntyre (2010: 36–40) utilize consonance as the cover term.

Assonance, also known as interior rhyme in Brooks and Warren (2004: 523–525), describes syllables with a common middle vowel, for example *live-with-will* and *come-love*. And this sound pattern needs to be distinguished from syllables with a common end vowel such as *die* and *why*, which form rhyme.

Thornborrow and Wareing (2000: 30–32), besides the previously discussed terms, introduce two more categories of rhyme—reverse rhyme and pararhyme. Reverse rhyme is characterized by syllables that share a common vowel and initial consonant, as opposed to the traditional rhyme with common vowel and final consonant, for instance, *with* and *will*. Pararhyme, on the other hand, deals with syllables that have identical initial and final consonants but different middle vowels, such as *live* and *love*.

In the aforementioned definitions, the different sound patterns are based on shared or identical sounds within syllables. Two additional points must be clarified here. Firstly, when all the sounds of words are the same, they create a repetition. Secondly, sound patterns can occasionally form from similar, rather than identical, sounds.

Example 3.4

These fruitful fields, these numerous flocks I see,
Are others' **g**ain, but **k**illing **c**ares to me.

(George Crabbe, *The Village*, I, 216–217)

In the second line, the words *killing* and *cares* share the same initial consonants, thus creating an instance of full alliteration. However, the word *gain* is also a part of this alliterative pattern involving *killing* and *cares*, serving to highlight the contrast in meaning between the first and second halves of the line. As demonstrated in Table 3.1, the consonants /g/ and /k/ are similar because they share the place and manner of articulation—the only difference being the vibration of vocal cords. This type of sound pattern is defined as loose alliteration by Short (2013: 108). The pair of words used to exemplify end rhyme, namely *love* and *prove*, only bear similar vowel sounds in modern English. Thus, such a sound pattern is more aptly classified as half-rhyme. However, if we distinctly categorize /ʌ/ and /uː/ as different vowels—the former being a middle vowel and the latter a back vowel—the pattern could also fall under the consonance category, given that only the terminal consonants are repeated.

3.3.2 Stress and metrical patterns

Rhyme occurs when two or more words use identical or similar speech sounds. As discussed above, the nature of these identical or similar sounds, along with their syllabic positions, define the types of rhyme. Furthermore, within words, tone groups, and sentences, some syllables bear stress while others do not. This systematic arrangement of stressed and unstressed syllables is known as a foot and serves as a method to establish rhythmic effect in language.

3.3.2.1 Different types of feet

S.T. Coleridge devised a verse entitled *Metrical Feet* to illustrate the different types of metrical feet, which can help us remember the name of different feet and their stress patterns:

Metrical Feet
(Stanza one)

Trochee **trips** from **long** to **short**;
From **long** to **long** in **so**lemn **sort**
Slow Spondee **stalks, strong foot**!, yet **ill a**ble
Ever to **come** up with the **Dac**tyl's **tri**syllable.
Iambics **march** from **short** to **long**.
With a **leap** and a **bound** the swift **A**napests **throng**.
One **syl**lable **long**, with one **short** at each **side**,
Amphibrachys **hastes** with a **state**ly **stride**—
First and **last** being **long**, **mid**dle **short**, Am**phi**macer
Strikes his **thun**dering **hoofs like** a **proud high**-bred **Ra**cer.

Table 3.3 summarizes the most commonly used feet used in English poetry, which are then briefly illustrated below.

Table 3.3 Foot type and stress pattern

Foot type	Style	Stress pattern	Syllable count
Iamb	Iambic	Unstressed + Stressed	Two
Trochee	Trochaic	Stressed + Unstressed	Two
Anapest or anapaest	Anapestic	Unstressed + Unstressed + Stressed	Three
Dactyl	Dactylic	Stressed + Unstressed + Unstressed	Three
Amphibrach	Amphibrachic	Unstressed + Stressed + Unstressed	Three
Amphimacer	Cretic	Stressed + Unstressed + Stressed	Three
Spondee	Spondaic	Stressed + Stressed	Two
Pyrrhic	Pyrrhic	Unstressed + Unstressed	Two

- **iamb**

an iambic foot contains two syllables, an unstressed syllable followed by a stressed one:

Example 3.5

And **palm** / to **palm** / is **ho**/ly **pal**/mers' **kiss**

- **trochee**

a trochaic foot contains two syllables as well, but in this case, the stressed syllable comes first, followed by an unstressed syllable:

Example 3.6

Willows / **whi**ten, / **as**pens / **qui**ver

- **anapest**

an anapestic foot consists of three syllables; two unstressed syllables are followed by a stressed one:

Example 3.7

Without **cause** / be he **pleased**, / without **cause** / be he **cross**;

- **dactyl**

a dactylic foot is similar to an anapest, except reversed—a stressed syllable is followed by two unstressed ones:

Example 3.8

One for the / **mas**ter, and / **one** for the / **dame**

- **amphibrach**

an amphibrachic consists of three syllables; a stressed syllable is in between two unstressed syllables:

Example 3.9

How **dear** to / my **heart** are / the **scenes** of / my **child**hood

- **amphimacer**

a cretic foot consists of three syllables; an unstressed syllable is in between two stressed syllables:

Spring

By William Blake

Sound the **Flute**!
Now it's **mute**.
Birds delight
Day and **Night**.
Nightingale
In the **dale**
Lark in **Sky**
Merrily
Merrily Merrily to **welcome in** the **Year**

- spondee and pyrrhic

a spondaic foot consists of two stressed syllables, and a pyrrhic foot comprises two unstressed syllables; lines of poetry rarely consist only either of spondees or pyrrhics:

Example 3.10

When the / **blood creeps** / and the / **nerves prick**

3.3.2.2 Different types of meter

A line can consist of varying numbers of feet. Lines with one foot are labeled as monometer, two feet as dimeter, three feet as trimeter, and four feet as tetrameter. Lines with five feet are identified as pentameter, with six feet as hexameter, with seven feet as heptameter, and with eight feet as octameter. When a line is described as being in iambic pentameter, it indicates that the line comprises five iambs. An exemplification of an iambic pentameter, where a sequence of an unstressed syllable followed by a stressed syllable is repeated five times, can be found in Shakespeare's *Romeo and Juliet*:

Example 3.11

For **saints** / have **hands** / that **pil**/grims **hands** / do **touch**

3.4 Metrical analysis of a poem

Sections 3.2 and 3.3 have introduced word stress, notional stress, logical stress, and metrical patterns. All of them play a role in the metrical analysis of poems, which are said to have the feature of musicality. Among them, word stress and notional stress are linguistic features, and logical stress depends on context and is a feature of language in use. However, metrical patterns are ideal and are assumed by poetic convention, and the musicality is realized by a hierarchy of recurrent "beats" and measures. They are all independent and interrelated to each other. Leech (2013: 79) proposes a four-leveled account of metrical form to explain the subtlety and expressiveness of prosodic effects in poetry:

(a) Performance	(individual, "instantial")
(b) Rhythm	(linguistic, "natural")
(c) Meter	(abstract, "mathematical")
(d) Musical scansion	(based on isochrony and a hierarchy of recurrent "beats" and measures)

According to Leech (2013: 71–79), meter is concerned with the pattern of mathematical regularity that underlies the rhythm, and rhythm is the realization of meter in actual language and indicates that the values which are given to syllables on this level have little to do with poetry but are simply the result of applying the word stress and notional stress rules. Sometimes different contextual considerations may allow us to stress the same sequence of words in more than one way. In such a case, a reading of the poem requires a choice between alternative renderings at the level of performance. The musical scansion is based on the notion of isochrony: the division of a piece of verse, in terms of psychologically perceived time, into equivalent units (or measures) marked off by a rhythmic "beat". Let's use the following stanza from Lord Byrant's poem to illustrate how the four levels work.

She Walks in Beauty, like the Night

By Goerge Gordon Byrant

SHE walks in beauty, like the night
Of cloudless climes and starry skies,
And all that's best of dark and bright
Meets in her aspect and her eyes;
Thus mellow'd to that tender light
Which Heaven to gaudy day denies.

By using the notations proposed by Leech (2013), the stanza can be scanned as follows:

(Meter) w s w s w s w s
Line 1 SHE walks in beauty, like the night
(Rhythm) x / x / x x x /

(Meter) w s w s w s w s

Line 2 Of cloudless climes and starry skies,
(Rhythm) x / x / x / x /

(Meter) w s w s w s w s
Line 3 And all that's best of dark and bright
(Rhythm) x / x / x / x /

(Meter) w s w s w s w s
Line 4 Meets in her aspect and her eyes;
(Rhythm) / x x / x x x /

(Meter) w s w s w s w s
Line 5 Thus mellow'd to that tender light
(Rhythm) x / x x / / x /

(Meter) w s w s w s w s
Line 6 Which Heaven to gaudy day denies.
(Rhythm) x / x(x) x / x / x /

Note: w = "weak", s = "strong", / = stressed syllable, x = unstressed syllable

The metrical analysis at the level of meter shows that the poem is in iambic tetrameter, with each line containing 4 iambs. The rhythmic analysis shows that only Lines 2 and 3 have a perfect match between the metrical pattern and the rhythmic beats. The other 6 lines all have some kind of tension created by the mismatch between the levels of meter and rhythm.

Baylor Concert Choir of Baylor School of Music released a performance of the poem in 2014, which provided an excellent musical scansion. The first stanza is as follows:

Line 1 SHE **walks** | in **beau**|ty, **like** | the **night**
Line 2 Of **cloud**|less **climes** | and **star**|ry **skies,**
Line 3 And **all** | that's **best** | of **dark** | and **bright**
Line 4 Meets **in** | her **as**|pect **and** | her **eyes;**
Line 5 Thus **mel**|low'd **to** | that **tend**|er **light**
Line 6 Which **Heaven** | to **gau**|dy **day** | **denies.**

The musical scansion is very close to the metrical scansion, and eases the tension between metrical scansion and rhythmic analysis by crossing the boundary between the two tone groups indicated by the comma in Line 1, by promoting the two unstressed syllables (i.e. /ɪn/ and /ənd/) to stressed ones and demoting the stressed syllable /miːts/ to an unstressed syllable in Line 4, and by promoting the unstressed syllable /tə/ in Line 5.

Marianne Faithfull, an English singer and actress, performed and released a reading of the poem in 2021. Her metrical scansion is different from the musical scansion.

Line 1 SHE **walks** | in **beau**ty, || like the **night** |
Line 2 Of **cloud**|less **climes** | and **star**|ry **skies**,
Line 3 And **all** | that's **best** | of **dark** | and **bright**
Line 4 (‸) **Meets** | in her **as**pect | and her **eyes**;
Line 5 Thus **mel**low'd | to that **tend**|er **light**
Line 6 Which **Hea**ven | to **gau**|dy **day** | de**nies**.

The first line is not an end-stopped one. When Marianne read the first two lines, she had a short pause after the word *beauty*, and finished *like the night of cloudless climes and starry skies* as one tone group. Her performance also employed several rhetorical devices. In the first line, there are two cases of substitution of feet: the second foot is amphibrachic and the third is anapestic, rather than iambic. In Line 4, the first foot is a defective one, where a bracketed caret is used to indicate a missing unstressed syllable; the second foot is arguably an anapest and the third foot is a standard anapest. In Line 5, the first foot is an amphibrach, and the second is an anapest. In Line 6, the first foot can be analyzed either as an iamb if /'hevn/ is regarded as one syllable or as an amphibrach if the pronunciation is said to contain two syllables.

Brooks and Warren (2004: 504–505) propose some practical notes on metrical scansion. As they don't distinguish the four levels as discussed above, their notes can actually be interpreted as guidelines for a reader to solve the tension between metrical scansion and rhythmic analysis when reading a poem.

1. Every foot we mark off should have one primary syllable and only one.

2. Every foot has one or more unaccented syllables. If it lacks any, the missing syllable should be indicated by a caret in order to show that the foot is defective.

3. Try to keep the treatment of variations, substitutions, and other literary devices as close as possible to the established metrical pattern.... Metrical feet do not necessarily correspond to words.

4. Remember that *sound*, not *spelling*, counts in scansion.

5. In determining the meter (kind of foot and number of feet to a line) in order to scan a poem, one should take the poem as a whole and not merely a line at a time, for the lines may not be metrically identical. One should try, thus, to get a sense of the basic pattern. Always one should read a poem aloud, at least several times, to establish the initial acquaintance. Any line of a poem, it must be remembered, may be irregular—even the first line.

3.5 Revisiting the translation of poems

With the introduction of phonetic and phonological concepts from Sections 3.2 to 3.4, we can now understand and appreciate Robert Frost's statement that poetry is what gets lost in translation. Firstly, Chinese is largely a mono-syllabic language, while English is largely polysyllabic. Thus, the number of Chinese characters cannot be directly translated into English syllables, and this requirement is better perceived as the requirement of the number of foot in English poetry. Out of the four English versions, Xu Yuanchong's translation, written in iambic pentameter, accurately captured the beauty of the original poem phonologically. Secondly, English and Chinese have different syllable structures and different suprasegmental features. When translating Chinese poems to English, preserving rhythmic patterns becomes crucial. While English meters depend on the combination of stressed and unstressed syllables, Chinese poetry relies on the combination of different tones. Therefore, maintaining the original rhythm in English translations of Chinese poetry can be challenging, and often requires a shift from tone-based rhythm to stress-based rhythm, as demonstrated in both Xu's first version and the last version published by Foreign Languages Press.

Exercises:

1. Make a list of sound patterns introduced in Section 3.3 and tell the differences among them.

2. Analyze the rhyme and meter in *The Road Not Taken* by Robert Frost.

Two roads diverged in a yellow wood,
And sorry I could not travel both
And be one traveler, long I stood
And looked down one as far as I could
To where it bent in the undergrowth;

Then took the other, as just as fair,
And having perhaps the better claim
Because it was grassy and wanted wear,
Though as for that the passing there
Had worn them really about the same,

And both that morning equally lay
In leaves no step had trodden black.

Oh, I kept the first for another day!
Yet knowing how way leads on to way
I doubted if I should ever come back.

I shall be telling this with a sigh
Somewhere ages and ages hence:
Two roads diverged in a wood, and I,
I took the one less traveled by,
And that has made all the difference.

3. Try to improve the following English translations with reference to the meters introduced in this chapter.

身如菩提树，心如明镜台。 时时勤拂拭，莫使染尘埃。	The body is like unto the *Bodhi-tree*, And the mind to a mirror bight; Carefully we cleanse them hour by hour Lest dust should fall upon them.
菩提本无树，明镜亦非台。 本来无一物，何处染尘埃。	Originally there was no Bodhi-tree, Nor was there any mirror; Since originally there was nothing, Whereon can the dust fall?

（冯友兰，2015：470–471）

4. It's a well-known fact that we currently live in an age of advertising where all brands, regardless of size, use slogans to differentiate themselves. While there are countless slogans in circulation today, the most effective ones succinctly capture a brand's essence, conveying its core purpose in as few words as possible. The following are some successful advertising slogans, please analyze the sound patterns they employ:

Harley Davidson—American by Birth. Rebel by Choice.
Walmart—Save Money. Live Better.
Energizer—Keeps going and going and going.
Blogger—Push button publishing.
Vodafone—Make the most of now.
Philips—Sense and Simplicity.
Panasonic—Ideas for Life.

Chapter 4

Words and Stylistic Analysis

4.1 Words and their syntagmatic and paradigmatic aspects

Words play a critical role as they form the fundamental linguistic elements required for meaningful communication. Wilkins (1972: 111) holds that "[W]ithout grammar very little can be conveyed; without vocabulary nothing can be conveyed." And Krasen matter-of-factly states that "[W]hen students travel, they don't carry grammar books, they carry dictionaries." (Lewis, 1993: iii) Words, due to their importance, are frequently used to denote utterances and even language itself. For example, in the following quote from Oscar Wilde's novel *The Picture of Dorian Gray*, words refer to what was said by Lord Henry in the first paragraph and they are more inclusive to refer to any language in use in the second.

> The few words that Basil's friend had said to him—words spoken by chance, no doubt, and with wilful paradox in them—had touched some secret chord that had never been touched before, but that he felt was now vibrating and throbbing to curious pulses.
>
> Music had stirred him like that. Music had troubled him many times. But music was not articulate. It was not a new world, but rather another chaos, that it created in us. Words! Mere words! How terrible they were! How clear, and vivid, and cruel! One could not escape from them. And yet what a subtle magic there was in them! They seemed to be able to give a plastic form to formless things, and to have a music of their own as sweet as that of viol or of lute. Mere words! Was there anything so real as words?

Furthermore, the quote brings to light some significant observations about language (probably in the form of words). Firstly, words have a music of their own (*have a music of their own as sweet as that of viol or of lute*), which has been discussed in Chapter 3. Secondly, languages give plastic forms to formless things and present the world to us in unique ways. The process of lexicalization, or giving form to experiences, is crucial in this conversion, because it produces words which language holds ready as denotations for required concepts. This lexicalization of experiences becomes particularly noticeable when words, placed in a new context, make new meanings, or when new words are created enabling users to conveniently discuss novel ideas. This is also evident when an experience is lexicalized in one language but not another. *The Report to the 20th National Congress of the Communist Party of China* is emblematic of this, summarizing the latest developments across all societal sectors, thereby providing numerous examples.

Example 4.1

树立大食物观，发展设施农业，构建多元化食物供给体系。
(We will adopt an all-encompassing approach to food, develop protected agriculture, and build a diversified food supply system.)

A word taking on a new meaning in a new context is demonstrated via the word 设施 in Example 4.1. Originally, according to《现代汉语词典》, 设施 refers to the facilities and equipment utilized for manufacturing, production or even for people's day-to-day living. However, when used as a modifier, it now has taken on the meanings of "protected" or "environmentally controlled". The compound word or nominal phrase, 设施农业, brings to life a discourse on modern agriculture that is driven by technology, marking a departure from the traditional agriculture dependent on climate and weather.

Example 4.1 also introduces a new word. We are already accustomed to terms like 世界观, 人生观, 价值观, all of which are listed in Chinese dictionaries such as the《现代汉语词典》. The term（大）食物观, however, is relatively new and yet to find its place in dictionary entries. Its lexical status stems from the altered viewpoints on food in contemporary society.

Example 4.2

推进粤港澳大湾区建设，支持香港、澳门更好融入国家发展大局，为实现中华民族伟大复兴更好发挥作用。
(We will continue to develop the Guangdong-Hong Kong-Macao Greater Bay Area and support Hong Kong and Macao in better integrating themselves into China's overall development and playing a greater role in realizing national rejuvenation.)

粤港澳大湾区 in Example 4.2 is another new word. Geographically, the area encompassing Guangdong, Hong Kong, and Macao has existed before and continues to exist presently. However, the official designation of 粤港澳大湾区 only emerged when the area gained political and economic significance.

Example 4.3

我们要坚持对马克思主义的坚定信仰、对中国特色社会主义的坚定信念，坚定道路自信、理论自信、制度自信、文化自信，以更加积极的历史担当和创造精神为发展马克思主义作出新的贡献，既不能刻舟求剑、封闭僵化，也不能照抄照搬、食洋不化。

(We must remain firm in our conviction in Marxism and socialism with Chinese characteristics and strengthen our confidence in the path, theory, system, and culture of socialism with Chinese characteristics. With a stronger sense of historical responsibility and creativity, we should make greater contributions to the development of Marxism. We should never act blindly without assessing how conditions have evolved or allow ourselves to become ossified or closed off, nor should we mechanically imitate others or indiscriminately absorb foreign ideas.)

Lexical gaps occur when a fully developed word or expression exists in one language but lacks a direct equivalent in another language. In Example 4.3, 刻舟求剑 is a Chinese idiom for which a direct counterpart in English is difficult to find. Therefore, the English translation needs to paraphrase the idiom to make its meaning accessible to English readers.

Thirdly, language is very expressive and has the rhetorical effect of touching our hearts and of triggering various emotional states. Both poems and public speeches are particularly impactful in this regard. In Example 4.4, the combination of 拼, 干, and 奋斗 effectively stirs up a sense of pride for our remarkable achievements and a deep satisfaction within our hearts.

Example 4.4

新时代的伟大成就是党和人民一道拼出来、干出来、奋斗出来的！

(The great achievements of the new era have come from the collective dedication and hard work of our Party and our people.)

This chapter is dedicated to exploring the rhetorical strength of words. Section 4.2 primarily focuses on the syntagmatic structure of words, while Section 4.3 delves into the paradigmatic categories that words can be grouped into. Section 4.4, on the other hand, grapples with lexical meaning, examining the more intricate syntagmatic and paradigmatic relations that words engage in when employed in varying contexts.

4.2 Morphemes and word-formation

4.2.1 Morphemes and figures of speech/sound

From a structural standpoint, word forms may comprise various elements. These elements are referred to as morphemes in linguistics, which are the smallest units of meaning or grammatical function. These elements have differential statuses and functions within the structure of words, and are thus classified into different categories as shown in Table 4.1.

Table 4.1 Categories of morphemes

Words	Elements	Categories of morphemes	Word-formation
teach	teach	free, lexical	–
teaching	teach	free, lexical, stem, root, base	
	-ing	bound, grammatical, inflectional	
teacher	teach	free, lexical, root, base	derivation
	-er	bound, derivational, grammatical	
teachers	teach	free, grammatical, root, base	derivation
	teacher	base, stem	
	-er	bound, derivational, lexical	–
	-s	bound, inflectional, grammatical	–

The first distinction is drawn between free and bound morphemes. Free morphemes can be used on their own, for example *teach*; while bound morphemes can appear only as parts of words, for instance *-ing*, *-er*, and *-s*.

As illustrated in Table 4.1, the bound morphemes are further classified into inflectional and derivational morphemes. Deviational morphemes are the ones used to build new words. For example, we can say that the new word *teacher* is derived from the verb *teach* by attaching the derivational morpheme *-er* to it. Inflectional morphemes mainly carry grammatical information, for example marking a verb's imperfective aspect—as the *-ing* in *teaching*, a noun's number like *-s* in *teachers*, and the like. Old English is rich in inflectional morphemes, but only eight of them are used in modern English:

(1) Jim*'s* two sister*s* are really different.

(2) Take time to deliberate; but when the time for action arrive*s*, stop think*ing* and go in.

(3) The writer lik*ed* joking and hasn't tak*en* things seriously.

(4) One is the loud*est* person in the house and the other is quiet*er* than a mouse.

In Sentence 1, the first underlined morpheme *-'s* attached to a noun marks the possessive case, and the second underlined morpheme *-s*, just like *s* in *teachers*, is used to indicate plural. In Sentence 4, the underlined *-er* and *-est* are used after adjectives to express the comparative and the superlative, and they can also be used after adverbs. In Sentences 2 and 3, the underlined four morphemes are used after verbs to mark the 3rd person singular and present tense (*-s*), present participle (*-ing*), past tense (*-ed*) and past participle (*-en*).

Another distinction is drawn between content/lexical morphemes and function/grammatical morphemes. Content/lexical morphemes express a concrete meaning or content, while function morphemes have more of a grammatical role. For example, the morpheme *teach*, *man* and *wife* can be considered content morphemes. On the other hand, the morpheme *to* in Sentence 2 belongs to the function category given that it is an infinitive marker.

The morphemes *teach*, *man*, *wife*, and *to* are all free morphemes. In a narrow sense, the distinction between content/lexical and function/grammatical morphemes only applies to those free morphemes (Yule, 2020: 73). In a broad sense, it also applies to bound morphemes. That is, content/lexical morphemes include both free morphemes that are nouns, adverbs, adjective, and verbs and bound morphemes that are bound roots and derivational affixes like *-er* in *teacher*. Function/grammatical morphemes can be free morphemes that are prepositions, pronouns, determiners, and conjunctions. Additionally, they can also be bound morphemes that are inflectional affixes such as *-ed* functioning to indicate past tense.

To analyze the structure of words, another three terms are frequently used. Their relationships can be diagrammed in Figure 4.1.

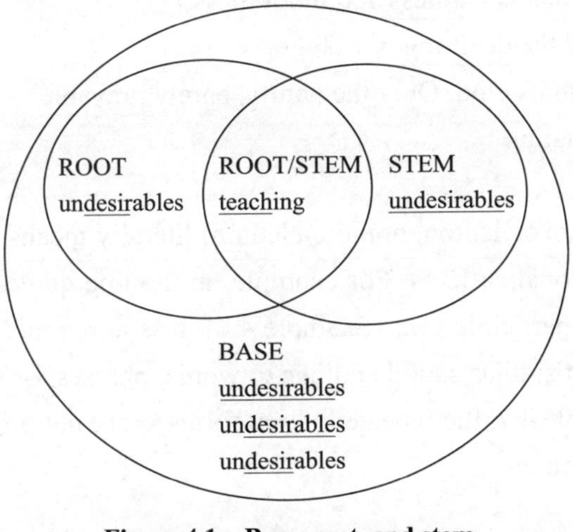

Figure 4.1 Base, root, and stem

A stem is of concern only when dealing with inflectional morphology and is what is left when inflectional morphemes have been removed. In the word *teaching*, *teach* is the stem; in the word *teachers*, *teacher* is the stem. A root is a form which is not further analyzable, either in terms of derivational or inflectional morphology. It is the part of word form that remains when all inflectional and derivational affixes have been removed. Accordingly, *teach* in the word *teaching* is both a stem and a root. While in the word form *teachers*, the stem is *teacher* and the root is *teach*.

Root and stem are the 'main body' of a word form. The bound morphemes attached to a root/stem are collectively referred to as affixes. Affixes can be classified according to their placement on the root/

stem: prefixes precede the root/stem (e.g., re + write), while suffixes follow the root/stem (e.g., teach + er, teach + ing).

A base is any form to which affixes of any kind can be added. This means that any root or any stem can be termed a base, but the set of bases is not exhausted by the union of the set of roots and the set of stems: a derivationally analyzable form to which derivational affixes are added can only be referred to as a base. That is, *desirable* can act as a base for prefixation to give *undesirable*, but in this process *desirable* could not be referred to as a root because it is analyzable in terms of derivational morphology, nor as a stem since it is not the adding of inflectional affixes which is in question.

The terms introduced above can help explain two figures of speech: polyptoton and homoeoteleuton. Polyptoton is defined as employment of the same word in various cases and is, linguistically speaking, the repetition of the root or stem of a word form. In T.S. Eliot's *The Dry Salvages* (Example 4.5), there are four different examples of polyptoton in the six lines quoted below:

Example 4.5

There is no end of it, the voiceless wailing,
No end to the **withering** of **withered** flowers,
To the movement of <u>pain</u> that is <u>painless</u> and motionless,
To the <u>dr</u> <u>ift</u> of the sea and the <u>dr</u> <u>ift</u> <u>ing</u> wreckage,
The bone's <u>prayer</u> to Death its God. Only the hardly, barely <u>prayable</u>
<u>Prayer</u> of the one Annunciation.

Homeoteleuton (also homoeoteleuton, homoioteleuton) literally means the use of similar endings, and the endings are mostly inflectional suffixes. For example, in the line quoted from Shakespeare's play, the repeated ending is the present participle *-ing* (Example 4.6). It is now more widely accepted as a figure of sound and defined as the use of similar sound endings to words, phrases, or sentences. But this definition is not strictly followed. In Example 4.7, the repeated plural forms *-s* are not pronounced the same and are still regarded as a case of homeoteleuton.

Example 4.6

My mother weeping, my father wailing, my sister crying, our maid howling, our cat wringing her hands.

(William Shakespeare, *The Two Gentlemen of Verona*, Ⅱ, iii)

Example 4.7

What objects are the fountains
Of thy happy strain?

What fields, or waves, or mountains?
What shapes of sky or plain?

4.2.2 Word-formation and neologisms

According to Mario Andrew Pei, an Italian-born American linguist, of all the words that exist in any language only a bare minority are pure, original, and unmixed roots. The majority are "coined" words, forms that have been in one way or another created, augmented, cut down, combined, and recombined to convey new needed meanings. He metaphorically interpreted language as a mint, and held that the language mint is a great manufacturing center, where all sorts of productive activities go on unceasingly.

The process of creating new words is referred to as word-formation. Word formations in English include compounding, derivation, back-formation, conversion, clipping, blending, acronym, and initialism.

Compounding is the process where at least two free morphemes or morpheme constructions are combined to produce a new word. The new word is a compound. For instance, the compound word *bathroom* is a combination of two morphemes—*bath* and *room*.

Derivation, in a narrow sense, refers to the process where a derivational morpheme is attached to an existing word. For example, the word *teacher* is derived from *teach* through the addition of *-er*. In a broad sense, in addition to the process discussed above, derivation also includes back-formation and conversion. In this case, derivation in the narrow sense is referred to as explicit derivation, and the other two are termed implicit derivation.

Back-formation refers to the process where a new word is created by deleting a recognized derivational morpheme from an originally older and more complex expression. For instance, *edit* is created by removing *-or* from the word form *editor*.

Conversion refers to the process of word formation that involves a change in lexical category. A good illustration is the verb *drive*, which can also be used as a noun.

Clipping refers to the process where a short form is used for a complex word by dropping some components of the complex word. In the process, usually either the first part or the end part is used, as in *ad(vertisement)*, *math(ematics)*, *(tele)phone*, and *(air)plane*. Occasionally, the middle part of a word is dropped to create an elliptical word: *news(paper)boy*.

Blending is similar to compounding in that two expressions are combined into a single new one. But it differs from compounding in that at least one expression goes through a shortening process. *Motel* is the combination of *mo(tor)* and *(ho)tel*, while *medicare* is the combination of *medi(cal)* and *care*.

Acronym and initialism share the same process where the first letters or syllables of word groups are written together. An acronym resulting from the process is pronounced as a full word (e.g., *radar* /'reɪdɑː(r)/ short for radio detection and ranging), while an initialism created through the process is pronounced letter by letter (e.g., *UN* short for the United Nations).

The new words resulting from the word-formation processes mentioned above are generally known as neologisms. They are created for various purposes, for example to fill a gap in their discourse, to create humor, or to define a situation in a new way.

Gap-filling examples are plentiful when a social change happens. For instance, when the Great Britain decided to withdraw from the European Union, *Brexit* was created in the form of blending (Br[itish] + exit) to talk about the departure. In fact, a group of words were created in the same way to imply some other withdrawals from EU (Example 4.8):

Example 4.8

Upcoming risky events in Europe: Brexit to be followed by Grexit, Departugal, Italeave, Fruckoff, Czechout, Oustria, Finish, Slovakout, Latervia, Byegium, until EU reach the state of Germlonely.

Poets and novelists are more skillful in creating new words for various purposes. In the following stanza from a poem by e.e. cummings (Example 4.9), the poet creates an adjective *moonly* out of the morphemes *moon* and *-ly,* and a new verb, *unbe,* out of the morphemes *un* and *be*. Both of them are derivatives, and they work to form an ABAB rhyme scheme:

Example 4.9

It is most mad and moonly
and less it shall unbe
than all the sea which only
is deeper than the sea.

James Joyce, best known for his *Ulysses*, also experimented with the relationship between morphological structures and meaning in his work. The following (Example 4.10) is from a rather daunting passage from *Finnegans Wake:*

Example 4.10

What a zeit for the goths! vented the Ondt, who, not being a sommerfool, was thothfully making chilly spaces at hisphex affront of the icinglass of his windhame, which was cold antitopically Nixnixundnix.

At first glance, this passage may seem like an intimidating jumble of words. Still, through detailed morphological analysis of the unfamiliar words, some sense can be derived, and it becomes an interesting linguistic puzzle.

Joyce's linguistic creativity frequently stems from his manipulation of morpheme combinations, which he takes from not just English but also other foreign languages. The word *sommerfool*, for example, combines two recognizable free morphemes—*sommer* from German, meaning "summer", and *fool*. The word *thothfully* seems to be a mixture of the free morphemes *thought* and *sloth,* topped off with the bound morphemes *-ful* and *-ly*. *Hisphex* and *windhame*, despite not being familiar English dictionary words, still adhere to possible English morphological combinations. *Antitopically* is formed from a combination of the morpheme *anti-,* the word *topic* and the bound morpheme *-al* and *-ly*.

The morphological analysis presented above prompts further semantic connections. For instance, there seem to be "hot" words (arguably *sommer* and *sloth*) and "cold" words (*chilly, icing,* and *cold*), as well as words to do with time and the weather: *summer, wind, chilly, cold* and *zeit* (the German word for *time*). *Vented* would also fit in this field if we consider that Joyce might be using it as an English word here, as in "to vent one's anger"; he might also be making a pun with the French word for *wind,* which is *vent,* by turning it into a past tense English verb form with the past tense morpheme *-ed*. In this way, we can begin to appreciate what Joyce is doing with the raw materials of language, and increase our understanding of the text too.

4.3 Categories of words and stylistics

The paradigmatic relation is built on classes of words, as the words from the same class are generally substitutable with each other. Based on different criteria, words can be classified into different categories. Three categorizations of words are introduced in this section.

4.3.1 Grammatical classification

As English learners, we are all familiar with English word classes based on their grammatical behavior. Indeed, discussing English becomes challenging without referencing these grammatical classifications. For example, Chapter 3 cannot make clear the rules governing the placement of sentence stresses if we don't have the established grammatical labels. Likewise, the process of word formation through conversion also relies on the pre-existing notion of word classes.

The most fundamental and commonly recognized distinction in English grammatical classification of words is that between nouns and verbs. 沈家煊 (2011: 75) diagramed the distinction and compared it with that in Chinese in Figure 4.2.

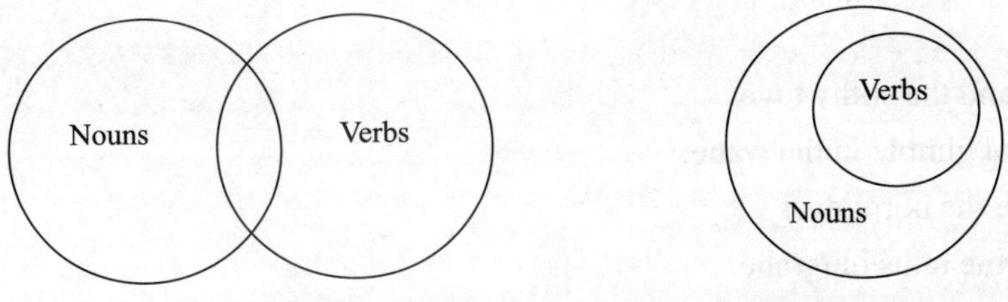

Figure 4.2 The relation between nouns and verbs in European languages (left) and that between Chinese nouns and verbs (right)

The varying relationships between nouns and verbs in Chinese and in European languages arise from the distinct levels of grammaticalization. As a European language, English exhibits a higher degree of grammaticalization in word classes than Chinese, resulting in more significant differences in the grammatical behavior of English nouns and verbs compared to their Chinese counterparts.

Example 4.11

a. 中国共产党领导人民打江山、守江山，守的是人民的心。
(As the Communist Party of China has led the people in fighting to establish and develop the People's Republic, it has really been fighting for their support.)

b. 我们全面加强党的 1 领导，明确中国特色社会主义最本质的特征是中国共产党 2 领导，中国特色社会主义制度的最大优势是中国共产党 3 领导，中国共产党是最高政治 4 领导力量，坚持党中央集中统一 5 领导是最高政治原则，系统完善党的 6 领导制度体系，……
(We have strengthened Party leadership in all respects. We have made clear that the leadership of the Communist Party of China is the defining feature of socialism with Chinese characteristics and the greatest strength of the system of socialism with Chinese characteristics, that the Party is the highest force of political leadership, and that upholding the centralized, unified leadership of the Party Central Committee is the highest political principle. We have made systematic improvements to the Party's leadership systems.)

In Example 4.11a, the word 领导 functions as a verb, while in Example 4.11b, the first occurrence of 领导 serves as a noun. It is evident that the noun and verb forms of this word display no morphological distinctions. However, when translated into English, the noun and verb exhibit both inflectional and derivational differences.

In the English translation of 4.11a, the verb *lead* is marked by the present perfect tense and assumes the morpheme of the past participle. Conversely, in the English translation of 4.11b, the noun *leadership* is employed, formed by adding the derivational morphemes *-er* and *-ship* to the root *lead*. As such, English verbs and nouns are morphologically marked.

Jabberwocky①
(Lewis Carroll)

'T was brillig, and the slithy toves
    Did gyre and gimble in the wabe:
All mimsy were the borogoves,
    And the mome raths outgrabe.

① This version is based on Carroll (1902).

"Beware the Jabberwock, my son!
  The jaws that bite, the claws that catch!
Beware the Jubjub bird, and shun
  The frumious Bandersnatch!"

He took his vorpal sword in hand:
  Long time the manxome foe he sought—
So rested he by the Tumtum tree,
  And stood awhile in thought.

And, as in uffish thought he stood,
  The Jabberwock, with eyes of flame,
Came whiffling through the tulgey wood,
  And burbled as it came!

One, two! One, two! And through and through
  The vorpal blade went snicker-snack!
He left it dead, and with its head
  He went galumphing back.

"And hast thou slain the Jabberwock?
  Come to my arms, my beamish boy!
O frabjous day! Callooh! Callay!"
  He chortled in his joy.

'T was brillig, and the slithy toves
  Did gyre and gimble in the wabe:
All mimsy were the borogoves,
  And the mome raths outgrabe.

Jabberwocky is known as a piece of nonsense writing. But the identification of nouns and verbs in terms of inflectional morphology can help us interpret the poem. The first stanza features five verbs: *was* in Line 1, *gyre* and *gimble* in Line 2, *were* in Line 3, and *outgrabe* in Line 4. The first three are identified as verbs based on the past tense inflection they adopt. Simultaneously, four nouns are present in the same stanza: *toves* in Line 1, *wabe* in Line 2, *borogoves* in Line 3, and *raths* in Line 4. Among them, *toves, borogoves* and *raths* are said to be nouns because all are inflected for number. But nouns sometimes can only be identified as nouns by taking into account the configurations into which they enter with other grammatical categories as the morpheme *-s* is also used after verbs to mark third person singular.

Firstly, nouns tend to be accompanied by determiners. These include articles and demonstratives, among other elements, which work to clearly identify the noun they precede—either through the context, the listener's knowledge, or reference to the speech situation. The determiner *the* is used four times in the first stanza, assisting in the identification of *toves, wabe, borogoves,* and *raths* as nouns.

Secondly, nouns are regularly modified by adjectives. Adjectives used in an attributive manner with nouns or those that are directed by a copular verb are characteristics of noun identification. Thus, *slithy* in Line 1, *mimsy* in Line 3, and *mome* in Line 4 are identified as adjectives. These enhancements, notably *slithy* in Line 1 and *mome* in Line 4, provide further evidence of *toves* and *raths* being nouns.

Lastly, nouns appear before verbs as subjects and after verbs as objects in an English sentence. In the first line, *the slithy toves* precedes the verbal phrase *did gyre and gimble*, functioning as the sentence's subject. This configuration also implies that if a noun is identified as a subject, a verb should follow. Thus, *outgrabe* in Line 4 is identified as a verb, adhering to this pattern.

From the previous analysis, it appears that Stanza 1 narrates the events involving a group of entities referred to as *toves* which possess a distinct characteristic—slithy. These toves are familiar to both speakers and listeners and are portrayed as spinning around in a specific location termed *wabe*. Also, associated creatures or things, called *borogoves*, exhibit the attribute of mimsiness. Furthermore, entities known as *mome raths* are described as engaging in an action expressed as *outgrabe*.

There are two other major word classes in English: adjectives, and adverbs. The relationships among nouns, verbs, adjectives and adverbs are diagrammed in Table 4.2. The line between nouns and verbs and between adjectives and adverbs are in bold, indicating that adjectives and adverbs are as clearly distinguished from each other as nouns and verbs are. And as shown by the arrangement in the table, just as adjectives are used to modify nouns, adverbs are used to modify verbs, specifying the manner of action. The word *awhile* in Line 4 of Stanza 3 is an adverb, and it is used to describe the extent of thinking. The compound *snicker-snack* in Line 2 of Stanza 5 is also an adverb, describing how the boy used the blade of his sword to kill the Jabberwock.

Table 4.2 Nouns, verbs, adjectives and adverbs in English

Nouns	Verbs
Adjectives	Adverbs

In addition to the four major word classes, English also has some minor word classes. Determiners are one of them. The others include conjunctions like *and* in Line 1, prepositions such as *in* in Line 2 of Stanza 1, pronouns like *that* in Line 2 of Stanza 2 and *he* in Lines 1 and 2 of Stanza 3.

The analyses of Stanza 1 of *Jabberwocky* and the quote from James Joyce's *Finnegans Wake* suggest some interesting points about the major and minor word classes and the derivational and inflectional morphemes.

Firstly, writers mainly experiment with the four major word classes when creating neologisms, while they seldom play with the minor ones. The reason is that the four main word classes are open classes and they readily accept new members. The minor ones are closed classes whose members are limited. Writers tend not to interfere with closed class words for the reason that they carry important grammatical information, and if writers did not put them in their usual position in a sentence, it would become practically impossible to interpret their texts.

Secondly, it is the derivational morphemes that writers use creatively, rather than the inflectional morphemes, which carry grammatical information such as tense and number. In *Jabberwocky* and *Finnegans Wake*, the neologisms are largely derivatives and their grammatical categories are made clear with the help of the inflectional morphemes.

4.3.2 Etymological classification

English is a language with many origins and has a long history of development. Table 4.3 offers a concise timeline of its development, documenting noteworthy events that has shaped English.

Table 4.3 A brief chronology of English[①]

55 BCE	Roman invasion of Britain by Julius Caesar.	Local inhabitants speak Celtic
CE 43	Roman invasion and occupation. Beginning of Roman rule of Britain.	
436	Roman withdrawal from Britain complete.	
449	Settlement of Britain by Germanic invaders begins.	
450–480	Earliest known Old English inscriptions.	Old English
1066	William the Conqueror, Duke of Normandy, invades and conquers England.	
c1150	Earliest surviving manuscripts in Middle English.	Middle English
1348	English replaces Latin as the language of instruction in most schools.	
1362	English replaces French as the language of law. English is used in Parliament for the first time.	
c1388	Chaucer starts writing *The Canterbury Tales*.	
c1400	The Great Vowel Shift begins.	
1476	William Caxton establishes the first English printing press.	Early Modern English
1564	Shakespeare is born.	
1604	*Table Alphabeticall*, the first English dictionary, is published.	

① This brief chronology was retrieved from the following website on December 26, 2024: https://www.englishclub.com/history-of-english/#google_vignette, and the dates have been confirmed by referring to Appendix 1 in McArthur (1998).

(Continued)

1607	The first permanent English settlement in the New World (Jamestown) is established.	Early Modern English
1616	Shakespeare dies.	
1623	Shakespeare's *First Folio* is published	
1702	The first daily English-language newspaper, *The Daily Courant*, is published in London.	
1755	Samuel Johnson publishes his English dictionary.	
1776	Thomas Jefferson writes the American Declaration of Independence.	
1782	Britain abandons its colonies in what is later to become the USA by signing a preliminary peace treaty with them.	
1828	Webster publishes his American English dictionary.	Late Modern English
1922	The British Broadcasting Corporation is founded.	
1928	*The Oxford English Dictionary* is published.	

When Julius Caesar invaded Britain in 55 BCE, the English language had not yet developed. Instead, the inhabitants, the Celts, spoke various Celtic languages, from which Welsh remains a contemporary descendant. Subsequently, in the 5th century, Britain saw the arrival and settlement of Germanic tribes such as the Angles, Saxons, and others. These groups brought with them distinct but related Germanic dialects, which evolved into what we now recognize as Old English. This early form of English, which was considerably different in both sound and spelling from the language we use today, was the dominant spoken form until around the year 1100. However, Old English did not become extinct. It is estimated that about half of the most frequently used words in Modern English have their origins in Old English. Examples of these enduring words include *be*, *strong*, *water* and numerous terms related to agriculture, such as *sheep*, *ox*, *earth*, *wood*, *field* and *work*.

Before the Norman Conquest by Duke William of Normandy, the Anglo-Saxon vocabulary was notably influenced by two major forces. The first of these was Christianity, which introduced approximately 400 to 500 words from Greek and Latin into the language. This influence is evident in words such as *angel*, *disciple* and *martyr*. The second significant influence came from the Vikings from Scandinavia, who brought with them numerous words, particularly those starting with the letters *sk*, such as *sky* and *skirt*.

Both Old Norse and Old English survived, which led to a language rich in synonyms, giving us pairs of words with similar meanings but different origins. For example, a child might be *reared* (English) or *raised* (Norse). Other notable pairs resulting from this confluence include *wish* (English) and *want* (Norse), *craft* (English) and *skill* (Norse), as well as *hide* (English) and *skin* (Norse).

With the Norman Conquest of England in 1066, the linguistic landscape of the country experienced a significant shift as the Normans introduced their Norman French language. As a result, three primary languages coexisted within the nation: French was spoken by the aristocracy, Latin was the language of the Church, and English remained the tongue of the general populace. This multilingual environment often led to the existence of multiple words for a single concept. For instance, the word *kingly* was of Anglo-Saxon origin, but with the influence of the Normans, new alternatives like *royal* and *sovereign* emerged in the lexicon.

Despite the dominance of French among the ruling class, it did not replace English; rather, over the ensuing three centuries, English absorbed French terms. By the end of the 15th century, a more complex and enriched language, known as Middle English, had evolved, "borrowing" around 10,000 words from French.

Beginning in the 16th century, as the British established contacts with numerous cultures around the globe, and with the British Empire eventually expanding to cover a quarter of the Earth's surface at its height, the English language naturally assimilated a multitude of foreign words. The extensive reach of the empire and its global dominance created a conducive environment for English to become a linguistic repository, enriching its lexicon with terms from a wide array of countries.

In the contemporary era, the English language continues to expand its vocabulary through the incorporation of terms from various languages. For instance, there has been a notable influx of words derived from Chinese, spurred by increasing global interest in Chinese culture, sports, entertainment, politics, and economics.

Words such as *Confucius*, *Laozi*, *Tao*, and *Tao Te Ching* have entered English usage, reflecting cultural influences. The rise in popularity of Chinese martial arts and cinema has seen terms like *Kungfu* and *Taichi* become common in English-speaking contexts.

In the realms of international politics and economics, the term *Lianghui,* which refers to the annual pair of meetings held by the Chinese government, is gaining currency among international media outlets, especially since its use by CNN. Furthermore, the monetary units *Jiao* and *Yuan,* integral to the Chinese economy, are now recognized in English dictionaries. *Yuan* is often used in English to denote China's currency, reflecting its international economic significance.

When there is a choice, there is meaning. Special rhetorical effect could be achieved if words of the right origin are used. Experienced orators often use Old English to arouse their audience's emotions. For example, during World War Ⅱ, Winston Churchill made his speech by using English words almost all coming from Old English, stirring the courage of his people against Hitler's armies positioned to cross the English Channel: "We shall fight on the beaches, we shall fight on the landing grounds, we shall fight in the fields and in the streets, we shall fight in the hills. We shall never surrender[①]."

4.3.3 Words in different registers and dialects

The linguistic landscape back in the three centuries after the Norman Conquest suggests another way

① The word *surrender* is an exception, which came from Norman French.

to classify words, that is, the domain or field in which they are used. In *The Report to the 20th National Congress of the Communist Party of China*, most words are political terms. Example 4.12 provides a good illustration.

Example 4.12

大会的主题是：高举中国特色社会主义伟大旗帜，全面贯彻新时代中国特色社会主义思想，弘扬伟大建党精神，自信自强、守正创新，踔厉奋发、勇毅前行，为全面建设社会主义现代化国家、全面推进中华民族伟大复兴而团结奋斗。

(The theme of this Congress is holding high the great banner of socialism with Chinese characteristics, fully implementing the Thought on Socialism with Chinese Characteristics for a New Era, carrying forward the great founding spirit of the Party, staying confident and building strength, upholding fundamental principles and breaking new ground, forging ahead with enterprise and fortitude, and striving in unity to build a modern socialist country in all respects and advance the great rejuvenation of the Chinese nation on all fronts.)

When some words or expressions are used across different domains or fields, special rhetorical effect can be achieved. In Example 4.13, 撸起袖子加油干 is a colloquial expression used in our daily life. Its usage in such a solemn context makes the speech friendly to the audience and helps to create an intimate relationship between President Xi and all the Chinese people.

Example 4.13

面对这些影响党长期执政、国家长治久安、人民幸福安康的突出矛盾和问题，党中央审时度势、果敢抉择，锐意进取、攻坚克难，团结带领全党全军全国各族人民撸起袖子加油干、风雨无阻向前行，义无反顾进行具有许多新的历史特点的伟大斗争。

(In the face of these acute problems and challenges, which undermined the Party's long-term governance, the security and stability of the country, and the wellbeing of the people, the Party Central Committee fully assessed the situation, made resolute decisions, and took firm steps. Under its leadership, the entire Party, the military, and the Chinese people were brought together. We rolled up our sleeves and got down to work, forging ahead with resolve to carry out a great struggle with many new features of our times.)

The language varieties used in different domains or fields are technically known as registers. A related term is dialect which refers to the language varieties used by a group of language users from a specific region. The dialectical varieties often do not have a written or standardized form, i.e. do not have officially standardized orthographic and grammatical rules. And the speakers are thus perceived to be illiterate or ill-educated.

Example 4.14

"What are you doing, clumsy, drunken fool?" the mother cried.

"Then tha should get the flamin' thing thysen. Tha should get up, like other women have to, an' wait on a man."

"Wait on you—wait on you?" she cried, "Yes, I see myself."

"Yis, an' I'll learn thee tha's got to. Wait on me. yes, tha sh'lt wait on me—"

"Never, milord, I'd wait on a dog at the door first."

(D.H. Lawrence, *Son and Lovers*, 1913)

Example 4.14 is part of a dialogue between Walter Morel, a coal miner, and his wife. The words used by the miner indicate that he was nearly illiterate and came from a working class. In contrast, the words used by his wife is closer to the standard English, indicating that she had a better upbringing. The words help to build the language users' identities.

4.4 Lexical semantics and stylistics

Meaning can be made at all levels of language. The meaning of words is called lexical meaning. The distinction between content and function words is largely based on the general classification of lexical meaning into the concrete experiential meaning and the abstract functional meaning. As stylistic analyses focus on the interplay between syntagmatic and paradigmatic dimensions of language, this section moves on to more delicate classifications of meaning.

4.4.1 Sense and reference

There is an anecdote published on June 17, 1965 in a Nebraska newspaper which acknowledged a Wisconsin newspaper:

Ken Thompson stopped in at Dick McDaniels' Pizza Palace the other night and ordered a pizza. When it was ready, Dick asked Ken if he wanted it cut in six or eight pieces.

Ken thought a while, and then said, "Better make it six pieces. I could never eat eight."

—Weyauwega (Wis.) Chronicle

Probably we will say Ken was not smart and would just laugh it off. But it is linguistically significant as it sheds light on the working of language or languages. Metaphorically, the pizza might be seen as representing the world or our experiences, which are interpreted and constructed through different languages. Essentially, languages partition the world or our experiences into varied segments, analogous to slicing a pizza into diverse piece counts.

To illustrate this point, consider how a day is temporally segmented in English contrasted with Chinese. According to *The Britannica Dictionary*, English typically divides a day into four segments: morning, afternoon, evening, and night. A more elaborate subdivision is outlined below.

Parts of the Day

Morning 5 am to 12 pm (noon)

- Early morning 5 to 8 am
- Late morning 11 am to 12pm

Afternoon 12 pm to 5 pm

- Early afternoon 1 to 3pm
- Late afternoon 4 to 5pm

Evening 5 pm to 9 pm

- Early evening 5 to 7 pm

Night 9 pm to 4 am

In China, the segmentation of the day is defined with greater intricacy, with some divisions echoing back to ancient times. The subdivisions listed below reflect those adopted by the alarm clock on my Honor smartphone.

凌晨 1:00 am to 6:59 am
早上 7:00 am to 8:59 am
上午 9:00 am to 11:59 am
中午 12:00 to 12:59
下午 1:00 pm to 4:59 pm
傍晚 5:00 pm to 6:59 pm
晚上 7:00 pm to 10:59 pm
半夜 11:00 pm to 0: 59 am

Envisioning the day as a pizza, the English language might segment it into four broad slices, whereas Chinese cuts it into eight more defined portions. Additionally, the size of these 'time slices' varies between the two languages. Some bilingual Chinese-English dictionaries render the Chinese term 上午 as *morning* in English. However, a closer examination of how each language delineates the sections of a day demonstrates that this translation might be imprecise: *morning* in English spans a longer period than 上午 in Chinese. This discrepancy is attributable to the fewer lexical items in English that specify different parts of a day compared to Chinese.

In linguistics, the concept of sense involves the meaning of a word derived from its relationship with other words (Cruse, 2014: 46–47). An associated notion is reference, which pertains to the entity or entities in the world that a particular word signifies (Cruse, 2014: 46). As for referential meaning, *morning* in English typically refers to the time from 5 am to 12 pm. In contrast, 上午 in Chinese conventionally refers to the period from 9 am to 11:59 am. This variance in referential meanings between the two terms illustrates a linguistic principle whereby sense influences and constrains reference.

The concept of sense is very important in textual interpretation. Example 4.15 is from《中庸》, and Example 4.16 is from Part eight of *The Report to the 20th National Congress of the Communist Party of China*.

Example 4.15

仲尼祖述尧、舜，宪章文、武，上律天时，下袭水土。辟如天地之无不持载，无不覆帱，辟如四时之错行，如日月之代明。万物并育而不相害，道并行而不相悖。小德川流，大德敦化，此天地之所以为大也！

Example 4.16

实施公民道德建设工程，弘扬中华传统美德，加强家庭家教家风建设，加强和改进未成年人思想道德建设，推动明大德、守公德、严私德，提高人民道德水准和文明素养。
(We will continue the civic morality campaign, carry forward traditional Chinese virtues, foster stronger family ties, values, and traditions, and raise the intellectual and moral standards of minors. We will build public commitment to the greater good, public morality, and personal integrity. These efforts will help raise public moral standards and enhance public civility.)

In Example 4.15, the sense of 大德 is based on its contrast with 小德. But in Example 4.16, the sense of 大德 is derived from its relation with 公德 and 私德. Consequently, the two words bear different interpretations.

4.4.2 Lexical field

The lexical items used to designate different parts of a day in English and in Chinese form a lexical set, and so do 大德, 公德 and 私德. This lexical set is technically known as lexical field (also semantic field), denoting a set of semantically related words whose meanings delimit each other and are said to cover a whole conceptual or objective field without gaps (similar to a mosaic) (Bussmann, 2000).

Since lexical fields predominantly consist of lexical items—words with concrete conceptual meaning, the examination of lexical fields within a text can illuminate its underlying themes. For example, the poem *Ironing* is structured around several lexical fields. A close analysis of these fields can provide valuable clues for interpreting the central theme of the poem.

Ironing

(Vicki Feaver, in O'Brien [1998])

I used to iron every thing:
my iron flying over sheets and towels
like a sledge chased by wolves over snow,

the flex twisting and crinkling
until the sheath frayed, exposing
wires like nerves. I stood like a horse

with a smoking hoof,
inviting anyone who dared
to lie on my silver-padded board,

to be pressed to the thinness
of dolls cut from paper.
I'd have commandeered a crane

if I could, got the welders at Jarrow
to heat me an iron the size of a tug
to flatten the house.

Then for years I ironed nothing.
I put the iron in a high cupboard.
I converted to crumpledness.

And now I iron again: shaking
dark spots of water onto wrinkled
silk, nosing into sleeves, round

buttons, breathing the sweet heated smell
hot metal draws from newly-washed
cloth, until my blouse dries

to a shining, creaseless blue,
an airy shape with room to push
my arms, breast, lungs, heart into.

Jeffries and McIntyre (2010: 59) conducted a detailed analysis and made some evidenced interpretation of the poem. The main lexical fields are summarized in Table 4.4.

Table 4.4 Lexical fields in *Ironing*

Lexical field	Lexical items
Human body	*arms, breast, lungs, heart, hoof, nerves*
Domestic linen and clothes	*sheets, towels, sleeves, blouse, silk, cloth, buttons*
Heavy industry	*iron, crane, welders, Jarrow, tug, hot metal, wires*
Smooth	*pressed, thinness, creaseless, flatten, airy, shape*
Wrinkled or untidy	*flex, twisting, crinkling, crumpledness, wrinkled, frayed*

Jeffries and McIntyre (2010: 59) note the most pronounced lexical fields in the poem *Ironing* as two sets of contrasting pairs: one contrasts "domestic linen and clothes" with "heavy industry", while the other juxtaposes "smooth" and "wrinkled or untidy". The poem unfolds in three sections, where the last part resolves the tension introduced in the initial two.

In the first section (Stanzas 1 to 5), the protagonist irons a variety of domestic items, signifying a stage in life consumed by tasks involving sheets and towels. The second section (Stanza 6) reflects a cessation of this activity, with no ironing occurring at all. The final section (Stanzas 7 to 9) sees a return to ironing, but this time it appears to be limited to her own clothing.

While the first part features the distinction between "domestic linen and clothes" and "heavy industry", it is unlikely that a poem about ironing has a heavy industry theme. A reading of the whole poem reveals that the real divide in the domestic sphere is between items that are communally owned and personal belongings. Additionally, a split exists in the field of smoothness—between absolute, almost vicious flatness and *an airy shape*, "the latter being three-dimensional and allowing for life to inhabit the cloth, as opposed to the earlier two-dimensional, and by implication, lifeless, pressing" (Jeffries and McIntyre, 2010: 59).

The semantic structure of *Ironing* cleverly sets up a dichotomy within its lexical fields, suggesting, for example, an assumption that fabric must be either flat or wrinkled, and then subverts this notion by suggesting there are other states fabrics can embody. Among these alternatives is a three-dimensional, yet smooth state that symbolizes a more nuanced view of life and vitality beyond the binary of "smooth" versus "wrinkled".

4.4.3 Sense relations between lexical items

Sense relations among lexical items are typically divided into two broad categories: paradigmatic and syntagmatic sense relations. Paradigmatic sense relations operate within the sets of choices, while syntagmatic sense relations are an expression of coherence constraints. Moreover, paradigmatic and syntagmatic sense relations function in tandem, syntagmatic relations delimiting the space within which paradigmatic relations operate (Cruse, 2014: 133). Within the context of stylistic analysis, paradigmatic sense relations hold considerable importance and can be subdivided further into two distinct types: those concerning identity and inclusion, and those involving opposition and exclusion.

4.4.3.1 Paradigmatic relations of identity and inclusion

Paradigmatic relations of identity and inclusion include hyponymy, meronymy, and synonymy. The first two are closely related to the notion of *lexical field*, and provide us a more delicate way to analyze a lexical field.

In Table 4.4, the first lexical set serves as an example of meronymy, referring to the part-whole relationship. Within this field, terms like *arms*, *breast*, *lungs*, *heart*, *hoof*, and *nerves* are meronyms (or partonyms) relating to their respective whole, the human body, which is the holonym. The subsequent fields in the same table demonstrate hyponymy, the semantic relationship denoting subordination, whereby a term represents a more specific instance within a broader category. For instance, in the second lexical field, *blouse* is a hyponym to the broader category of *domestic clothes*, signifying its more specific nature. Conversely, *domestic clothes* functions as a hypernym (or superordinate) to *blouse*, indicating the broader category to which *blouse* belongs.

Lexical items entering the sense relations of hyponymy and meronymy usually form a system, construing a specific semantic domain. As a document that summarizes the national achievements over a fixed period of time and that outlines the missions and strategies for the future developments, *The Report to the 20th National Congress of the Communist Party of China*, offers plentiful examples.

Example 4.17

我们开展了史无前例的反腐败斗争，以“得罪千百人、不负十四亿”的使命担当祛疴治乱，不敢腐、不能腐、不想腐一体推进，“打虎”、“拍蝇”、“猎狐”多管齐下，反腐败斗争取得压倒性胜利并全面巩固，消除了党、国家、军队内部存在的严重隐患，确保党和人民赋予的权力始终用来为人民谋幸福。

(We have waged a battle against corruption on a scale unprecedented in our history. Driven by a strong sense of mission, we have resolved to “offend a few thousand rather than fail 1.4 billion” and to clear our Party of all its ills. We have taken coordinated steps to see that officials do not have the audacity, opportunity, or desire to be corrupt, and we have used a combination of measures to “take out tigers,” “swat flies,” and “hunt down foxes,” punishing corrupt officials of all types. We have achieved an overwhelming victory and fully consolidated the gains in our fight against corruption. All this has helped remove serious hidden dangers in the Party, the country, and the military and ensured that the power granted to us by the Party and the people is always exercised in the interests of the people.)

In Example 4.17, corrupt officials, denoted by the Chinese terms 贪官污吏, are metaphorically described using the words 虎 (tiger), 蝇 (fly), and 狐 (fox), illustrating the different natures of corruption. In comparison, our society is characterized by the components 党 (party), 国家 (state), and 军队 (military). While both groups may be represented similarly in Figures 4.3 and 4.4, they embody different relational contexts; the former depicts a hyponymic relationship, where 虎, 狐, and 蝇 are specific instances of the general concept of corrupt officials. On the other hand, the latter illustrates a meronymic relationship, where 党, 国家, and 军队 are parts that constitute the whole that is society.

When combined, these relationships suggest that the battle against corruption is broad and encompasses various types of corrupt officials within the essential institutions of society. Notably, both 贪官污吏 and 社会 are enclosed in brackets in Figures 4.3 and 4.4 to indicate that their respective overarching terms—the hyperonym for corrupt officials and the holonym for parts of society—are not explicitly stated in the text. Moreover, sometimes a language may not provide a direct hyperonym or holonym, which, as discussed in Section 4.1, leads to lexical gaps, signifying areas where the vocabulary does not have a specific word to describe a particular concept or idea.

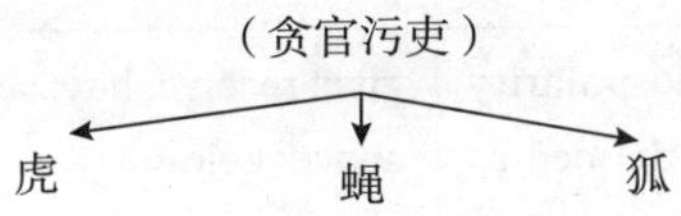

Figure 4.3 Corrupt officials

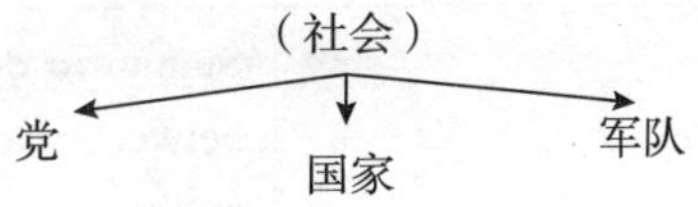

Figure 4.4 Society

Synonymy is the semantic relation of sameness or (strong) similarity in meaning (Bussmann, 2000). This relation can be illustrated by that between 不忘 and 牢记 in Example 4.18, both of which are translated as *never forget* in the English version.

Example 4.18

全党同志务必不忘初心、牢记使命，……

(It is imperative that all of us in the Party never forget our original aspiration and founding mission, …)

4.4.3.2 Paradigmatic relations of opposition and exclusion

As illustrated in Figures 4.3 and 4.4, a superordinate has more than one immediate hyponym and a holonym has more than one meronym. The relation between hyponyms and meronyms is that of exclusion.

Opposition can be classified into two categories: conventional and discursive opposition. Conventional opposition is the object of study in linguistics, and discursive opposition is the contribution made by stylistics.

Table 4.5 provides a summary of conventional opposition.

Table 4.5 Different types of opposites

Opposition		Definition	Examples
Complementarity		Complementarities partition a conceptual area into two mutually exclusive compartments.	dead: alive, true: false, continue: stop
Antonymy	Polar	A single scale is involved, with a zero at one end and extending indefinitely in the other direction.	heavy: light
	Equipollent	Two scales are involved, pointing in opposite directions, with their zeroes adjacent to one another.	hot: cold
	Overlapping	Two scales are involved here, but they overlap, with the zero of the negative scale situated halfway up the positive scale.	good: bad
Reversion		Movement (or more generally, change) in opposite directions.	rise: fall, advance: retreat
Conversion		Semantic opposition denoting the polarity between two-place predicates and defined as an equivalence relation.	give: receive, buy: sell, father: son, above: below

Opposition is frequently employed in literary works. In the poem *Mean Time*, Duffy masterfully combines a pair of reversives *shorten-lengthen* with two complementary pairs *endless-finite* and *day-night*. In the process, the poet creates a new, converse relationship for this context, which accurately characterizes the Winter Solstice as a time marked by a decrease in daylight and an extension of night:

> These are the shortened days
> and the endless nights.

Duffy selectively utilizes one element from each oppositional pair—*lengthen-shorten* and *endless-finite*—to construct a paradigmatic relationship that blends contrasting concepts for the reader. This stylistic choice confronts readers with the tangible process of days dwindling in length, while nights grow ostensibly limitless, though the actual lengthening of nights is only inferred. Consequently, the poem communicates a dual sensation of symmetry and asymmetry: days that seem increasingly brief are counterbalanced by nights that feel never-ending. This depiction grasps the essence of winter in the northern hemisphere, where despite the known symmetrical progression of seasons, the perceptual experience can feel disproportionately gloomy (Jeffries, 2014: 62).

Jeffries (2014: 2–3) introduces the concept of discursive opposition, which pertains to oppositions formed within specific textual contexts. She illustrates this concept with an example that features an image of a black man underscored by a provocative slogan:

Labour says he's black. Tories say he's British.

The slogan adopts a parallel structure: X says Y is Z, where "X" represents political parties (Labor and Conservative), and "Z" denotes the attributes *black* and *British*. This setup leads readers to anticipate a dichotomy between the descriptors "black" and "British" in the concluding segments of each sentence.

The advertisement's parallel structure and traditional party oppositions cunningly craft "black" and "British" as binaries. The implied message is that Labor's identification of the man as "black" negates his "Britishness," suggesting an either/or scenario regarding racial and national identity. Contrarily, the Conservative standpoint is framed as inclusive and non-biased, implying they do not see race ("color blind") and therefore consider everyone as "British" irrespective of ethnicity.

Jeffries (2014: 3) posits that the constructed opposition between "black" and "British" is indicative of an underlying assumption that these identifiers might be mutually exclusive—an individual cannot be both "black" and "British". The presence of this opposition subtly caters to the biases of those who may harbor racist sentiments, as it reinforces the notion of incompatibility between racial identity and national belonging.

4.4.3.3 Homonymy and polysemy

In the study of linguistics, alongside the paradigmatic sense relations previously described, we also encounter concepts like homonymy and polysemy, which delve into the nuanced ways in which words can have different meanings.

Homonymy concerns itself with words that share the same phonological (sound) and orthographic (spelling) forms but carry distinct meanings. An example is the word *meter,* which can denote either a measure of length or a device for recording measurements; they are pronounced and spelled identically but do not share related meanings.

Polysemy, on the other hand, describes a single word that bears multiple meanings, closely interrelated by extension or metaphor. For instance, *green* can mean fresh, inexperienced, or the color green, with each sense originating from a shared conceptual root.

Homonymy and polysemy are distinct from one another in that homonyms have meanings that are usually unrelated semantically, whereas the meanings in polysemy are related.

It's important to note that words may share the same spelling or pronunciation, but not necessarily both. Homographic words have the same orthography but may differ in meaning and pronunciation, such as the two pronunciations of *wind*—to *wind* a clock (verb) contrasts with a gust of *wind* (noun).

Conversely, homophonic words are pronounced the same but have different orthographies and meanings, exemplified by pairs such as *pray* (to make a religious request) and *prey* (an animal hunted for food), or *course* (a path or direction) and *coarse* (rough texture).

4.4.4 Seven types of meaning

In Section 4.4.3, it has been demonstrated that sense relationships essentially pertain to the connections between concepts. However, it's important to recognize that conceptual meaning represents only a fraction of the full spectrum of lexical meaning. According to Leech (1974: 10–27), there are six additional types of meaning that complement conceptual meaning. These are collectively summarized in Table 4.6.

Table 4.6 Seven types of meaning

1. CONCEPTUAL MEANING		Logical, cognitive, or denotative content
ASSOCIATIVE MEANING	2. CONNOTATIVE MEANING	What is communicated by virtue of what language refers to.
	3. SOCIAL MEANING	What is communicated of the social circumstances of language use.
	4. AFFECTIVE MEANING	What is communicated of the feelings and attitudes of the speaker/writer.
	5. REFLECTED MEANING	What is communicated through association with another sense of the same expression.
	6. COLLOCATIVE MEANING	What is communicated through association with words which tend to occur in the environment of another word.
7. THEMATIC MEANING		What is communicated by the way in which the message is organized in terms of order and emphasis.

Based on Leech's (1974: 10–27) own analysis of the seven categories of meaning, they are briefly introduced and illustrated here. CONCEPTUAL MEANING is sometimes also called "denotative" or "cognitive" meaning, and is commonly accepted as the central factor in linguistic communication. This form of meaning is frequently analyzed by drawing on distinctive features, similar to those used in phonetic descriptions. To illustrate, the word *woman* can be analytically represented by the features +HUMAN, –MALE, and +ADULT. This analytical approach differentiates it from the word *boy*, which can be characterized as +HUMAN, +MALE, and –ADULT.

CONNOTATIVE MEANING is the communicative value an expression has by virtue of what it refers to, over and above its purely conceptual content. In other words, connotative meaning is based on the "real world" experience one associates with an expression when one uses or hears it. While the word *woman* is primarily defined by its conceptual components (+HUMAN, –MALE, +ADULT), there are numerous non-definitive attributes typically associated with a woman that individuals learn to recognize. These attributes can be physical (like "biped", "having a womb"), psychological (such as "gregarious", "subject to maternal instinct"), or even stereotypical traits ("capable of speech", "experienced in cookery", "skirt-or-dress-wearing") that may not always universally apply.

Furthermore, connotative meaning encompasses perceived characteristics influenced by specific perspectives or biases held by individuals, groups, or entire societies. Historically, women have been ascribed a variety of qualities—both negative ("frail", "prone to tears", "cowardly", "emotional", "irrational", "inconstant") imputed by patriarchal views, as well as positive ("gentle", "compassionate", "sensitive", "hard-working"). It's important to note that connotative meanings are not static; they shift with time and vary across different cultures. For example, a century ago, "not wearing trousers" was a significant connotative aspect of womanhood in European contexts, while in some non-Western societies today, womanhood may imply attributes that differ from Western conceptualizations.

It's also clear that connotative meanings can differ among individuals within the same linguistic community. To an English speaker with misogynistic views, the word *woman* may invoke unfavorable connotations that wouldn't occur to someone with feminist viewpoints.

SOCIAL MEANING pertains to the insights conveyed by language use regarding the societal context in which it occurs. In part, the social meaning of a text is "decoded" through the recognition of varying styles and levels within a language, which inform us about the social and geographical background of the speaker or the nature of the relationship between the interlocutors. Certain words or accents, categorized as dialectal, can reveal the user's origin, while other linguistic cues might inform us about the dynamics between a speaker and listener, such as formality or intimacy.

Advertisers often utilize language that harbors specific associations with their intended audience. For instance, a record store in Lancaster named *Ear 'Ere* cleverly aligns itself with a demographic that typically drops the "h" in their pronunciation—a widespread trait often marginalized by educational institutions. In this name, the words *hear* and *here* are homophones, as is *ear* when articulated without the initial *h*. This allows the name to playfully double as *hear it here*, referring to the act of listening to music at the store, and echo the phrase *hear hear*, traditionally used to express agreement during discussions in British Parliament. Thus, the store's name engages with social meaning by leveraging linguistic nuances to foster a sense of belonging with a particular community.

AFFECTIVE MEANING addresses the way language expresses a speaker's personal emotions, attitudes toward the listener, or feelings about the subject being discussed. It is often explicitly conveyed through the conceptual or connotative content of the words used. A direct expression, such as *You're a vicious tyrant and a villainous reprobate, and I hate you for it!* leaves no ambiguity about the speaker's negative feelings towards the individual addressed.

Considering the affective meaning in advertising, like in an estate agent's ad, the emotion or attitude intended to be conveyed becomes more obvious when compared to a neutral description. For example, an ad stating *A superb family detached home, close to amenities, full of character* is designed to evoke positive emotional responses by using complimentary adjectives and invoking a sense of convenience and charm. If this description were neutralized to *A house that is separate from others and near shops*, the affective allure would be substantially diminished, focusing solely on practical features without emotional appeal.

For a comprehensive treatment of affective meaning within linguistic studies, one can refer to Martin and White (2005), which offers a more detailed examination of how affect is communicated through language.

REFLECTED MEANING is the meaning which arises in cases of multiple conceptual meaning, when one sense of a word forms part of our response to another sense. In Example 4.19, *giving the bride away* is a phrase that traditionally means a father handing over his daughter to the groom during a wedding ceremony—an idiom rooted in cultural practice. However, when juxtaposed with the information about the high average cost of weddings, the phrase also invokes its literal sense of giving something away at no cost, which creates a humorous contrast because weddings are obviously expensive. This incongruity between the idiomatic and literal meanings gives rise to a reflected meaning that comments on the irony of the situation.

In Example 4.16, the word 大德 acquires a new sense when forming a system with the other two items 公德 and 私德, but it also has the reflected meaning derived from its original contrast with 小德.

Example 4.19

The average cost of a wedding is now £7,359. And they still call it giving the bride away.

COLLOCATIVE MEANTNG consists of the associations a word acquires on account of the meanings of words which tend to occur in its environment. This aspect of meaning is not about isolated words but how they combine and interact in linguistically customary ways. Although *pretty* and *handsome* both essentially refer to aesthetic appeal or being "good-looking," they are differentiated by the range of nouns with which they are likely to co-occur or (to use the linguist's term) collocate:

pretty	handsome
girl	boy
boy	man
woman	car
flower	vessel
garden	overcoat
color	airliner
village	typewriter
etc.	etc.

The ranges may well, of course, overlap: *handsome woman* and *pretty woman* are both acceptable, although they suggest a different kind of attractiveness because of the collocative associations of the two adjectives. Further examples are quasi-synonymous verbs such as *wander* and *stroll* (*cows* may *wander*, but may not *stroll*) or *tremble* and *quiver* (one *trembles* with *fear*, but *quivers* with *excitement*).

As reflected meaning and collocative meaning, affective meaning and social meaning all have more in common with connotative meaning than with conceptual meaning; they all have the same open-ended, variable character, and lend themselves to analysis in terms of scales or ranges, rather than in discrete either-this-or-that terms. Thus, they are brought together under the heading of ASSOCIATIVE MEANNING in Table 4.6.

The final category of meaning is THEMATIC MEANING, or what is communicated by the way in which a speaker or writer organizes the message in terms of ordering, focus, and emphasis. This meaning is not made by a single lexical item but by the syntactic structure, and it is introduced here for the purpose of completeness. Example 4.20a is about Mrs Bessie Smith, while Example 4.20b is about the first prize.

Example 4.20

a. Mrs Bessie Smith donated the first prize.

b. The first prize was donated by Mrs Bessie Smith.

4.4.5 Rhetorical devices based on lexical meaning

A lot of rhetorical devices are usually said to be based on lexical items. In fact, they arise from playing with lexical meaning. With the concepts introduced above, the rhetorical devices can be analyzed and classified as follows (张德禄，张国，张淑杰，等, 2016: 34–39) (see Table 4.7).

Table 4.7 Rhetorical devices

Play with meaning	Rhetorical devices	Semantic concepts
Meaning transference	Simile, metaphor, personification	Lexical/semantic field
	Synecdoche, metonymy	Meronymy
Contradiction in logic	Oxymoron, paradox	Antonymy
Meaning extension and contradiction	Hyperbole, meiosis (litotes)	Antonymy
Meaning conversion	Irony	Polysemy, homonymy, antonymy
Semantic correlation	Pun	Homonymy, polysemy, reflected meaning

Meaning transference refers to the phenomenon where a word's meaning is extended or transferred either within its current semantic domain or to a different semantic field altogether. This can happen through various rhetorical and figurative devices.

Synecdoche and metonymy are examples of meaning transference within the same semantic domain. Synecdoche, closely related to meronymy, involves using a part to refer to a whole or vice versa (e.g., "wheels" for "car"), while metonymy involves using a word closely associated with a concept to stand in for the concept itself (e.g., "the White House" to refer to the U.S. President or presidential actions).

On the other hand, simile, metaphor, and personification represent cross-domain transference, where the meaning moves between unrelated semantic fields. A simile directly compares two distinct things by connecting them with words such as "like" or "as" (e.g., "as brave as a lion"), a metaphor implies the comparison by stating one thing is another (e.g., "time is a thief"), and personification gives human characteristics to non-human entities (e.g., "the wind whispered through the trees"). These figures of speech transfer meaning from one realm (literal or conceptual) to another to enhance understanding, provide emphasis, or create imagery.

Contradiction in logic occurs when terms that are logically opposed to each other, known as antonyms, are juxtaposed. When this juxtaposition of contradictory terms results in a single word or phrase that presents an apparent contradiction, it is known as an oxymoron. An example of an oxymoron is the phrase *living death*, which combines the contradictory concepts of life and death.

On the other hand, when contradictory terms are combined in a manner that produces a statement which conflicts with itself on a logical level, this creates a paradox. A paradox is a statement that appears to be self-contradictory or illogical, but on closer examination may reveal an underlying truth. The statement "It was the best of times; it was the worst of times" is paradoxical because it asserts two opposing evaluations of the same time period, inviting the reader to explore a deeper complexity within the context.

In the opening stanza of Carol Rumens' poem *Song of the Non-existent*, various literary devices are at play that demonstrate meaning transference and the use of logical contradiction to create evocative imagery.

This is the hour between dog and wolf, when the first
Anxiety walks across to the polished counter,
And the sky becomes lighter and darker at the same time,
And the moon, if it shows, is a pale, inessential detail

The phrase *the hour between dog and wolf* presents a time that is neither day nor night, evoking an ambiguous, transitional moment. Traditionally, the dog could represent domesticity and daylight while the wolf might symbolize wildness and night. Placing these nouns where one might expect a reference to a specific time of day leads the reader to infer that twilight is suggested here. This expression relies on metonymy, as it uses creatures associated with day and night to represent the time of day.

When Rumens describes *anxiety* as walking across to the polished counter, the emotion (which is abstract) is given the physical action of an animate being. This is an example of personification, where an inanimate concept is described with life-like qualities, in this case, imbuing anxiety with humanlike agency and movement.

Lastly, describing the sky as *becoming lighter and darker at the same time* juxtaposes antonyms to create an oxymoron that captures a complex visual phenomenon. It suggests the paradoxical nature of dusk, a time when the fading light of day mixes with the encroaching darkness of night, creating a layered interplay of light.

Every one of these lines contributes to the overall atmosphere of the poem, which is charged with contradictions and rich, ambiguous imagery that goes beyond the literal meanings of the words.

Meaning extension and contradiction refer to what are traditionally known as overstatement and understatement, which, in rhetoric, are referred to as hyperbole and meiosis. Hyperbole is a rhetorical device involving exaggerated language intended to provoke a strong emotional response or create a sense of emphasis that could lead to a reevaluation or heightened perception of the subject. An example of hyperbole is the phrase *dead tired*, which does not literally mean deceased but rather extremely exhausted.

Meiosis is a broader category of understatement that subtly downplays the significance of something in order to convey a point. Within this category is litotes, a specific type of meiosis that makes use of negation to emphasize the opposite quality, often with ironic or humorous effect. For instance, the statement *He is not the wisest man in the world* employs litotes to suggest that the person is far from wise, potentially implying that he is quite foolish, without directly stating it.

Irony often involves using language that signifies the opposite, typically for humorous or emphatic effect. It is characterized by expressions that may seem ambiguous or contradictory, but through context and tone, point to a meaning that is different from, and often the opposite of, what is said. This is usually achieved by employing polysemy (a single word having multiple meanings), homonymy (different words that sound alike but have different meanings), or antonymy (using words that are opposite in meaning).

For example, saying *You are charming* when the person's behavior is actually unpleasant can be an instance of irony. The literal compliment is contradicted by the speaker's tone or the context of the situation, signaling that the intended message is in fact "You are mean." This ironic use of language relies on the listener's ability to recognize the dissonance between the words used and the situation at hand to understand the true meaning behind the statement.

A pun is a form of wordplay that exploits multiple meanings of a term or terms with similar sounds but different meanings for an intended humorous or rhetorical effect. The example provided from Xu Yuanchong's translation of Chairman Mao's poem exemplifies this play on words through the clever use of homophones—words that are pronounced the same but have different meanings.

The line *To face the powder, not powder the face* displays a pun where the word *powder* and *face* are used in two different semantic ways. *Powder* in the first instance is used as a noun to represent gunpowder, suggesting action or confrontation usually in the context of conflict or war. In the second instance, *powder* is used as a verb that means to apply a cosmetic powder to the face, a common beauty practice. Similarly, *face* is used first as a verb which could imply to confront or deal with a challenging situation bravely, and then as a noun indicating the front part of the head where makeup would be applied.

The artful juxtaposition in this pun serves not only as a means for evoking humor but also as a tool for highlighting contrast between the seriousness of warfare compared with the trivial act of applying makeup, thereby conveying a deeper message within the poem. The pun, therefore, is not merely for entertainment but also enables a layered understanding of the underlying themes the poet wishes to express.

Exercises:

1. What are the concepts used to analyze the structure of words? Are they applicable to the analysis of Chinese words?

2. English new words have been constantly invented for the convenience of communication. Please analyze the word formation of the following latest coinages: *bedgasm*, *chairdobe*, *textpectation*, *cellfish*, *errorist*, *hiberdating*, *youniverse*, *onlineness*. You can add more to this list as new coinages are being made right now. And you are encouraged to invent new words by and for yourself.

3. Find any two texts preferably from two genres or two writers with different styles, and make a comparison of the words used in them in terms of their classes. If there are any differences, try to provide an explanation.

4. In Section 4.3.1, the first stanza of *Jabberwocky* is interpreted based on an analysis of nouns and verbs used in it. Please try to figure out the meaning of the other stanzas by analyzing the classes of words used in them.

5. *love is more thicker than forget* is a famous love poem by e.e. cummings. Its words and grammar are very simple, but its theme is elusive. Please analyze it using the concepts explained in this chapter.

love is more thicker than forget
more thinner than recall
more seldom than a wave is wet
more frequent than to fail

it is most mad and moonly
and less it shall unbe
than all the sea which only
is deeper than the sea

love is less always than to win
less never than alive
less bigger than the least begin
less littler than forgive

it is most sane and sunly
and more it cannot die
than all the sky which only
is higher than the sky

Chapter 5

Sentence and Stylistic Analysis

5.1 From word to sentence and from lexis to grammar

Chapter 4 extensively covers an array of subjects concerning words, including word formation, word classes, lexical meaning, sense relations between words, and rhetorical devices primarily resulting from the play of (components of) words. As language users, we are aware that we combine words to create sentences in our communication. This section delves into the process and implications of forming sentences through the arrangement of words.

5.1.1 Units between word and sentence

In Examples 5.1a and 5.1b, a Chinese sentence from *The Report to the 20th National Congress of the Communist Party of China* is presented, along with its English translation. However, a sentence is not merely a simple linear string of words, as depicted in Figures 5.1a and 5.1b.

Example 5.1a

制造业规模、外汇储备稳居世界第一。

Example 5.1b

China's manufacturing sector is the largest in the world, as are its foreign exchange reserves.

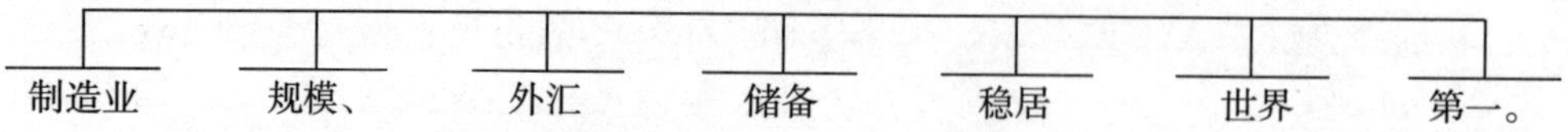

Figure 5.1a Example 5.1a

China's manufacturing sector is the largest in the world, as are its foreign exchange reserves.

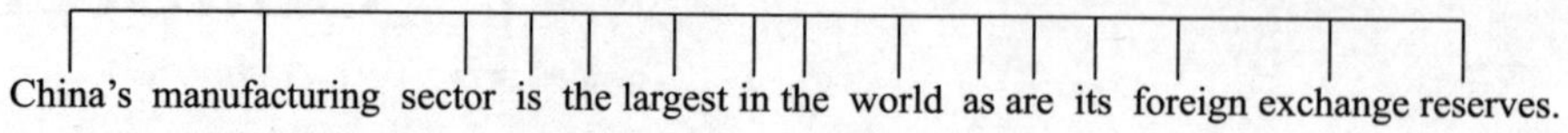

Figure 5.1b Example 5.1b

Considering a sentence as a mere collection of words implies that all words have an equal significance in contributing to the formation of a sentence. However, this viewpoint falls short of capturing the complex structure of a sentence. Halliday (2008: 310) holds that describing a sentence as a construction of words is rather like describing a house as a construction of bricks, without recognizing the walls and the rooms as intermediate structural units. Similarly, there exist intermediary units between sentences and words. Figure 5.1a' illustrates that the sentence is immediately composed of three units, denoted as (1), (2), and (3). These units differ in terms of their components. The first unit comprises two sub-units, each containing two words. The second unit consists of a single word, and the third unit comprises two words. While Figure 5.1b' represents the English translation of 5.1a, it demonstrates a more complex structure with an additional level above the units marked by bracketed numbers.

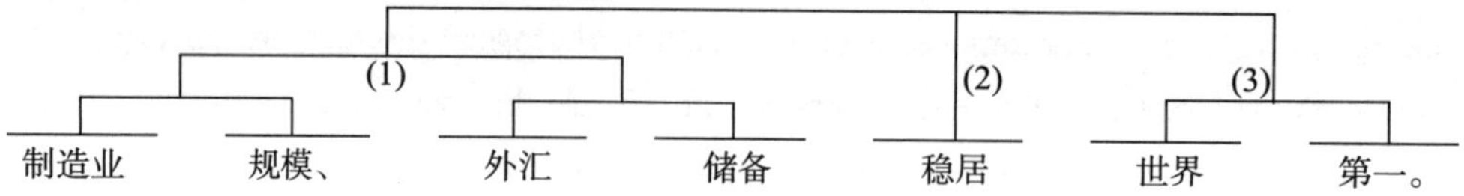

Figure 5.1a' Example 5.1a

China's manufacturing sector is the largest in the world, as are its foreign exchange reserves.

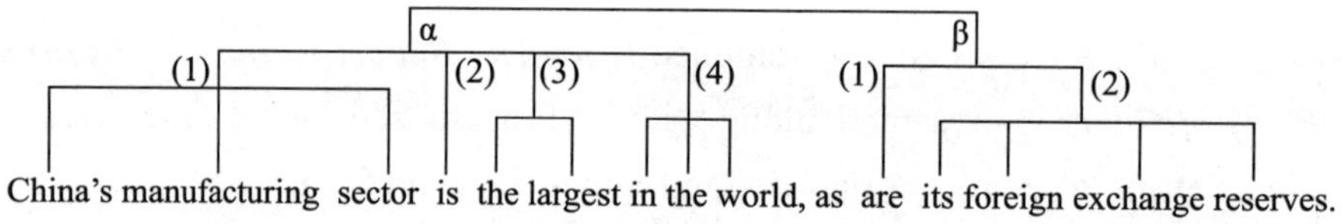

Figure 5.1b' Example 5.1b

When analyzing language from a structuralist perspective, the units directly below the sentence [identified as α and β in Figure 5.1b'] are referred to as clauses. Additionally, the units below the clause [marked as (1), (2), (3), and (4) in Figures 5.1a' and 5.1b'] are collectively known as phrases according to Crystal (1995: 217).

Functional linguistics posits that the connections between clauses and phrases, as well as between phrases and words, are structural relationships. This means that a clause is formed structurally from phrases, and a phrase is formed structurally from words. However, the relationship between a sentence and a clause is non-structural. Instead, clauses are linked to one another in clause complexes through projection and logico-semantic relations (Halliday, 2008: 363) (see Figure 5.8 in Section 5.4.2.1). For instance, clause α and clause β are linked together through a comparison. Therefore, a clause is considered the largest structural unit.

Additionally, functional linguistics categorizes the unit referred to as phrases above into two types: word groups and phrases. A word group is an extension of a single word, while a phrase is a contraction of a clause. In Example 5.1a, 制造业规模, 外汇储备, and 世界第一 can all be contracted into single words, so they are considered word groups. Similarly, in Example 5.1b, *China's manufacturing sector*, *the largest*, and *its foreign exchange reserves* are also word groups because each of them has a head word. Figures 5.1a and 5.1b also contain 3 immediate units of clause which just consist of one word each: Unit (2) in Figure 5.1a' (稳居), Unit (2) in Clause α and Unit (1) in Clause β in Figure 5.1b' (*is* and *are*). These units are also considered word groups because they are expandable. For example, 稳居 could be expanded into 稳居在, and *is* and *are* can be expanded into *has been* and *have been*. On the other hand, Unit (4) in Figure 5.1b' (i.e., *in the world*) is an example of a phrase for the reason that none of the three words in it can be chosen to stand for the whole unit.

Crystal (1995: 217) employs the term "level", while Halliday (2008: 31–32) employs the term "rank", to describe the various types of units mentioned earlier. Halliday (2008: 32) visualizes the relationships between clauses, word groups/phrases, words, and morphemes in terms of ranks in Figure 5.2.

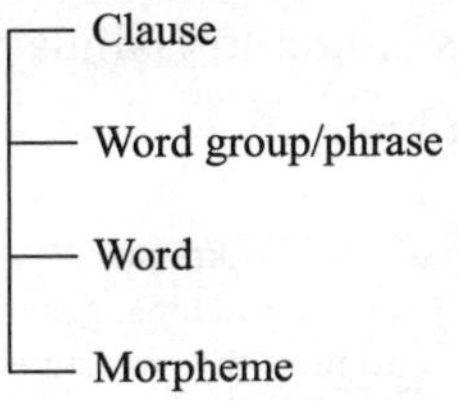

Figure 5.2 Ranks of linguistic units

Referring to Figure 5.2, Example 5.1a can be described as a sentence composed of one clause, which in turn consists of three word groups. The first word group is a word group complex, where two word groups of equal status are combined. Each of these word groups is made up of two words. The second word group consists of a single word, while the third word group consists of two words.

Example 5.1b presents a clause complex where two clauses are linked through a comparison relation. The first clause is comprised of three word groups and one phrase. The first word group consists of three words, the second word group consists of one word, and the third word group consists of two words. Additionally, the phrase in the first clause consists of three words. The second clause, on the other hand, consists of two word groups. The first word group consists of one word, and the second word group consists of four words. Furthermore, the words in these examples can be further analyzed in terms of their constituent morphemes.

5.1.2 Lexico-grammar as a stratum of language

Structurally, words are the basic, indivisible unit of language that can stand alone, while clauses, as mentioned above, are the largest structural unit. Beyond this basic distinction between words and clauses, linguists often make a further distinction between lexis and grammar. While words and clauses serve as fundamental components of language, lexis and grammar are two means whereby language makes meaning (Sinclair, 2004: 175).

Grammar is closely associated with clauses. Just as specific rules must be followed when building a house, such as placing the walls, roof, windows, and doors in their designated positions, rules must also be followed when constructing a clause. These rules govern the combination of morphemes to form words, the combination of words to form word groups or phrases, and the combination of word groups or phrases to form clauses. The systematic study of the rules governing morpheme combination is known as morphology (refer to Chapter 4 for more details). The rules that govern the combination of words and word groups or phrases are collectively referred to as grammar. These abstract rules are finite, yet they give rise to infinite clauses, which combine non-structurally to generate infinite sentences.

Grammar provides patterns of organization, and lexis produces items that fill places in the patterns. Lexical items are abstract linguistic units which might be words or combinations of words, and they have a direct connection with meaning (Sinclair, 2004: 131–133).

The proposed language model by Halliday, McIntosh and Strevens (1964) (refer to Chapter 2 for more details) introduces lexico-grammar as a stratum of language that construes the stratum of discourse and is realized by the stratum of phonology. According to Halliday (2008: 43–44), lexis and grammar are two poles of a single continuum, as illustrated in Figure 5.3.

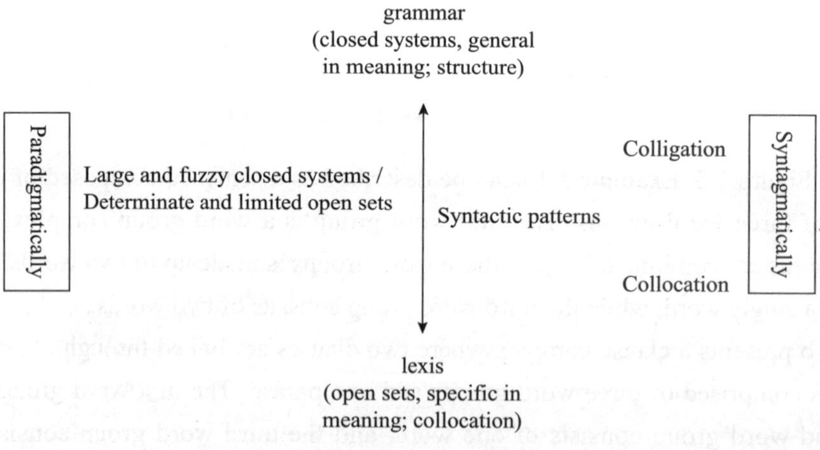

Figure 5.3 The lexico-grammar cline

According to Halliday (2008: 43–44), different techniques evolve to describe the two ends of the continuum: dictionary and thesaurus for lexis, the grammar book for grammar, and either of these techniques may be extended all the way along the continuum. For example, lexis, if approached from the end of grammar, can be referred to as the most delicate grammar.

Paradigmatically speaking, grammar tends to take the form of closed systems where meaning is derived from valeur. On the other hand, lexical items typically form open sets, with each item carrying a specific meaning. However, there exist intermediate categories, which can be considered as relatively large and fuzzy closed systems from a grammatical viewpoint, or somewhat definitive and limited open sets from a lexical perspective. For instance, prepositions, temporal and other specialized adverbs, and various types of conjunctions fall within this intermediate category (Halliday, 2008: 45).

Syntagmatically speaking, grammar generates syntagmatic structures, while lexical items exhibit collocational relationships with one another. Halliday (2008: 45) locates patterns in between structures and collocations around the midpoint, such as *take + pride/pleasure/delight + in ...-ing*. Sinclair (2004: 174) introduces various lexical structures that can be considered as points between grammatical structure and lexis, including collocation and colligation. Collocation refers to the regular co-occurrence of words, while colligation refers to the co-occurrence of words with specific grammatical choices.

Both collocation and colligation greatly contribute to stylistic analyses. For example, in Chapter 4, the analysis of the nonsensical writing *Jabberwocky* heavily relies on colligation. The presence of the determiner *the* before nouns such as *toves, wabe, borogoves,* and *raths* contributes to their identification. Furthermore, collocative meaning in Section 4.4.4 is unattainable without the presence of collocation.

Moreover, Chapter 4 has discussed the presence of lexical gaps which results from different lexicalization across languages. The translation of collocations serves as additional evidence to showcase the prevalence of different lexicalization. This is illustrated through Examples 5.2a and 5.2b. In the original version (Example 5.2a), the last three clauses utilize the same Chinese verb 发展. However, in the English version (Example 5.2b), the Chinese verb is translated into three different verbs (namely, *develop*, *cultivate*, and *support*), each collocating with a distinct nominal word group. This discrepancy implies that the concept represented by a single lexical item in Chinese is expressed by three distinct lexical items in English.

Example 5.2a

巩固和完善农村基本经营制度，发展新型农村集体经济，发展新型农业经营主体和社会化服务，发展农业适度规模经营。

Example 5.2b

We will consolidate and improve the basic rural operation system, develop new rural collective economies, cultivate new types of agribusiness and commercial agricultural services, and support appropriately scaled agricultural operations.

5.2 Syntactic ambiguity and different grammatical approaches

Intentional ambiguity adds an element of enjoyment to the use of language. Jeffries and McIntyre (2010: 54–55) and Leech (2013: 34–35) highlight ambiguity as a defining feature of poetic style. And even certain tests designed for non-native speakers intentionally include numerous ambiguous sentences for playful purposes. Ambiguity, to some extent, is intertwined with the creative use of language. Here are a few Chinese examples illustrating how humorous or creative efforts can be achieved through intentional ambiguity.

Example 5.3 下雨天留客天留我不留。

Example 5.4 这辆自行车没锁。

Example 5.5 鸡吃过了。

Example 5.6 以前喜欢一个人，现在喜欢一个人。

Ambiguity occurs due to a variety of reasons, one of which is the creation of the same sentence through different grammatical rules. In fact, disambiguating a sentence involves clarifying the distinct grammatical rules that govern the combination of words within the sentence. Linguists have invested significant efforts in uncovering the grammatical rules that govern word combinations. This section will introduce four approaches to analyzing clauses, offering insights into their structures and functions.

5.2.1 Component and Immediate Constituent Analysis (IC Analysis)

Section 5.1 clarifies that a sentence may contain one clause or a clause complex, and a clause consists of word groups or phrases. We can apply Immediate Constituent Analysis (IC analysis, a fundamental technique in syntactic analysis, involving breaking down a sentence, a clause or a word group/phrase into its immediate constituents) to determine the number of clauses and the number of word groups or phrases in each sentence.

Regarding Example 5.3, multiple analyses are possible①, which are illustrated below:

1. 4 clauses

Example 5.3' 下雨 | 天 || 留客 | 天 || 留 | 我 || 不留

2. 3 clauses

① The analyses in this section don't adopt the analytical method of binary cutting because it has been found that some linguistic expressions cannot be simply divided into two halves.

Example 5.3” 下雨天 || 留客天 | 留 || 我 | 不留

3. 3 clauses

Example 5.3’” 下雨天 || 留客天 | 留 || 我不 | 留

3. 2 clauses

Example 5.3”” 下雨天 || 留客天 | 留我 || 不留

In these analyses, the single vertical bar ‘|’ signifies the boundary of the linguistic unit at the primary level of division; whereas, the double vertical bar ‘||’ denotes the boundary of the linguistic unit at the secondary level of division. In Example 5.3’, the first-level linguistic unit is recognized as a clause, and the example comprises four such clauses. The first clause contains one verb phrase, while the other three clauses consist of two phrases each: the first being a noun phrase and the second being a verb phrase.

In both Examples 5.3” and 5.3’”, the first-level linguistic unit is also a clause, and both of them comprises three clauses each. The first clause in the two examples is the same, comprising two noun phrases. However, the second and third clauses differ in the two examples. In Example 5.3”, the second clause consists of a verb phrase followed by a noun phrase, and the third clause is a negated verb phrase. In Example 5.3’”, the second clause consists of a verb phrase plus a noun phrase followed by a clause particle which indicates the clause is an interrogative one, and the third clause is a verb phrase.

In Example 5.3””, the first-level linguistic unit is again a clause. And two clauses can be identified. The first clause remains the same as in Examples 5.3” and 5.3’”. The second clause contains two verb phrases.

Applying IC analysis allows us to break down the sentence and its clauses into its immediate constituents, identifying the hierarchical relationships between the constituents. The various analyses of Example 5.3 highlight the potential for different hierarchical constructions with distinct meanings from the same string of words, and thus disambiguate its ambiguity.

5.2.2 Parts of speech and Constituent Structure Grammar

Example 5.4 presents another sentence with ambiguity. However, an analysis based on immediate constituents reveals that there is only one way to analyze it into its constituents. The first-level linguistic unit is a phrase and there are two phrases in this example. Each phrase contains two words. This implies that constituent analysis alone is not sufficient to disambiguate this sentence.

Constituent structure grammar proves to be a better approach. By clarifying the grammatical class of the phrases, as demonstrated in Section 5.2.1, we are already adopting the perspective of constituent structure grammar. Additionally, this approach requires us to label each word in the phrase. By analyzing Example 5.4 and labeling the grammatical class of each word, we can identify two different ways to analyze the sentence (refer to Figure 5.4a and Figure 5.4b).

Example 5.4 这辆 || 自行车 | 没 || 锁。

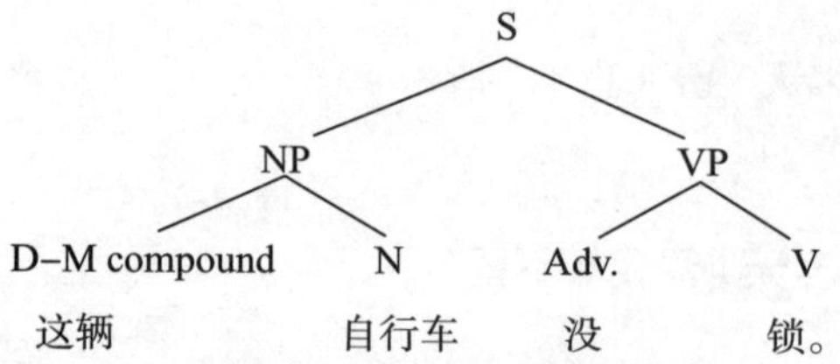

Figure 5.4a Example 5.4

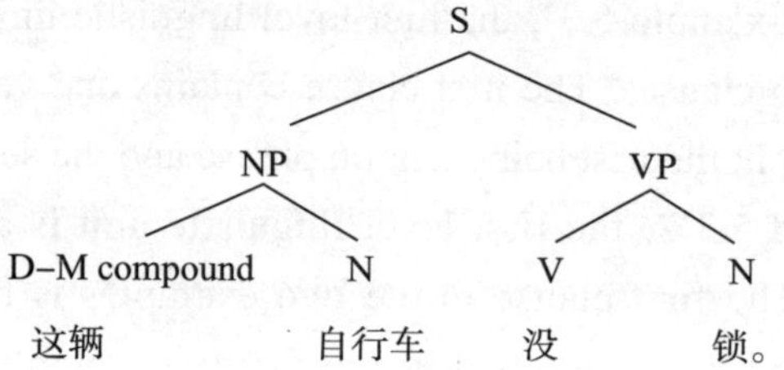

Figure 5.4b Example 5.4

In Figures 5.4a and 5.4b, the notation used is as follows:

- S represents the sentence.
- NP stands for noun phrase.
- VP stands for verb phrase.
- D-M compound refers to a determinative measure compound.
- N represents a noun.
- V represents a verb.

By employing these notations, we can visually represent the hierarchical structure and grammatical classes of the constituents within Example 5.4. The analyses depicted in Figure 5.4a and Figure 5.4b demonstrate that the same string of words can make different meanings when the words are assigned different grammatical classes, despite the fact that this string maintains a single hierarchical structure. This highlights the significance of considering the grammatical class of each word in understanding the semantic nuances and interpretations afforded by a sentence. By assigning distinct grammatical classes to the words within the same syntactic framework, we can derive multiple interpretations and uncover the influence of word class on meaning.

5.2.3 Surface and Deep Structures and Transformational Generative Grammar

The IC analysis of Example 5.5 reveals that the sentence consists of one clause, which is composed of two phrases. Approaching the analysis from the viewpoint of constituent structure grammar, we observe that the first phrase is a noun phrase, comprising a single noun. The second is a verb phrase, consisting of a verb followed by a phrase particle. The sentence is concluded with a clause particle. Both analyses indicate that this sentence possesses only one hierarchical structure wherein each constituent element can be assigned to a single grammatical class. However, despite this structural clarity, the sentence remains ambiguous.

Example 5.5' 鸡 | 吃过了。

Figure 5.5 presents one version of syntactic theory proposed by transformational generative grammar.

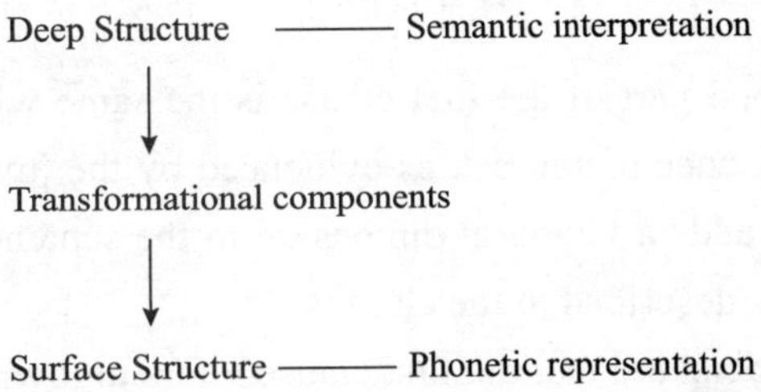

Figure 5.5 The theoretical model of the standard theory of syntax (Chomsky, 1965: 135–136)

The theoretical model partly aims to explain the relationship between the underlying meaning of a sentence (deep structure) and its actual surface form (surface structure). Deep structure refers to the abstract representation of a sentence that captures its underlying meaning and grammatical relations. It results from applying phrase structure rules to generate hierarchical structures. Deep structure represents the essential meaning and relationships between words and phrases, independent of specific linguistic features or word order. Surface structure, on the other hand, refers to the actual arrangement of words and phrases in a sentence, including features like word order, inflections, and function words. It is the visible and audible form of a sentence that is produced during verbal or oral communication.

According to transformational generative grammar, the transformational rules operate on the deep structure to generate the surface structure. Transformations handle operations such as movement, deletion, insertion, and substitution, which account for the syntactic variations we observe in different sentences with the same underlying meaning and the same visible and audible form of a sentence with different underlying meanings as well.

The sentence in Example 5.5 can have two possible deep structures. In one deep structure, the first noun phrase functions as the subject, and the second verb phrase functions as the predicate. In another deep structure, the first noun phrase functions as the object, while the second verb phrase functions as the predicate. Subject and object are syntactic roles that determine the syntactic relationships between different elements within a sentence.

This analysis highlights that syntactic roles, in conjunction with the syntactic structure and grammatical class, play a crucial role in constructing meaning. Depending on the assigned syntactic roles, the interpretation and intended meaning of the sentence can differ significantly.

5.2.4 Different functional roles and Systemic Functional Grammar

Example 5.6 consists of two clauses, both exhibiting the same hierarchical structures (see Example 5.6'). Within these clauses, each phrase and word can be assigned to a single grammatical class. Moreover, the phrases in both clauses serve identical syntactic roles, functioning as an adjunct, predicate, and object. This parallelism in syntactic patterns enhances the overall structural coherence and grammatical unity throughout the sentence.

Example 5.6' 以前 || 喜欢 ||| 一个人，| 现在 || 喜欢 |||① 一个人。

However, although the second part of the first clause is the same with the second part of the second clause, the two second parts introduce a contrast, as evidenced by the juxtaposition of the words 从前 (in the past) and 现在 (now) which adds a temporal dimension to the sentence, implying a shift or change in circumstances between the events described in the clauses.

Native Chinese speakers understand that the first clause refers to loving a specific individual, while the second clause implies a preference for being alone. How is it possible that the two second parts which are structurally and grammatically the same make different meanings? Systemic Functional Grammar (SFG) offers an explanation.

According to SFG, the two clauses functionally construe a mental figure, which is a configuration of three semantic roles, that is, Senser②, mental Process, and Phenomenon. The semantic role of Phenomenon can be realized by a nominal group construing a thing, an act or a fact (see more details in Section 5.4.2.2). Therefore, 一个人 in a mental figure can be interpreted as either a specific individual or the state of being alone. This flexibility is attributed to the same semantic role of Phenomenon, allowing for the different meanings to be made within the context of the clause.

In conclusion, the meaning making of a sentence relies on various elements, including its hierarchical structure, the grammatical class of its constituents, the syntactic roles assigned to its constituents, and the semantic roles carried by its constituents.

5.3 Descriptive Grammar and Stylistic Analysis

Section 5.2 just provides four grammatical frameworks that have been developed to explain the rules governing the formation of hierarchical structures, the combination of phrases and words belonging to different grammatical classes, and the combination of phrases fulfilling distinct syntactic and semantic roles. In fact, linguists have proposed several other frameworks for syntactic analysis, including case grammar, construction grammar, and cognitive grammar. While all of these approaches are capable of

① It indicates the third-level division.

② In SFG, functional labels have their initial letters capitalized.

providing accurate descriptions of language, they differ in their explanatory power. Some frameworks, such as TG grammar, SFG, and Cognitive Grammar, strive for explanatory adequacy and are extensively studied by linguists in the field of linguistics. It means that they are the primary focus of research conducted by university professors. On the other hand, there are grammatical frameworks that are designed for language learners and users and are content with their descriptive adequacy. These frameworks are referred to as descriptive grammar. However, the line between these types of grammar is not always clear-cut, as descriptive grammar often incorporates new developments and findings from linguistic research. In the area of stylistic analysis, various grammatical frameworks have been utilized. Due to the limitation of space, it is not possible to provide a detailed introduction to all of them in a chapter of a coursebook. Consequently, this section will primarily concentrate on descriptive grammar and its application in stylistic analysis. The subsequent section will introduce SFG, which aims to explain why language is the way it is from a functional perspective, and examine how it contributes to stylistic analysis.

Quirk et al. (1985) have produced a comprehensive and detailed guide to the descriptive grammar of the English language. This work combines descriptive analysis, functional explanations, corpus-based research, and insights from generative linguistics to offer readers a deep understanding of English structures and usage patterns in authentic language contexts. The concepts and analyses presented in this section draw heavily on Quirk et al. (1985), which serves as an invaluable resource for those seeking a thorough exploration of English grammar.

5.3.1 Clause structure

In Quirk et al.'s (1985) descriptive grammar, a clause consists of several structural elements, namely Subject (S), Verb (V), Object (O), Complement (C), and Adverbial (A). Based on these elements, Quirk et al. (1985) identify seven basic clause structures:

1. SV: Subject + Verb
2. SVA: Subject + Verb + Adverbial
3. SVC: Subject + Verb + Complement
4. SVO: Subject + Verb + Object
5. SVOO: Subject + Verb + Two Objects
6. SVOC: Subject + Verb + Object + Complement
7. SVOA: Subject + Verb + Object + Adverbial

These structural elements and basic clause structures, along with their variations, provide a systematic framework for analyzing texts. Below, we employ these structural elements and refer to the basic clause structures to analyze the poem *The Unprofessionals*, which is written by U. A. Fanthorpe, describing the actions of individuals, likely relatives and friends, who visit someone's house during a time of great distress. The patterns are summarized in Table 5.1.

Table 5.1 Clause types in *The Unprofessionals*

<table>
<tr><th>Type</th><th>A(dverbial)</th><th>S(ubject)</th><th>V(erb)</th><th>O(bject)</th><th>C(omplement)</th><th colspan="2">A(dverbial)</th></tr>
<tr><td>SV</td><td></td><td>the worst thing</td><td>happens</td><td></td><td></td><td colspan="2"></td></tr>
<tr><td>SVO</td><td></td><td>That</td><td>uproots</td><td>the future</td><td></td><td colspan="2"></td></tr>
<tr><td>SVOA</td><td></td><td>you</td><td>must live for</td><td>That</td><td></td><td colspan="2">every hour of your future</td></tr>
<tr><td>SV</td><td></td><td>They</td><td>come</td><td></td><td></td><td colspan="2"></td></tr>
<tr><td>C</td><td></td><td></td><td></td><td></td><td>Unorganised, inarticulate, unprofessional</td><td colspan="2"></td></tr>
<tr><td>SVAAA</td><td></td><td>They</td><td>come</td><td></td><td></td><td>sheepishly</td><td rowspan="3">From tea to tea, from Anadin to Valium</td></tr>
<tr><td>(S)VAAA</td><td></td><td></td><td>sit</td><td></td><td></td><td>with you</td></tr>
<tr><td>VOAA</td><td></td><td></td><td>holding</td><td>hands</td><td></td><td></td></tr>
<tr><td>VA</td><td></td><td></td><td>Sleeping</td><td></td><td></td><td colspan="2">on put-you-ups</td></tr>
<tr><td>VO</td><td></td><td></td><td>answering</td><td>the phone</td><td></td><td colspan="2"></td></tr>
<tr><td>VAA</td><td></td><td></td><td>Coming</td><td></td><td></td><td colspan="2">in shifts, spontaneously</td></tr>
<tr><td>VAA</td><td></td><td></td><td>Talking</td><td></td><td></td><td colspan="2">sometimes
About wallflowers, and fishing, and why</td></tr>
<tr><td>VO</td><td></td><td></td><td>Dealing with</td><td>Kleenex and kettles</td><td></td><td colspan="2"></td></tr>
<tr><td>VO</td><td></td><td></td><td>Doing</td><td>the washing up and the shopping</td><td></td><td colspan="2"></td></tr>
<tr><td>AAVOAA</td><td rowspan="2">Like civilians in a shelter, under bombardment</td><td></td><td>Holding</td><td>hands</td><td></td><td colspan="2" rowspan="2">Through the immortality of all the seconds,
Until the blunting of time.</td></tr>
<tr><td>AAVOCAA</td><td></td><td>sitting</td><td>it</td><td>out</td></tr>
</table>

The Unprofessionals

(U. A. Fanthorpe)

When the worst thing [S] happens [V],
That [S] uproots [V] the future [O],
That [O] you [S] must live for [V] every hour of your future [A],

They [S] come [V],
Unorganised [C], inarticulate [C], unprofessional [C];

They [S] come [V] sheepishly [A], sit [V] with you [A], holding [V] hands [O],
From tea to tea [A], from Anadin to Valium [A],
Sleeping [V] on put-you-ups [A], answering [V] the phone [O],
Coming [V] in shifts [A], spontaneously [A],

Talking [V] sometimes [A],
About wallflowers, and fishing, and why [A]
Dealing with [V] Kleenex and kettles [O],
Doing [V] the washing up and the shopping [O],

Like civilians in a shelter [A], under bombardment [A],
Holding [V] hands [O] and sitting [V] it [O] out [C]
Through the immortality of all the seconds [A],
Until the blunting of time [A].

5.3.2 Structural elements and phrases

To respect the tradition, the unit below clause is referred to as phrase. Quirk et al. (1985: 60) identify five formal categories of phrase: noun phrase, verb phrase, adjective phrase, adverb phrase, and prepositional phrase. The analysis summarized in Table 5.1 shows that there are complex relationships between structural elements and phrases. Quirk et al. (1985: 60) diagram the complex relationships in Figure 5.6.

Among the five formal categories, the verb and noun phrases are considered the most important phrasal categories for functional reasons. As shown by Figure 5.6, the verb phrase operates as the V element of a clause, i.e., the most central and indispensable part of the clause. The noun phrase is more important because of its multi-functionality. Figure 5.6 shows that it can function as any of the clause elements except V.

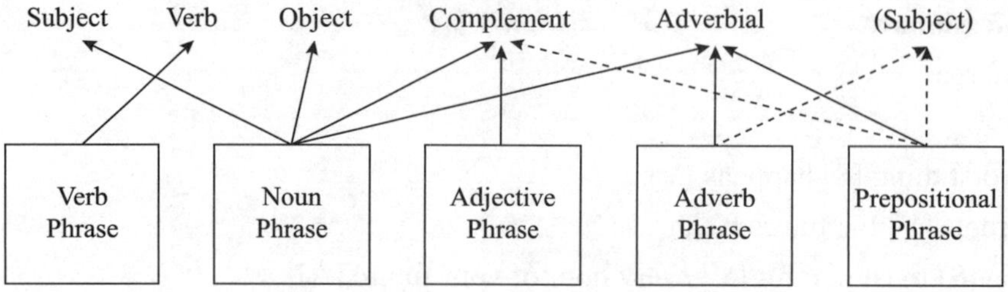

Figure 5.6 Phrases as clause elements

Table 5.1 illustrates the categorization of verb phrases into two groups: finite verb phrases (the first six) and non-finite verb phrases (the remaining nine). A finite verb phrase contains different kinds of grammatical information. Firstly, the **lexical verb** or **main verb** carries the meaning content, which in Table 5.1 are respectively *happen*, *uproot*, *live for*, *come*, *come*, and *sit*. Secondly, the finite verb phrase provides information about **tense**. In Table 5.1, all of the verb phrases are marked for the present tense. Thirdly, finite verb phrases also convey information about modality, which reflects the speaker's attitude towards the statement. Modality encompasses degrees of possibility, certainty, doubt, as well as information about obligation, permission, or suggestion. For instance, the verb phrase *must live for* in Table 5.1 includes the auxiliary *must*, indicating a high degree of possibility. Lastly, finite verb phrases can also carry information about **aspect**, which indicates whether an action or state is completed or ongoing. The first six verb phrases in Table 5.1 are all in the simple aspect①.

Non-finite verb phrases are less informative than finite verb phrases, as they are either in the form of an infinitive, in the form of a gerundive, or in the form of a past participle. All the nine non-finite verb phrases in Table 5.1 are in the form of a gerundive.

As shown in Figure 5.6, noun phrases can function as the S element, O element, C element, and A element. All the phrases functioning as the S and O elements in Table 5.1 are noun phrases, and *every hour of your future* functioning as the A element is also a noun phrase. These noun phrases can be analyzed in Table 5.2.

The analysis reveals that a noun phrase must have one and only one head. Additionally, a noun phrase can refer explicitly to a specific person or thing through a name (e.g., *Kleenex* in Table 5.2) or less explicitly through pronouns (e.g., *that*, *you*, *they*, and *it* in Table 5.2), where the context or co-text provides the necessary information about their referents.

A noun phrase can also refer more generally to something in the world by using common nouns, such as *kettles* and *hands* in Table 5.2. In such cases, it often becomes necessary to qualify or differentiate it from other similar entities. This can be achieved through modification, whereby the noun phrase is made more specific or elaborate. Nouns are frequently preceded by determiners, such as *the* and *every* in Table 5.2. Additionally, nouns can be further modified by adding information before the head itself, as seen with *worst* in Table 5.2. They can also be postmodified by adding information after the noun, such as *of your future* in Table 5.2.

① Quirk et al. (1985: 189) uses "simple" to describe a verb phrase totally unmarked for aspect.

Table 5.2 Noun phrases in *The Unprofessionals*

Determinative	Premodifier	Head	Postmodifier
		that	
		you	
		they	
		it	
		Kleenex and kettles	
		hands	
the		future	
the		phone	
the the		washing up and shopping	
the	worst	thing	
every		hour	of your future

Table 5.1 provides a summary of the analysis of each clause in *The Unprofessionals*. However, it is important to note that the clauses in the table do not hold equal status. In the first stanza, the clauses in the second and third lines actually function as postmodifiers of the noun *thing*.

Table 5.2 also has two examples where *and* is used to connect two nominal elements, namely *Kleenex and kettles* and *the washing up and the shopping*. In these instances, *and* serves to combine two distinct noun phrases. These examples demonstrate instances of noun phrase complex, where multiple noun phrases are connected using a coordinating conjunction.

5.3.3 Clause types and sentence types

A sentence is basically a unit of written language. Figures 5.1a' and 5.1b' demonstrate that a sentence can consist of either a single clause or multiple clauses. When a sentence comprises only one clause, it is referred to as a simple sentence; whereas, a sentence with multiple clauses is known as a multiple sentence (Quirk et al., 1985: 987).

Just as verb phrases within a clause can be either finite or non-finite, the clauses that make up a sentence can also be categorized as finite or non-finite clauses. Multiple sentences can be formed by combining finite clauses with one another or with non-finite clauses.

The initial nine lines of *The Unprofessionals* illustrate the complexity of multiple sentences. Firstly, a distinction can be made between compound and complex sentences. A compound sentence consists of two or more coordinated main clauses; the coordinated clauses are in a paratactic relationship (i.e., they are equal in status). A complex sentence has a main clause and one or more subordinate clauses. This distinction is evident in the following two sentences, which are rephrased from the two parts of the first nine lines, separated by a semicolon:

- When the worst thing happens, they come.
- They come sheepishly and sit with you.

Both sentences comprise only finite clauses. The first sentence is a complex one, with the first clause subordinate to the second. On the other hand, the second sentence is a compound one, which consists of two finite clauses joined by the coordinating conjunction *and*.

The original version of the second sentence is quite intricate, as it utilizes four non-finite clauses to provide further details about what *They* do after they come. All four non-finite clauses function as subordinate clauses, rendering the section following the semicolon a sentence that contains both coordinated and subordinate clauses.

The original version of the first sentence is even more complex. Firstly, the fifth line can be interpreted as a non-finite clause that could be expanded to *which is unorganized, inarticulate, and unprofessional*—a relative clause. Secondly, the two clauses in the second and third lines serve as post-modifiers to the noun *thing*. Consequently, these two clauses are not immediate components of the sentence but are ranked lower as part of the noun phrase. As a result, the original version of the first sentence consists of a main clause, a subordinate finite clause, a subordinate non-finite clause, and two down-ranked clauses.

5.3.4 An interpretation of *The Unprofessionals*

The analysis of *The Unprofessionals* goes beyond introducing descriptive notions for English sentence analysis, and has already conducted a systematic syntactic examination in Section 5.3.3. Jeffries (2014) interprets the poem as an affectionate account of the support people offer each other during challenging times. Her interpretation is extensively supported by systematic linguistic evidence. In the interest of pedagogy, her analysis and interpretation are introduced below, with additional linguistic evidence provided and terminologies adjusted to align with the concepts introduced above when applicable.

According to Jeffries (2014), the initial stanza of the poem aims to evoke a sense of unease in the reader. This uneasiness arises from the first stanza's deviation from the default relationship between information and clause structure. In English, information structure is typically connected to clause structure and can be understood through the following principles:

1. The predicator (i.e., verbal element) is pivotal to the sense of the clause;

2. Earlier clause elements normally contain given information;
3. Later clause elements normally contain new information;
4. There is therefore normally a correlation between given information and short clause elements, and between new information and longer clause elements;
5. If default clause structure is used, this means that grammatical subjects will be shorter on the whole than objects and complements;
6. Optional adverbials (adjuncts, disjuncts, and so on) will occur more readily towards the end of a clause, particularly if they are lengthy;
7. The predicator (verbal element) will occur relatively early in the clause;
8. Deviation from default syntax (such as fronting, passivization, cleft structures) will tend to uphold the principles of information structure as listed in 1–6.

Based on the aforementioned principles, the stylistic assumption is that readers have certain expectations when it comes to sentence structure. Any deviation from these expectations can elicit conscious or subconscious reactions from readers. In the opening three-line stanza of *The Unprofessionals*, the entire stanza consists of an adverbial subordinate clause, which is syntactically optional. The sentence would still be grammatically correct without this clause. Moreover, the clause is notably lengthy for an optional initial element and thus deviates from Principle 6 mentioned above. This deviation might frustrate the reader. It is unclear at this point what the sentence is specifically about or what action takes place within it. All we gather from this stanza is that it establishes the context of *when the worst thing happens*. As analyzed earlier, this adverbial clause itself is complex, as it contains two down-ranked clauses that provide further details about *the worst thing*. These details convey that this event irrevocably alters one's life (*That uprooting the future*) and demands their constant attention for every moment of their future (*That you must live for every hour of your future*). It is important to note that the context established in this stanza is general (*When*), applicable to an unknown or generalized individual, with the second-person pronoun assumed to refer to anyone. The context does not explicitly state what the "thing" is, leaving the reader to identify it as the "worst thing" they are most familiar with. Consequently, the reader may experience a sense of unease about the ominous possibilities that could befall anyone. Notably, this effect is achieved through a hypothetical adverbial clause that is categorical rather than modal—the use of *When* indicates that the worst thing will undoubtedly occur. Furthermore, the down-ranked clauses that function as post-modifiers to the noun *thing* also contribute to the categorical nature of the description, emphasizing that everything will be forever changed.

In the second stanza, the shortest in the poem, a sense of undermined relief is evoked. This feeling of relief stems from the introduction of the main clause and the deictic feature of the finite verb phrase *come*. When the first stanza concludes, the reader is left without a syntactic resolution in terms of a grammatical subject and verb. In Line 4, Stanza 2, *They come*. In a metalinguistic sense, the word [t]hey functions as the anticipated grammatical subject; while within the poem, it refers to the visitors. Although the identity of the visitors is not explicitly stated, the relief derived from finally reaching the subject may cause readers to overlook the lack of explicitness about referents. The focus shifts more towards the alleviation of frustration rather than the specific identity of "They". The brevity and directness of the main clause elements, after the preceding anticipation, may lead readers to believe that the problem at hand, whatever it may be, is resolved, as the syntax now feels complete. It is worth noting that the verb *come* is spatially deictic, indicating movement towards the deictic center of the person experiencing the crisis. As readers, we are positioned in that same space, potentially deepening our empathy. After the prolonged wait for the relief of companionship, there is no adverbial following the verb. "They" simply come without any specific purpose or action.

However, this relief is not absolute; it is undermined. The main clause *They come* occupies a line on its own, reinforcing the sense that the syntax is now complete. Nevertheless, additional optional elements of the sentence are provided in Line 5, specifically *Unorganized, inarticulate, unprofessional*. In the previous analysis, these adjectives were considered to form a non-finite clause. However, there exists a structural ambiguity here, as these three adjectives could also be analyzed as post-modifiers of *they*. When taking collocation into account, the situation becomes more complex. The last two adjectives, *inarticulate* and *unprofessional*, are typically used to describe a person, while the first adjective, *unorganized*, is a more natural collocate of *coming to visit*. This grammatical ambiguity and the mixed collocation likely contribute to undermining the initial relief felt when someone (*They*) arrived to offer assistance in the dire situation. Readers, along with the person at the center of the crisis, may perceive that help has finally arrived after a seemingly endless wait. However, naturally, this arrival cannot undo the crisis; instead, it offers mere presence.

Uneasiness in Stanza 1 is followed by undermined relief in Stanza 2, which is followed by comfort in Stanza 3. The comfort arises from the activities construed by non-finite clauses, and it continues throughout the remaining stanzas. The third stanza initiates with a variation of the main clause from Stanza 2, *They come sheepishly*, which is immediately followed by another coordinated main clause (*sit with you*). In contrast to the main clause in Stanza 2, which is preceded by a lengthy subordinate adverbial clause and followed by three multi-syllabic adjectives, this time the main clause is introduced promptly, with the manner of their arrival appended (*sheepishly*). Subsequently, the reader is provided with the first real piece of information about what happens in the following main clause (*sit with you*). This central part of the poem marks a significant turning point since the 'unprofessionals' have now arrived, and their various activities fill the remaining syntactic structure of the poem with subordinate non-finite clauses denoting repetitive actions over an extended period:

> holding hands, / From tea to tea, from Anadin to Valium,
> Sleeping on put-you-ups,
> answering the phone,
> Coming in shifts, spontaneously,

These activities, strung out as they are across the time-frame of the crisis, seem pointless but comforting.

The comfort experienced remains subtle, yet still intertwined with a touch of awkwardness. This awkwardness mainly stems from skillful punctuation and the retrospective interpretation of *Talking* in the first line of the fourth stanza. The "unprofessionals" occupy time and space with their activities, and the accumulation of these non-finite clauses continues into the fourth stanza with three additional clauses structured similarly:

> Talking sometimes, / About wallflowers, and fishing, and why
> Dealing with Kleenex and kettles,
> Doing the washing up and the shopping,

It is worth noting that the first of these three clauses presents a slightly unconventional arrangement. The adverbial *sometimes* appears to conclude the clause, while the topics of discussion (*wallflowers, fishing, and why*) are added almost as an afterthought. This syntactic arrangement takes the reader in and out of a sense of syntactic security, seemingly mirroring the experience of the person in the poem who is alternately comforted and reminded of the crisis. In a way, the addition of the retrospective three-part list of discussed topics alters the nature of the verb *talk*. Initially, in the process of online reading, the apparently complete non-finite clause *Talking sometimes* constructs the verb as intransitive, lacking objects, and only requiring an adverbial to indicate when the talking may occur. However, following the comma, the inclusion of the prepositional phrases seems to transform the verb into one that necessitates adverbial completion, supplying the content of what is being talked about. This shift, from mere talking to talking about specific things, echoes the talking itself. Initially, the talking itself is the whole point with the purpose of breaking the silence (remember these people are inarticulate). Pragmatically speaking, the talking is a locutionary act. But once the silence has been broken, the topics transition from unrelated subjects with no connection to the crisis (like "wallflowers" and "fishing") to the fundamental question of "why" the worst thing has happened. The sequencing, the gaps, and the transition from talking for the sake of talking to talking about the issue at the forefront of everyone's thoughts hold significance. The comma after *sometimes* creates a pause that the reader, like the "unprofessionals" themselves, must navigate in order to progress with the reading process. It acts as an awkward moment within a room engulfed in grief.

Following this slightly lengthier subordinate clause, we resume the busyness encapsulated in the earlier clauses. The visitors, having mentioned the significant question (*why*), perceive that they can now take more active measures, engaging in practical efforts to assist, such as managing household affairs. The fact that there are no further main clauses lends an air of unreality to the situation. These activities are incessant and ongoing, failing to move things forward, yet they consume time.

The poem concludes with a sense of resignation, which arises from the continued use of non-finite clauses in the final stanza. The final stanza continues the pattern, though with a subordinate clause-complex based on another pair of non-finite clauses (*Holding hands and sitting it out*). However, in this instance, there are additional adverbials preceding and following the clause complex:

- Like civilians in a shelter, under bombardment,
- Through the endless passage of every second, until time becomes dull.

The first of these adverbials functions as a comparison, likening the visitors to people in a war. Similar to the opening clauses of the poem, this adverbial extends the waiting time for the reader, who is yet to know whether there will be a final, resolving main clause or if the string of "*-ing*" clauses will persist. The following line, however, confirms the latter, and the string is succeeded by two concluding lines consisting of prepositional phrases functioning as adverbials, each emphasizing the lengthy duration required for healing. By this point, even the verbs have vanished, replaced by noun phrases denoting time (*immortality*, *all the seconds*, *time*) and a nominalization of a verb (*the blunting*) representing the process through which time heals. By the end of the poem, approximately eleven and a half lines have passed since encountering a main verb. Although the potential frustration experienced by the reader from the earlier subordinate clauses may be less apparent in the lengthy series of adverbial clauses following the main verb, it nevertheless may instill a resigned feeling that time is not moving on and there will be no further syntactic relief.

5.3.5 Syntactic foregrounding from the perspective of descriptive grammar

5.3.5.1 Syntactic deviation

Section 5.3.4 provides a summary of the principles underlying the default structure of a clause, which also applies to sentence structure. However, due to various reasons, the default structure of both clause and sentence is often deviated, resulting in periodic sentences, elliptical sentences, and inverted sentences.

A periodic sentence is structured in a way that withholds the main idea or point until the end, thus creating suspense or emphasis. It typically consists of clauses or phrases that precede the main clause, providing additional information or building up the context. A good example is the first four lines of the poem *The Unprofessionals* (quoted as Example 5.7), where the main clause is preceded by three lengthy subordinate clauses. If the main clause were placed at the beginning (see Example 5.7'), the sentence would have a more conventional structure. Such a sentence, with the main idea or point at the beginning, is referred to as a loose sentence.

Example 5.7

When the worst thing happens,
That uproots the future,
That you must live for every hour of your future,
They come,

Example 5.7’

They come,
When the worst thing happens,
That uproots the future,
That you must live for every hour of your future,

An elliptical sentence is structured in a way that omits certain words or parts of a sentence that are grammatically necessary. The omitted words can usually be easily recovered from the co-text, but there could still be multiple ways to complete the sentence. Lines 4 and 5 of *The Unprofessionals*, quoted here as Example 5.8, provides an illustration. It could be understood as *They come, which is unorganised, inarticulate, unprofessional* or *They come, who is unorganised, inarticulate, unprofessional*. Elliptical sentences can add stylistic variation and conciseness to writing. However, they also require careful interpretation to ensure clarity in meaning.

Example 5.8

They come,
Unorganised, inarticulate, unprofessional;

An inverted sentence is a structure where the typical subject-verb-object/complement order is reversed. In an inverted sentence, the verb or auxiliary verb appears before the subject. This inversion is often employed to create a more poetic or dramatic effect or to emphasize a specific element of the sentence. In Example 5.9, the verb *took* comes before the subject *the angry witch* to maintain the metrical pattern of iambic pentameter. This inversion adds a rhythmic quality to the line. Short (2013: 134) refers to this type of structure as “poetic grammar.”

Example 5.9

Then tooke the angrie witch her golden cup
Which still she bore, replete with magick artes;

(Edmund Spenser, *The Faerie Queene*, I, viii, 14)

In addition to the unusual syntactic arrangements mentioned above, a sentence can also deviate through grammatical violations, which means that the sentence does not follow the established grammatical rules of the language. In Example 5.10, the two lines deliberately violate the established grammatical rules of English by combining the comparative form with the word *more*. This intentional grammatical deviation highlights cummings’ artistic approach to language and illustrates his unique poetic style.

Example 5.10

love is more thicker than forget
more thinner than recall

(e.e. cummings, *love is more thicker than forget*)

5.3.5.2 Syntactic overregularity

Chapters 3 and 4 have introduced various figures of speech that involve sound patterns and artistic use of lexical items. Besides such figures of speech at the phonological and lexical levels, there are also figures of speech at the syntactic level, which arise from the repetition of certain grammatical structures. Leech (2013: 20) states that although figures of speech can be categorized according to different language levels, they sometimes emerge from a combination of different language levels. The following five figures of speech are examples of figures that are based on the repetition of certain grammatical structures, while also involving other factors: parallelism, antithesis, chiasmus, anaphora and epistrophe.

Parallelism refers to the repetition of syntactically similar constructions in coordinated sentences, clauses or phrases (cf. Bussmann, 2000). For instance, in Example 5.11, the parallelism in the second line is achieved through the repetition of the phrase structure *from ... to ...*. In Example 5.12, both the Chinese and English versions achieve parallelism by repeating the same syntactic structures. The repeated structure in Chinese is S + V + Conj. + negated V. The repeated structure in English is S + V + A + Subordinate clause.

Example 5.11

They come sheepishly, sit with you, holding hands,
From tea to tea, from Anadin to Valium,

Example 5.12

万物并育而不相害，道并行而不相悖。
(An ancient Chinese philosopher observed that "all living things may grow side by side without harming one another, and different roads may run in parallel without interfering with one another.")

Antithesis and parallelism are similar because they both involve the repetition of the same structure. However, antithesis requires that the items filling the repeated structure have opposite meanings. In Example 5.13, the underlined parts in the Chinese and English versions both achieve parallelism through the repetition of the same syntactic structure four times. When considering the meanings of the four subjects and their following verbs, the first two subjects and their following verbs are in opposition to the last two. In this case, it is an example of antithesis.

Example 5.13

完善干部考核评价体系，引导干部树立和践行正确政绩观，推动干部能上能下、能进能出，形成能者上、优者奖、庸者下、劣者汰的良好局面。

(We will improve the system for assessing officials' performance and see that officials have a correct understanding of what it means to perform well. We should also see that officials can be demoted as well as promoted and dismissed as well as recruited, thereby creating an environment in which the competent are elevated, the outstanding are rewarded, the mediocre are demoted, and the incompetent are dismissed.)

Chiasmus also involves the repetition of the same structure, but it requires the items in the repeated structure to be in reverse order. In Example 5.14, chiasmus is achieved by adopting the pattern of AB-BA.

Example 5.14

江山就是人民，人民就是江山。

(This country is its people; the people are the country.)

There are two additional syntactic figures of speech that involve the repetition of the initial or ending element of a structure. When the initial elements are repeated in successive clauses or sentences, it is called anaphora. On the other hand, when the ending elements are repeated in consecutive clauses or sentences, it is known as epistrophe or antistrophe.

Anaphora can be demonstrated in Example 5.15, where the adverbial phrase *one hundred years later* is repeated at the beginning of each sentence. This repetition emphasizes the passage of time and the ongoing struggles faced by the Negro.

Epistrophe is illustrated in Example 5.16, where the three underlined Chinese verb phrases all end with the same word. This repetition at the end of each phrase creates a rhythmic effect and draws attention to the collective efforts of the Party and the people in achieving great accomplishments in the new era.

Example 5.15

But one hundred years later the Negro still is not free. One hundred years later, the life of the Negro is still badly crippled by the manacles of segregation and the chains of discrimination.

(Martin Luther King, *I Have a Dream*)

Example 5.16

新时代的伟大成就是党和人民一道拼出来、干出来、奋斗出来的！

(The great achievements of the new era have come from the collective dedication and hard work of our Party and our people.)

5.4 Functional grammar and functional stylistic analysis

Chomsky (e.g. 1966) proposes three criteria crucial for evaluating and developing linguistic theories, namely observational adequacy, descriptive adequacy, and explanatory adequacy, and gives a psychological account of the three levels of adequacy. For him, observational adequacy refers to the ability of a linguistic theory to account for and accurately describe the observable linguistic data. Descriptive adequacy, on the other hand, focuses on the competence of a linguistic theory in describing the underlying knowledge or mental representation of language that speakers possess. And explanatory adequacy is concerned with providing a deeper understanding of the cognitive mechanisms and processes that give rise to language. TGG, the third syntactic framework introduced in Section 5.2, is one version of the linguistic theory put forward by Chomsky to achieve the explanatory adequacy from a psychological perspective. Systemic Functional Grammar (SFG), introduced as the fourth syntactic framework in Section 5.2, can be said to achieve explanatory adequacy functionally by showing that the structure of language is determined by the function it serves. This grammar is more informative than descriptive grammar, and has a much more powerful toolkit to analyze clauses and sentences.

The stylistic analysis of *The Inheritors* from a functional perspective by Halliday (1971) is widely regarded as a classic in the field, making it an unparalleled resource for teaching purposes. *The Inheritors* recounts the story of a small group of Neanderthal people, self-identified as *the people*, whose world is invaded by a more advanced tribe that the Neanderthals initially refer to as *others* and later as *the new people*.

Throughout the majority of the novel, the narrative focuses on the Neanderthal people and their perspective on the invading tribe. A significant portion of the story centers around Lok, the central character, who spends an extended period hiding in a tree to observe the activities of the invaders. The account of their actions, including work, rituals, and play, is presented within the confines of Lok's limited comprehension. Consequently, understanding the events and motives often necessitates considerable interpretation on the part of the reader.

Halliday's analysis begins with an excerpt from this part of the story (see the Appendix 5.1). To illustrate the differences between descriptive and functional analyses, the excerpt is analyzed from both approaches.

5.4.1 The stylistic analysis of *The Inheritors* from the perspective of descriptive grammar

With the framework introduced in Section 5.3, the excerpt is analyzed in Table 5.3:

Table 5.3 Descriptive analysis of *The Inheritors*

Sentence types	Clause type	A	S	V	O	C	A
simple	SVA		The bushes	twitched			again
compound	SVA		Lok	steadied			by the tree
	(S)V			and gazed			
complex	SVO		A head and a chest	faced	him		
	(SV)C					half-hidden	
simple	SVCA		There	were		white bone things	behind the leaves and hair
complex	SVOAA		The man	had	white bone things		above his eyes and under the mouth so that his face was longer than a face should be.
compound	SVAA		The man	turned			sideways in the bushes
	(S)VAA			and looked			at Lok along his shoulder
compound	SVA		A stick	rose			upright
	SVCA		and there	was		a lump of bone	in the middle
simple	SVA		Lok	peered			at the stick and the lump of bone and the small eyes in the bone things over the face

(Continued)

Sentence types	Clause type	A	S	V	O	C	A
complex	ASVO	Suddenly	Lok	understood	that the man was holding the stick out to him but neither he nor Lok could reach across the river		
complex	SVA		He	would have laughed			if it were not for the echo of the screaming in his head
simple	SVCA		The stick	began to grow		shorter	at both ends
simple	ASVA	Then	it	shot out			to full length again
simple	SVO		The dead tree by Lok's ear	acquired	a voice		
simple	verbless		"Clop!"				
compound	SV		His ears	twitched			
	SVA		and he	turned			to the tree
complex	ASVO	By his face	there	had grown	a twig:		
	(SV)C					a twig that smelt of other, and of goose, and of the bitter berries that Lok's stomach told him he must not eat	

(Continued)

Sentence types	Clause type	A	S	V	O	C	A
simple	SVOA		This twig	had	a white bone		at the end
compound	SVCA		There	were		hooks	in the bone
	SVA		and sticky brown stuff	hung			in the crooks
compound	SVO		His nose	examined	this stuff		
	(S)VO			and did not like	it		
simple	SVA		He	smelled			along the shaft of the twig
compound	SVC		The leaves on the twig	were		red feathers	
	(S)VOA			and reminded	him		of goose
simple	SVCA		He	was		lost	in a generalized astonishment and excitement
compound -complex	SVA		He	shouted			at the green drifts across the glittering water
	(S)VO			and heard	Liku crying out in answer		
	(S)VO			but could not catch	the words		
complex	SVAA		They	were cut off			suddenly as though some-one had clapped a hand over her mouth

(Continued)

Sentence types	Clause type	A	S	V	O	C	A
compound	SVA		He	rushed			to the edge of the water
	(S)VA			and then rushed			back
compound -complex	ASVAA	On either side of the open bank	the bushes	grew			thickly in the flood
	SVA		they	waded out			until at their farthest some of the leaves were opening under water
	SV		and these bushes	leaned over			
simple	SVOCA		The echo of Liku's voice in his head	sent	him	trembling	at this perilous way of bushes towards the island
compound -complex	SVAA		He	dashed			at them where normally they would have been rooted on dry land
	SV		and his feet	splashed			
compound	SVOA		He	threw	himself		forward
	(S)VAA			and grabbed			at the branches with hands and feet
complex	SVO		He	shouted:	"I am coming!"		

The findings of the analysis are reported in Table 5.4. The excerpt consists of a total of 30 sentences. Out of these, 11 sentences are simple sentences, 9 are compound sentences, 7 are complex sentences, and the remaining 3 are compound-complex sentences. The 11 simple sentences are made up of 10 main clauses and 1 verbless clause. The 9 compound sentences contain a total of 18 main clauses. In the 7 complex sentences, there are 7 main clauses, 12 subordinate clauses①. Lastly, the 3 compound-complex sentences consist of 8 main clauses and 3 subordinate clauses. Altogether, there are 43 main clauses, 15 subordinate clauses, 1 minor clause, and 59 clauses in total in this excerpt according to descriptive grammar.

Table 5.4 A summary of the descriptive analysis

Sentences	Structure of main clause	Number	Total
Simple (11)	SVA	3	11
	ASVA	1	
	SVCA	3	
	SVO	1	
	SVOA	1	
	SVOCA	1	
	Verbless clause	1	
Compound (9)	(S)②V	2	18
	(S)VA	6	
	(S)VAA	3	
	SVC	1	
	SVCA	2	
	(S)VO	2	
	(S)VOA	2	
Complex (7)	$SVA_{(C)}$③	1	7
	$SVAA_{(C)}$	1	
	$SVO_{(C)}$④	2	

① Among them, 2 clauses are nonrestrictive post-modifying clauses: one is *half-hidden*; the other is *a twig that smelt of other, and of goose, and of the bitter berries that Lok's stomach told him he must not eat*. The analysis of the function of this type clause in a sentence can be found in Quirk et al. (1985: 1118–1120).

② The brackets mean what is included in the brackets is omitted and is retrievable from the co-text.

③ $A_{(C)}$ means the adverbial element can either be a subordinate clause or a phrase.

④ $O_{(C)}$ means the object is either a subordinate clause or a phrase.

(Continued)

Sentences	Structure of main clause	Number	Total
Complex (7)	$ASVO_{(C)}$	2	7
	$SVOAA_{(C)}$	1	
Compound-complex (3)	SV	2	8
	$SVA_{(C)}$	2	
	$SVAA_{(C)}$	1	
	ASVAA	1	
	$(S)VO_{(C)}$	2	

It is important to note that in descriptive grammar, subordinate clauses are treated as components of the main clauses within the same sentence. Therefore, a stylistic analysis based on descriptive grammar would focus on the main clauses. As far as this excerpt is concerned, the stylistic analysis can be conducted from two perspectives. The first aspect pertains to information organization. Out of the 43 main clauses examined, only 4 of them feature an initial adverbial phrase. Interestingly, among these four clauses, only one (i.e. *On either side of the open bank* in *On either side of the open bank the bushes grew thickly in the flood*) contains a lengthy prepositional phrase preceding the subject. This deviation somewhat contradicts Principle 6 in Section 5.3.4. However, an examination of the clause in relation to its context suggests that the prepositional phrase *on either side of the open bank* is likely used for cohesion purposes, as it establishes a meronymic relationship with *the water* mentioned in the preceding sentence. Similarly, the adverbial elements *then* in *Then it shot out to full length again* and *by his face* in *By his face there had grown a twig* serve similar cohesion functions. The sole exception is the adverb *suddenly* in *Suddenly Lok understood that the man was holding the stick out to him but neither he nor Lok could reach across the river*, which has an iconic effect. Its unexpected appearance at the beginning of the clause indeed surprises the reader. The remaining 39 main clauses, however, adhere to the principles outlined in Section 5.3.4, highlighting a default relationship between information structure and clause structure. This foregrounding of default clausal structure possibly implies that the events narrated are not particularly dramatic. Nevertheless, considering that the excerpt describes Lok's fearful encounter with an invader, such default structures might indicate Lok's limited cognitive abilities or his limited comprehension of the happenings.

The second aspect to consider is the structure of sentences and clauses. According to the statistics presented in Table 5.4, about 37% of the sentences fall into the category of simple sentences, while another 30% are compound sentences comprising coordinated clauses. This means that a total of 67% of the sentences possess a straightforward structure. Complex sentences, which involve hierarchical and somewhat intricate structures, make up 23% of the total. The most complex structures arise from compound-complex sentences, which account for only 10%. An index frequently utilized for text analysis is the average sentence length. The Ellegård norm for sentence length stands at 17.8 (refer to Exercise 5), whereas the average sentence length in this excerpt is 13.7, significantly below the norm. If we subject this excerpt to a readability assessment, the Flesch Reading Ease score is 89.6, while the Flesch-Kincaid Grade Level is 3.9. This indicates that the prevalent use of simple sentence structures and shorter average sentence length contributes to the excerpt's easy comprehensibility, making it suitable for readers at a fourth-grade level. Once again, this basic level of literacy implies Lok's limited cognitive abilities.

Upon examining the various clause structures, it becomes evident that the subject, object, and complement play critical roles within a clause. Out of the 43 main clauses, 23 follow the basic structure of subject plus verb with one or two optional adverbials, 6 main clauses adopt the structure of subject plus verb plus complement with optional adverbials, and 14 main clauses adhere to the structure of subject plus verb plus object with optional adverbials.

Quirk et al. (1985: 754) provide a summary of the semantic roles associated with each structural element in Figure 5.7. Upon analyzing the main clauses, it is observed that only one of them exhibits the semantic arrangement of Agent + Affected, as depicted in the clause *He threw himself forward*. However, even in this clause, the agent is the one affected. This suggests that the excerpt describes a world where individuals neither act upon others nor experience any effects from others. When these individuals are unfortunately invaded by others, we probably can't help feeling sympathetic towards them. Section 5.1.2 has made it clear that lexis and grammar form a continuum. The grammatical impoverishment is actually accompanied by underlexicalization, which is defined as "the absence, in a character's or narrator's verbal repertoire, of fairly common lexical items, which readers are likely to expect to be familiar to a competent language user" (Semino, 2014). For example, Lok didn't have the word *arrow* to denote what is referred to as stick or twig in the excerpt. The absence implies that Lok's world doesn't have the weapon and is vulnerable to the invasion of 'the man'.

5.4.2 *The Inheritors* and functional stylistic analysis

The analysis in the last part of Section 5.4.1 only focuses on the semantic roles of agent and affected. To conduct a more comprehensive analysis that is meaning-oriented, it is necessary to examine the semantic role of each structural element in all main clauses. However, the list of semantic roles in Figure 5.7 does not include the roles played by verbs, and it does not specify the combination of these roles. To address these limitations, this section will introduce SFG (Systemic Functional Grammar), which offers a more systematic approach to analyzing clause meaning from a functional perspective.

5.4.2.1 Clauses in functional stylistic analysis

Descriptive grammar, as mentioned earlier, initially distinguishes between simple sentences and multiple sentences. It further categorizes multiple sentences into compound and complex sentences. In the stylistic analysis within descriptive grammar, the main focus is on main clauses, considering subordinate clauses as structural elements of main clauses within the same sentence. SFG provides a more intricate system to analyze multiple sentences, as depicted in Figure 5.8. Additionally, the functional approach incorporates a broader examination of so-called subordinate clauses in the stylistic analysis.

Type	*S*	O_i	O_d	C_S	C_O	*A*	*Example*
SVC	aff			attrib			*She's happy.*
	agent			attrib			*He turned traitor.*
	loc			attrib			*The Sahara is hot.*
	temp			attrib			*Last night was warm.*
	event			attrib			*The show was interesting.*
	it			attrib			*It's windy.*
SVA	aff					loc	*He was at school.*
	agent					loc	*She got into the car.*
	pos					loc	*He is lying on the floor.*
	event					temp	*The meeting is at eight.*
SV	agent						*He was working.*
	pos						*She is standing.*
	aff						*The curtains disappeared.*
	ext						*The wind is blowing.*
	it						*It's raining.*
SVO	agent		aff				*He threw the ball.*
	ext		aff				*Lightning struck the house.*
	pos		aff				*He is holding a knife.*
	instr		aff				*The stone broke the window.*
	recip		aff				*She has a car.*
	agent		recip				*We paid the bus driver.*
	instr		recip				*The will benefits us all.*
	agent		loc				*They climbed the mountain.*
	loc		aff				*The bus seats thirty.*
	agent		cog				*They fought a clean fight.*
	agent		result				*I wrote a letter.*
	agent		event				*They had an argument.*
	agent		instr				*He nodded his head.*
SVOC	agent		aff		attrib		*He declared her the winner.*
	ext		aff		attrib		*The sun turned it yellow.*
	instr		aff		attrib		*The revolver made him afraid.*
	recip		aff		attrib		*I found it strange.*
SVOA	agent		aff			loc	*He placed it on the shelf.*
	ext		aff			loc	*The storm drove the ship ashore.*
	instr		aff			loc	*A car knocked it down.*
	recip		aff			loc	*I prefer them on toast.*
SVOO	agent	recip	aff				*I bought her a gift.*
	agent	aff	event				*She gave the door a kick.*
	agent	recip	result				*She knitted me a sweater.*

KEY: aff(ected), agent(ive), attrib(ute), cog(nate), event(ive), ext(ernal causer), instr(ument), (prop) *it*, loc(ative), pos(itioner), recip(ient), result(ant), temp(oral)

Figure 5.7 Semantic roles in a clause (Quirk et al., 1985: 754)

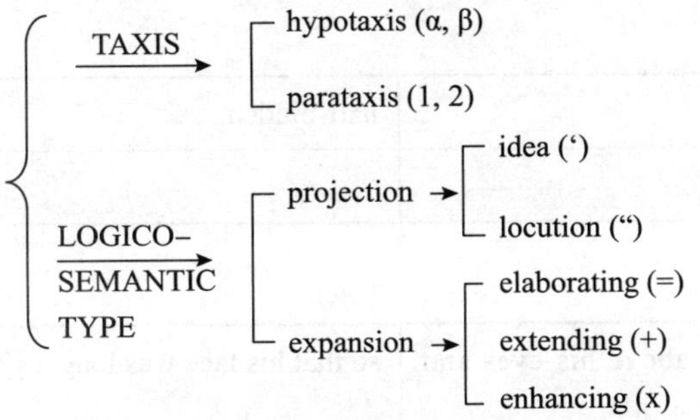

Figure 5.8 The systems of clause complexing (adopted from Halliday, 2008: 373)

In Figure 5.8, the system of taxis presents two options. Hypotaxis represents the relationship between a dependent clause and its dominant clause, while parataxis represents the relationship between two clauses of equal status. This distinction aligns with the differentiation between subordination and coordination (Quirk et al., 1985: 1040–1041). To annotate a hypotactic sentence, SFG suggests using the Greek letter α for the dominant clause, and subsequent Greek letters for the dependent clauses. For a paratactic sentence, the annotation involves using the number 1 for the initial coordinate clause, and subsequent natural numbers for the continuing coordinate clauses.

The subsystem of the logico-semantic type in Figure 5.8 employs the term of projection to address what is discussed as "reporting" in Quirk et al. (1985). It distinguishes between the wordings and ideas projected by the primary clause, also known as the projecting clause. And SFG employs single quotes to indicate ideas and double quotes to indicate wordings.

The feature of expansion in the subsystem discusses three ways in which the secondary clause expands the primary clause, which are explained by Halliday (2008: 378) as follows (see Table 5.5).

Table 5.5 Elaborating, extending, and enhancing

Elaborating: "i.e., for example, viz."	one clause expands another by elaborating on it (or some portion of it): restating in other words, specifying in greater detail, commenting, or exemplifying
Extending: "and, or"	one clause expands another by extending beyond it: adding some new element, giving an exception to it, or offering an alternative
Enhancing: "so, yet, then"	one clause expands another by establishing around it: qualifying it with some circumstantial feature of time, place, cause or condition

The three relationships are indicated by using "=", "+" and "x".

Since the compound sentences (i.e., paratactic clause-complexes in SFG's terms) in Table 5.3 have a clear structure, our analysis will focus on the complex sentences and compound-complex sentences with reference to the systems of clause complexing.

(1)

A head and a chest faced him,	half-hidden.
α	=β

(2)

The man had white bone things above his eyes and under the mouth	so that his face was longer [[than a face should be]].
α	xβ

(3)

Suddenly Lok understood	that the man was holding the stick out to him	but neither he nor Lok could reach across the river
α	‘β	
	1	+2

(4)

He would have laughed	if it were not for the echo of the screaming in his head.
α	xβ

(5)

By his face there had grown a twig:	a twig	[[that smelt of other, and of goose, and of the bitter berries	that Lok’s stomach told him	he must not eat]]
α	=β			

(6)

He shouted at the green drifts across the glittering water	and heard [[Liku crying out in answer]]	but could not catch the words.
1	+2	+3

(7)

They were cut off suddenly	as though someone had clapped a hand over her mouth.
α	xβ

(8)

On either side of the open bank the bushes grew thickly in the flood;	they waded out	until at their farthest some of the leaves were opening under water;	and these bushes leaned over.
1	+2		
	α	xβ	

(9)

He dashed at them	where normally they would have been rooted on dry land	and his feet splashed.
1		
α	xβ	

(10)

He shouted:	"I am coming!"
1	"2

As previously mentioned, within the framework of descriptive grammar, the 10 sentences reanalyzed here consist of 15 main clauses and 15 subordinate clauses. For the purpose of stylistic analysis, only the 15 main clauses are examined, while the 15 subordinate clauses are treated as embedded clauses within the main clauses.

The analysis of the 10 multiple sentences from the perspective of SFG differs from the analysis within the framework of descriptive grammar in two significant ways. Firstly, in the framework of descriptive grammar, reported clauses are treated as part of the reporting clause. However, in SFG, projected clauses are either treated as independent clauses with the same status as the projecting clause (as seen in the tenth sentence), or as dependent clauses that also contribute to the textual development (as seen in the third sentence). In both cases, the projected clauses are analyzed separately in functional stylistic analysis.

Secondly, within the framework of SFG, only clauses that function as participants (e.g., Sentence 6) or as constituents within a group structure, which itself is a constituent of a clause, are analyzed as embedded clauses. For example, in Sentence 2, the clause *than a face should be* modifies the head *longer*. In Sentence 5, the clause complex *that smelt of other, and of goose, and of the bitter berries that Lok's stomach told him he must not eat* modifies the head *twig*. Moreover, clauses that are said to function as adverbials in the main clause within the framework of descriptive grammar are treated as dependent clauses that expand the dominant clauses within the framework of SFG. These expanding clauses are also analyzed separately in functional stylistic analysis, such as the β clauses in Sentences 1 and 2.

In total, out of the 30 clauses in the 10 sentences, 25 clauses are subject to functional stylistic analysis, excluding the 5 embedded clauses marked by double square brackets. In contrast, a descriptive stylistic analysis focuses on the 15 main clauses. Therefore, a functional stylistic analysis examines an additional 10 clauses compared to a descriptive stylistic analysis.

5.4.2.2 Transitivity system and the analysis of *The Inheritors*

The excerpt contains a total of 54 clauses that can be subjected to functional analysis. Of these, 11 are from the 11 simple sentences, 18 are from the 9 compound sentences, and the remaining 25 are from the multiple sentences analyzed in Section 5.4.2.1. In Halliday's (1971) influential paper, an earlier version of SFG was used to analyze these clauses by categorizing them into types such as action, location/possession, mental process, attribution, and others. The modern version of SFG proposes a transitivity system consisting of six processes for analyzing English clauses, as shown in Figure 5.9.

The system of TRANSITIVITY is based on a functional understanding of our lived experience. Halliday (2008: 170) explains that our experience can be seen as a continuous flow of events or actions. These events are segmented into units of change by the grammatical unit of clause. Each unit of change is represented as a figure, which can be categorized as happening, doing, sensing, saying, being, or having. Every figure consists of a process that unfolds over time, with participants involved in the process in one way or another. In addition, there may be circumstances of time, space, cause, manner, etc.

The TRANSITIVITY system serves as the grammatical framework for identifying and classifying these different figures, ultimately providing a way to interpret and organize our experiential world into six distinct process types. Each process type offers its own model or schema for understanding and representing specific domains of experience as particular kinds of figures.

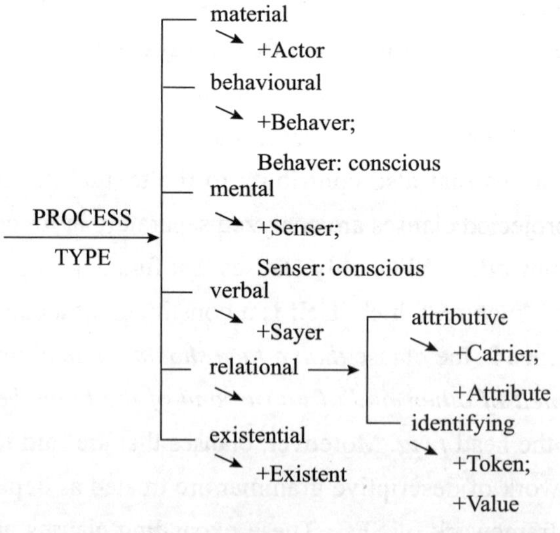

Figure 5.9 TRANSITIVITY[①] represented as system network (Halliday, 2008: 173)

① In SFG, the name for a system has all their letters capitalized in small capital letters.

The excerpt contains 26 "material" clauses, which are concerned with our experience of the material world. In a "material" clause, there is always one participant known as the Actor, who initiates the unfolding of the process through time, resulting in an outcome that differs from the initial phase of the process. This outcome may solely impact the Actor, making them the sole participant inherent in the process. Such a "material" clause represents a happening, which is traditionally referred to as an intransitive clause. Alternatively, the process may extend beyond the Actor to affect another participant known as the Goal, who is impacted in some way by the unfolding process. This type of "material" clause represents a doing, traditionally known as a transitive clause. In addition to the Actor and the Goal, there are several other participant roles that may be involved in a "material" clause, including Scope, Recipient, Client, Attribute, and Initiator. The 26 "material" clauses in the excerpt are analyzed as follows.

(1)

The bushes	twitched	again.
Actor	Process: material	Circumstance

(2)

Lok	steadied	by the tree
Actor	Process: material	Circumstance

(3)

The man	turned	sideways in the bushes
Actor	Process: material	Circumstance

(4)

A stick	rose	upright
Actor	Process: material	Circumstance

(5)

the man	was holding	the stick	out to him
Actor	Process: material	Goal	Circumstance

(6)

neither he nor Lok	could reach	across the river.
Actor	Process: material	Circumstance

(7)

it	shot out	to full length again
Actor	Process: material	Circumstance

(8)

His ears	twitched
Actor	Process: material

(9)

he	turned	to the tree.
Actor	Process: material	Circumstance

(10)

sticky brown stuff	hung	in the crooks
Actor	Process: material	Circumstance

(11)

His nose	examined	this stuff
Actor	Process: material	Goal

(12)

They	were cut off	suddenly
Goal	Process: material	Circumstance

(13)

someone	had clapped	a hand	over her mouth
Actor	Process: material	Goal	Circumstance

(14)

He	rushed	to the edge of the water
Actor	Process: material	Circumstance

(15)

(he)	rushed	back
Actor	Process: material	Circumstance

(16)

On either side of the open bank	the bushes	grew	thickly	in the flood
Circumstance	Actor	Process: material	Circumstance	Circumstance

(17)

they	waded out
Actor	Process: material

(18)

at their farthest	some of the leaves	were opening	under water
Circumstance	Actor	Process: material	Circumstance

(19)

these bushes	leaned over
Actor	Process: material

(20)

The echo of Liku's voice in his head	sent	him	trembling	at this perilous way of bushes towards the island
Initiator	Pro-	Actor	-cess	Circumstance

(21)

He	dashed	at them
Actor	Process: material	Circumstance

(22)

normally	they	would have been rooted	on dry land
Circumstance	Goal	Process: material	Circumstance

(23)

his feet	splashed
Actor	Process: material

(24)

He	threw	himself	forward
Actor	Process: material	Goal	Circumstance

(25)

(he)	grabbed	at the branches with hands and feet
Actor	Process: material	Circumstance

(26)

"I	am coming!"
Actor	Process: material

The excerpt has 5 "mental" clauses, which pertain to our experience of the world of our own consciousness. In a "mental" clause, there is always a human or human-like participant referred to as the Senser, who engages in sensory experiences such as feeling, thinking, wanting, or perceiving. Grammatically, the Senser is pronominally identified using pronouns such as *he* or *she*, not *it*. The Senser often interacts with another participant known as the Phenomenon, which is felt, thought, wanted, or perceived. The Phenomenon, unlike participants in a "material" clause, can be a thing, an act, or a fact. Additionally, within the broader category of "mental" clauses, there are four distinct sub-types of sensing: "perceptive", "cognitive", "desiderative", and "emotive". The following analysis breaks down the 5 "mental" clauses into their respective sub-types.

(1)

Suddenly	Lok	understood
Circumstance	Senser	Process: cognitive

(2)

His nose	did not like	it
Senser	Process: emotive	Phenomenon: thing

(3)

(The leaves on the twig)	reminded	him	of goose
Phenomenon	Process: cognitive	Senser	Circumstance

(4)

(he)	heard	[[Liku crying out in answer]]
Senser	Process: perceptive	Phenomenon: act

(5)

(he)	could not catch	the words
Senser	Process: perceptive	Phenomenon: thing

The excerpt contains 11 "relational" clauses, which are used to establish relationships between two entities. The English language has a systematic construction of relational processes. There are three primary types of relational relations: "intensive", "possessive", and "circumstantial". An "intensive" relational process establishes an equivalence relationship, denoting an "x is y" connection between two entities. A "possessive" relational clause signifies an "x has y" type of connection between entities. On the other hand, a "circumstantial" relational clause pertains to relationships of time, place, manner, cause, accompaniment, role, matter, or angle between two entities.

Each of the three relational types has two modes: "attributive" and "identifying". The "attributive" mode represents the abstract relationship of class-membership, with the member serving as the Carrier and the class as the Attribute. The "identifying" mode signifies the abstract relationship of identity, where both halves of the clause refer to the same entity. However, an "identifying" clause is not a tautology. The two halves, referring to the same entity, differ in terms of abstraction. The more abstract half is the Value and the more concrete half is the Token. The 11 "relational" clauses are analyzed into their respective sub-categories as follows.

(1)

A head and a chest	faced	him
Value	Process: circumstantial	Token

(2)

(which)	(is)	half-hidden
Carrier	Process: intensive	Attribute

(3)

The man	had	white bone things	above his eyes and under the mouth
Carrier	Process: possessive	Attribute	Circumstance

(4)

his face	was	longer [[than a face should be]].
Carrier	Process: intensive	Attribute

(5)

it	were not	for the echo of the screaming in his head
Carrier	Process: circumstantial	Attribute

(6)

The stick	began to grow	shorter	at both ends
Carrier	Process: intensive	Attribute	Circumstance

(7)

The dead tree by Lok's ear	acquired	a voice
Carrier	Process: possessive	Attribute

(8)

(which)	(is)	a twig [that smelt of other, and of goose, and of the bitter berries that Lok's stomach told him he must not eat]
Carrier	Process: intensive	Attribute

(9)

This twig	had	a white bone	at the end
Carrier	Process: possessive	Attribute	Circumstance

(10)

The leaves on the twig	were	red feathers
Carrier	Process: intensive	Attribute

(11)

He	was	lost	in a generalized astonishment and excitement
Carrier	Process: intensive	Attribute	Circumstance

"Material", "mental" and "relational" processes are the three principal types of processes. These processes characterize our physical world, world of consciousness, and the world of abstract relations, respectively. Additionally, there are three subsidiary process types located at the boundaries between the principal types. These subsidiary types are "behavioral" (at the boundary between material and mental), "verbal" (at the boundary between mental and relational), and "existential" (at the boundary between relational and material) processes.

In brief, "behavioral" clauses construe human physiological and psychological behavior, such as breathing, coughing, smiling, dreaming, and staring. In a "behavioral" clause, the participant who is performing the behavior is labeled as the "Behaver". There are 6 "behavioral" clauses in the excerpt.

(1)

(Lok)	gazed.
Behaver	Process: behavioral

(2)

(the man)	looked	at Lok along his shoulder
Behaver	Process: behavioral	Circumstance

(3)

(Lok)	peered	at the stick and the lump of bone and the small eyes in the bone things over the face
Behaver	Process: behavioral	Circumstance

(4)

He	would have laughed
Behaver	Process: behavioral

(5)

He	smelled	along the shaft of the twig
Behaver	Process: behavioral	Circumstance

(6)

He	shouted	at the green drifts across the glittering water
Behaver	Process: behavioral	Circumstance

"Verbal" clauses, on the other hand, are clauses of saying. The participant who is uttering or expressing something in a "verbal" clause is termed the "Sayer". And there is only one "verbal" clause in the excerpt.

He	shouted:
Sayer	Process: verbal

"Existential" clauses represent the existence or occurrence of something. In an "existential" clause, the entity or event that is said to exist or happen is simply labeled as the "Existent". Four "existential" clauses are identified in the excerpt.

(1)

There	were	white bone things	behind the leaves and hair.
	Process: existential	Existent	Circumstance

(2)

there	was	a lump of bone	in the middle
	Process: existential	Existent	Circumstance

(3)

By his face	there	had grown	a twig
Circumstance	Circumstance	Process: existential	Existent

(4)

There	were	hooks	in the bone
	Process: existential	Existent	Circumstance

The number of occurrence for each process type is summarized in Table 5.6.

Table 5.6 Different types of clauses in the excerpt

Clause type	Material	Mental	Relational	Behavioral	Verbal	Existential	Minor
Number	26	5	11	6	1	4	1

5.4.2.3 Thematic structure and the analysis of *The Inheritors*

According to SFG, a clause serves three distinct functions simultaneously: as a representation, a message, and an exchange. The previous section has introduced the transitivity system, which focuses on the clause as a representation. In this section, we will explore the clause as a message, while the clause as an exchange is left for readers to explore by themselves.

The structure of a clause that carries the "message" meaning is referred to as the thematic structure, which follows the pattern "Theme + Rheme". The Theme serves as the starting point of the message, locating and orienting the clause within its context. The Rheme, on the other hand, comprises the remaining part of the message where the Theme is further developed.

In the previous section, we learned that a clause, in its representational function, consists of three functional components: the process, the participants, and any circumstantial elements. The principle of thematic structure rules that the Theme includes one and only one of these functional components. In other words, the Theme of a clause concludes with the first constituent that can be classified as a participant, circumstance, or process. This constituent is then referred to as the topical Theme. A thematic analysis of the excerpt can be summarized as follows, adopting Halliday's (2008: 104–105) format:

Paragraph 1	
Paragraph Theme (from clause 1)	The bushes
Clause Themes	
Free clause	The bushes
Free clause	Lok
Free clause	and (Lok)
Free clause	A head and a chest
Bound clause	/
Free clause	There were
Free clause	The man
Bound clause	so that his face
Free clause	The man
Free clause	and (the man)
Free clause	A stick
Free clause	and there was
Free clause	Lok
Free clause	Suddenly
Bound clause	[understanding] that the man
Bound clause	[understanding] and neither he nor Lok

Free clause	He
Bound clause	if it
Free clause	The stick
Free clause	Then it
Paragraph 2	
Paragraph Theme (from clause 1)	The dead tree by Lok's ear
Clause Theme	
Free clause	The dead tree by Lok's ear
Paragraph 3	
Paragraph 4	
Paragraph Theme (from clause 1)	His ears
Clause Themes	
Free clause	His ears
Free clause	and he
Free clause	By his face
bound clause	/
Free clause	This twig
Free clause	There were
Free clause	and sticky brown stuff
Free clause	His nose
Free clause	and (he)
Free clause	He
Free clause	The leaves on the twig
Free clause	and (the leaves on the twig)
Free clause	He
Free clause	He
Free clause	and (he)
Free clause	and (he)
Free clause	They
Bound clause	as though someone
Free clause	He
Free clause	and (he)
Free clause	On other side of the open bank

Free clause	they
Bound clause	until at their farthest
Free clause	and these bushes
Paragraph 5	
Paragraph Theme (from clause 1)	The echo of Liku's voice in his head
Clause Themes	
Free clause	The echo of Liku's voice in his head
Free clause	He
Bound clause	where normally
Free clause	and his feet
Free clause	He
Free clause	and (he)
Free clause	He
Paragraph 6	
Free clause	"I"

5.4.2.4 An interpretation of *The Inheritors* from a functional perspective

The thematic analysis helps to reveal the main contents and the development of the excerpt. Paragraph by paragraph, the development proceeds as follows:

(1) The bushes ... Lok ... (Lok) ... A head and chest ... There were (to introduce something new) ... The man ... (the man) ... A stick ... and there was (more details about the stick) ... Lok ... Suddenly (Lok) understood the man ... neither he nor Lok ... He (Lok) ... The stick ... Then it ...

(2) The dead tree by Lok's ear

(3) "Clop!"

(4) His (Lok's) ears … he (Lok) … By his (Lok's) face … a twig … The twig … There were (more details about the twig) … and sticky brown stuff … His (Lok's) nose … He (Lok) … The leaves on the twig … He (Lok) … He (Lok) … (he) … They (Liku's words) … He (Lok) … (he) On each side of the open bank (the bushes) … they (the bushes) … and these bushes …

(5) The echo of Liku's voice in his head … He (Lok) … his feet … He (Lok) … and (he) … He …

(6) "I (Lok) …"

The six paragraphs describe Lok's encounter with an invading man. The first paragraph sets the scene by describing the bushes in the setting, and then introduces the invading man, specifically his head, chest, and overall presence. It also mentions the arrow shot by the invading man towards Lok, which is a stick from Lok's perspective, and provides a detailed description of the arrow stick, emphasizing its form, structure, and flying process. The second paragraph mentions that the arrow stick hits a dead tree near Lok's ear, producing a "clop" sound (see Paragraph 3).

The fourth paragraph reinterprets the arrow as a twig in the tree and shifts focus to Lok's examination of it. Lok then tries to connect with Liku, hearing Liku's cries but abruptly losing them. The paragraph also describes Lok's attempt to reach Liku and the obstacles of the bushes in his way, which are mentioned again.

The fifth paragraph highlights Lok's renewed attempts to find Liku and ends with his shouting. The words of his shouting are given in the sixth paragraph: "I...".

In Section 5.4.1, the stylistic analysis based on the information structure, sentence and clause structures, and the semantic roles of structural elements reveals that the Neanderthal people have a limited cognitive ability. The thematic analysis brings into our attention Lok's inability to recognize an arrow, mistakenly recognizing it as a stick when it was in flight and a twig when it struck a tree. This analysis suggests that the Neanderthal people were removed from modern society and unfamiliar with the weaponry employed by the invaders. Furthermore, the functional analysis of the clauses in the passage, particularly in terms of their representational meaning, provides further insights.

A participant can be classified as a main participant if it precedes the process (i.e., acts as the subject within the framework of descriptive grammar) or if it is directly involved in the process. The distribution of the main participants across different types of clauses in the excerpt is presented in Table 5.7. It highlights the main participants and their respective frequencies.

Table 5.7 The main participants in each clause type①

Main participants	Material	Mental	Relational	Behavioral	Verbal	Existential	Total
Lok or his body parts	13	5	1	5	1	0	25
Arrow either as a stick or as a twig	3	0	4	0	0	4	11
The man or his body parts	3	0	4	1	0	0	8
Bushes (including trees)	6	0	1	0	0	0	7
Liku's cries	2	0	0	0	0	0	2
someone	1	0	0	0	0	0	1
it	0	0	1	0	0	0	1
Total	28	5	11	6	1	4	55

① The sixth "material" clause has "neither he nor Lok" as the Actor, which means both "he" and "Lok" are the main participants in the clause. In the 22nd "material" clause, *The eco of Liku's voice* is in the position of subject and "Lok" is the actor; therefore, both of them are main participants.

Based on a functional analysis with reference to an earlier version of SFG, Halliday (1971) gave a summary of the features of the language in the excerpt. One of them is there is one participant only. Our analysis based on the updated model of SFG helps elaborate this feature. According to the table, the predominant main participants in the passage are Lok (or his body parts), the arrow either as a stick or as a twig, the man (or his body parts), and the bushes (including trees), accounting for 51 out of the total 55 main participants identified. The bushes serve as a main participant as they feature the setting in which the encounter takes place. Lok, the man, and the arrow are main participants because the encounter involves their interaction, with the man shooting the arrow towards Lok.

When we examine the interactions among the three key participants involved in the event where the invading man shoots an arrow at Lok, we note a lack of active engagement between them. For example, in our examination of the material clauses with Lok, his body parts, the arrow in its entirety or a part of it, the man, or his body parts as main participants, most only involve a single participant, and only very few have processes that extend beyond their Actors. Specifically, of the thirteen clauses featuring Lok as the main participant, only two describe actions that impact something else: *His nose examined this stuff*, and *He threw himself forward*. Among the three clauses where the invader is the main participant, just one depicts an action impacting another, namely, *the man was holding the stick out to him*. Notably, it is the sole clause that includes the man, the arrow, and Lok, even though Lok is only referenced as part of the setting. Only one out of the six clauses with the bushes as the main participant depicts action extending to another element: *normally they would have been rooted on dry land*. Lastly, all three clauses that center around the arrow or its components involve only that item. In the four "material" clauses that have a process that extends beyond their Actors, there is no direct interaction between Lok and the invading man, and their interaction is mediated through the stick: the man held the arrow stick out to Lok and Lok smelt the arrow stick.

Within the five "mental" clauses, Lok is positioned as the Senser in the first three. In the first of these, he understands that neither he nor the invading man can cross the river. In the remaining two mental clauses, Lok's emotional response to the arrow is highlighted, and he is prompted to recall something else.

Out of the eleven "relational" clauses, only two involve two of the three participants: the first relational clause presents the spatial relationship between Lok and the invading man, and the third one outlines the ownership between the man and the arrow.

Regarding the "behavioral" clauses, which typically focus on a single participant, three out of six instances include one of the three main participants with another mentioned in the circumstantial components: the second clause, with the invading man as the Behaver, has Lok in its circumstantial component, and the third and fifth clauses, with Lok functioning as the Behaver, have a part of the arrow stick in their circumstantial elements.

"Existential" clauses inherently involve just one participant. Of the four clauses, one specifically situates the arrow in relation to Lok.

Lastly, in the only 'verbal' clause, Lok, acting as the Sayer, is the sole participant mentioned.

The detailed analysis above probably gives a better support to Halliday's (1971) more lengthy discussion of the linguistic features of the excerpt:

> [I]n this language, processes are seldom represented as resulting from an external cause; in those instances where they are, the "agent" is seldom a human being; and where it is human being, it is seldom one of the people. Whatever the type of process, there tends to be only one participant; any other entities are involved only indirectly, as circumstantial elements (syntactically, through the mediation of a preposition). It is as if doing was as passive as seeing, and things no more affected by actions than by perceptions: their role is as in clauses of mental process, where the object of perception is not in any sense "acted on"—it is in fact the perceiver that is the "affected" participant, not the thing perceived—and likewise tends to be expressed circumstantially (e.g. *Lok peered at the stick*). There is no effective relation between persons and objects: people do not bring about events in which anything other than they themselves, or parts of their bodies, are implicated.

The linguistic features reported above help create "an atmosphere of ineffectual activity: the scene is one of constant movement, but movement which is as much inanimate as human and in which only the mover is affected—nothing else changes" (Halliday, 1971). The interpretation based on the analysis is "the inherent limitations of understanding, whether cultural or biological, of Lok and his people, and their consequent inability to survive when confronted with beings at a higher stage of development" (Halliday, 1971).

Exercises:

1. What is descriptive grammar? What is functional grammar? What are the differences between stylistic analyses based on the two grammatical frameworks?

2. What are the differences among the six processes identified in Systemic Functional Grammar?

3. The following sentences are all ambiguous. Analyze them by using either the descriptive grammar or the functional grammar to show your understanding of the ambiguities involved.
   1) Please make her dress fast.
   2) They are visiting scholars.
   3) She couldn't bear children.
   4) The magician made the princess a fog.
   5) The seniors were told to stop demonstrating.

4. Section 5.3 has analyzed the poem *The Unprofessionals* at the syntactic level, please try to analyze its foregrounded phonological and lexical features by employing concepts introduced in Chapters 3 and 4.

5. The following is a passage from *The Great Gatsby*, which likely leaves readers impressions of opulence, lavishness and generality. The following table gives the Ellegård norm for sentence length and the major grammatical word classes, and compares them with *The Great Gatsby* passage in total and paragraph by paragraph. It can be found that the average sentence length for the passage (33.9 words) is approximately twice the Ellegård norm, indicating some complexity of style. Please make a detailed analysis of each sentence and noun and verb phrases as well in the passage by using concepts introduced in Section 5.3 and try to find out how the reading impressions are supported by the linguistic analysis.

	Average sentence length	Nouns/%	Main verbs/%	Adjectives/%	Adverbs/%
Ellegård norm	17.8	27.2	12.1	7.4	5.3
Whole text	33.9	28.5	11.3	10.3	5.6
Paragraph 1	32.3	28.9	10.3	12.3	3.1
Paragraph 2	49.3	30.0	8.5	11.5	4.6
Paragraph 3	36.3	27.5	14.7	10.1	9.2
Paragraph 4	24.0	26.4	12.5	5.6	5.6

(Short, 2013: 337)

(1) At least once a fortnight a corps of caterers came down with several hundred feet of canvas and enough colored lights to make a Christmas tree of Gatsby's enormous garden. (2) On buffet tables, garnished with glistening hors-d'oeuvre, spiced baked hams crowded against salads of harlequin designs and pastry pigs and turkeys bewitched to a dark gold. (3) In the main hall a bar with a real brass rail was set up, and stocked with gins and liquors and with cordials so long forgotten that most of his female guests were too young to know one from another.

(4) By seven o'clock the orchestra has arrived, no thin five-piece affair but a whole pitful of oboes and trombones and saxophones and viols and cornets and piccolos and low and high drums. (5) The last swimmers have come in from the beach now and are dressing upstairs; the cars from New York are parked five deep in the drive, and already the halls and salons and verandas are gaudy with primary colors and hair shorn in strange new ways and shawls beyond the dreams of Castile. (6) The bar is in full swing and floating rounds of cocktails permeate the garden outside until the air is alive with chatter and laughter and casual innuendo and introductions forgotten on the spot and enthusiastic meetings between women who never knew each other's names.

(7) The lights grow brighter as the earth lurches away from the sun and now the orchestra is playing

yellow cocktail music and the opera of voices pitches a key higher. (8) Laughter is easier, minute by minute, spilled with prodigality, tipped out at a cheerful word. (9) The groups change more swiftly, swell with new arrivals, dissolve and form in the same breath; already there are wanderers, confident girls who weave here and there among the stouter and more stable, become for a sharp, joyous moment the center of a group and then excited with triumph glide on through the sea-change of faces and voices and color under the constantly changing light.

(10) Suddenly one of these gypsies in trembling opal, seizes a cocktail out of the air, dumps it down for courage and moving her hands like Frisco dances out alone on the canvas platform. (11) A momentary hush; the orchestra leader varies his rhythm obligingly for her and there is a burst of chatter as the erroneous news goes around that she is Gilda Gray's understudy from the Follies. (12) The party has begun.

6. The following passage is another excerpt from *The Inheritors*, please make a comparative stylistic analysis from the perspective of Systemic Functional Grammar of this passage and the one in Appendix 5.1, which has already been analyzed in Section 5.4.

The sail glowed red-brown. Tuami glanced back at the gap through the mountain and saw that it was full of golden light and the sun was sitting in it. As if they were obeying some signal the people began to stir, to sit up and look across the water at the green hills. Twal bent over Tanakil and kissed her and murmured to her. Tanakil's lips parted. Her voice was harsh and came from far away in the night.

"Liku!"

Tuami heard Marlan whisper to him from by the mast.

"That is the devil's name. Only she may speak it."

Now Vivani was really waking. They heard her huge, luxurious yawn and the bear skin was thrown off. She sat up, shook back her loose hair and looked first at Marlan then at Tuami. At once he was filled again with lust and hate. If she had been what she was, if Marlan, if her man, if she had saved her baby in the storm on the salt water—

"My breasts are paining me."

If she had not wanted the child as a plaything, if I had not saved the other as a joke—

He began to talk high and fast.

"There are plains beyond those hills, Marlan, for they grow less; and there will be herds for hunting. Let us steer in towards the shore. Have we water—but of course we have water! Did the women bring the food? Did you bring the food, Twal?"

Twal lifted her face towards him and it was twisted with grief and hate.

"What have I to do with food, master? You and he gave my child to the devils and they have given me back a changeling who does not see or speak."

The sand was swirling in Tuami's brain. He thought in panic: they have given me back a changed

Tuami; what shall I do? Only Marlan is the same—smaller, weaker but the same. He peered forward to find the changeless one as something he could hold on to. The sun was blazing on the red sail and Marlan was red. His arms and legs were contracted, his hair stood out and his beard, his teeth were wolf's teeth and his eyes like blind stones. The mouth was opening and shutting.

"They cannot follow us, I tell you. They cannot pass over water."

(Golding, 1961: 228–229)

Chapter 6

Discourse and Narrative Stylistics

6.1 Discourse and text

The terms "discourse" and "text" are sometimes used interchangeably in stylistic analyses. However, they are different in terms of abstraction involved. "Discourse" generally refers to language in use. It is also sometimes defined more elaborately; for example, Gee (2005: 21) defines discourse as "ways of combining and integrating language, actions, interactions, ways of thinking, believing, valuing, and using various symbols, tools, and objects to enact a particular sort of socially recognizable identity". On the other hand, "text" typically refers to a written or printed record, but it can also encompass the verbal representation of all communicative acts (Brown and Yule, 1983: 6). Despite their interconnectedness, this chapter adopts the broadest sense of "discourse" to refer to language in use, while using the term "text" inclusively to refer to a printed record or a verbal transcript of an oral communicative act.

《文心雕龙》, a famous book written by 刘勰 in 6th century China, presents our folk knowledge about a text. It states that characters, which are the written forms of words in Chinese, are combined to form sentences, sentences are combined to form textual sections, and sections are combined to produce a complete text.[①]

Chapter 5 has clarified that words are structural components of a clause, and they are initially combined to form phrases or word groups, which are then combined to form a clause. Both a single clause and a clause-complex can form a sentence. Is the relationship between a sentence and a text segment, and

---

① "夫人之立言，因字而生句，积句而成章，积章而成篇。篇之彪炳，章无疵也；章之明靡，句无玷也；句之清英，字不妄也；振本而末从，知一而万毕矣。"（刘勰，2012）

between a text segment and a text, similar to the relationship between a word and a sentence? Since a text segment, as the name suggests, acts as an intermediate unit between a sentence and a text, this section will focus on discussing the relationship between a sentence and a text. The discussion of the intermediate unit will be reserved for Section 3, where a specific text type (i.e., narrative texts) will be explored in detail.

Table 6.1 provides a comparison between linguistic expressions and discourses/texts. The column on the left contains linguistic expressions that are commonly found in dictionaries, grammar books, or textbooks. The column on the right demonstrates how these linguistic expressions are used in various contexts, resulting in three different discourses. In the first multi-modal discourse, the text "EXIT" is presented alongside a sign depicting a person running out of a door. This combination of text and visual representation conveys the message of an exit. The second multi-modal discourse features the text "NO SMOKING" positioned below a symbol prohibiting smoking. This combination effectively communicates the message of a smoking ban. In the third discourse, a "Six Word Stories" is presented, which stands somewhat independently from the other information on the same web page.

This comparison highlights two key points regarding the relationship between a text and a sentence. Firstly, a text is not defined by size or length. As evidenced in Table 6.1, the three verbal texts presented in the multi-modal discourses vary significantly in length. They range from a single-word sentence, to a one-phrase sentence, or to five sentences all composed of noun phrases. In reality, a text can be of a wide range of lengths, such as the extensive word count found in textbooks like this one.

Table 6.1 Linguistic expressions vs. discourses/texts①

Linguistic expressions	Discourses/Texts
exit	
No smoking.	
lovers friends best friends strangers	

① The "Six Word Stories" is retrieved from: www.sixwordstories.net/2014/03/strangers-friends-best-friends-lovers-strangers/.

Secondly, the relationship between a sentence and a text differs from that of a part to a whole. For instance, when the last sentence is removed from the six-word story in Table 6.1, the remaining ones still make sense. It becomes a different story, one with a happy ending.

Halliday and Hasan (1976: 1–2) provide a comprehensive explanation of the nature of a text and the relationship between a text and a sentence:

> A text is a unit of language in use. It is not a grammatical unit, like a clause or a sentence; and it is not defined by its size. A text is sometimes envisaged to be some kind of super-sentence, a grammatical unit that is larger than a sentence but is related to a sentence in the same way that a sentence is related to a clause, a clause to a group and so on: by CONSTITUENCY, the composition of larger units out of smaller ones. But this is misleading. A text is not something that is like a sentence, only bigger; it is something that differs from a sentence in kind.
>
> A text is best regarded as a SEMANTIC unit: a unit not of form but of meaning. Thus it is related to a clause or sentence not by size but by REALI ZATION, the coding of one symbolic system in another. A text does not CONSIST OF sentences; it is REALIZED BY, or encoded in, sentences. If we understand it in this way, we shall not expect to find the same kind of STRUCTURAL integration among the parts of a text as we find among the parts of a sentence or clause. The unity of a text is a unity of a different kind.

6.2 Discourse, genre and ideology: A functional approach

6.2.1 A framework for discussion

Chapter 2 has introduced the framework for discourse analysis from a functional perspective. In that framework (see Figure 2.3), language is stratified into three levels: grammar, discourse, and social context. Martin (1992: 496) proposes a more elaborate model to account for language and its semiotic environment (see Figure 6.1).

In this elaborated model, social context is further stratified into three strata, namely ideology, genre, and register. When conducting a stylistic analysis, it becomes crucial to take into account ideology and genre as they enable us to systematically examine the thematic meaning and textual structure of the analyzed text.

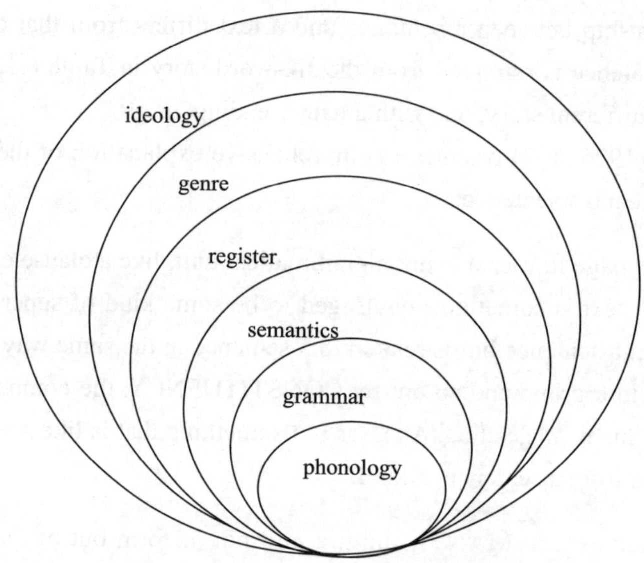

Figure 6.1 Language and its semiotic environment

6.2.2 Ideology

Ideology operates in an implicit way, but in two different means. One is the indiscriminate means based on shared meanings. This is best summarized in Lemke's (1995: 2) summary of the core insight of ideology: "there are certain common meanings we have learned to create and take for granted as common sense, which, however, support one social group's power to dominate another." This summary highlights the indiscriminate function of ideology based on shared meanings, which can be exemplified by the pair of words: *bachelor* and *spinster*. *Bachelor* conceptually refers to an unmarried male adult, while *spinster* conceptually refers to an unmarried female adult. In Chapter 4, we discussed that words have both conceptual and associative meanings such as connotative meaning. *Bachelor* has been used as a brand name for cigarettes, possibly due to its positive connotations of freedom and the pleasures of single life. On the other hand, *spinster* cannot be used as a brand name, at least in the present time, due to its negative connotations suggesting undesirability, loneliness, or inability to find a partner. This contrast reflects and construes the ideology of male dominance. It is important to note that societal attitudes evolve over time, and the negative connotations associated with *spinster* are gradually diminishing.

Ideology also has a discriminatory function based on different varieties of meanings. According to Martin and Rose (2007: 3–21), all native speakers of a language share a range of meaning-making resources, but there exist certain varieties of meanings that are not equally distributed. These varieties of meanings are, for example, constructed in the written discourses of contemporary social institutions, such as the sciences, government and education. Extensive efforts have been made to investigate how access to meaning is conditioned by factors like generation, gender, class, incapacity and ethnicity. Two influential theories have been developed to explore how access to meaning is influenced by the factor of social class. One is the code theory by Bernstein (1971). He proposes a distinction between "elaborated code" and "restricted code". The elaborated code is characterized by more complex and explicit language use, typically associated with formal situations and education. The restricted code, on the other hand, involves simplified and context-bound language, often associated with informal communication within specific social groups. He also pointed out that the two codes are closely related to social class. The elaborated code is mainly employed by families with a middle-class background, while the restricted code is used by families of lower classes. The two concepts are thus influential in understanding the relationship between language and social class. The other is Turner's sociological research on human emotions. He has explored how emotions are influenced by social factors and how they shape social interactions and relationships. Turner (2007: 188) holds that "individuals in lower social classes should, on average, reveal considerably more anger, sadness, fear, shame, guilty, and alienation than those in upper social classes".

6.2.3 Genre

The different varieties of meaning are conceptualized as genres from a functional perspective (Martin and Rose, 2008: 18). The Sydney School uses the term "genre" to refer to different types of texts that enact various types of social contexts, and defines a genre as a staged, goal-oriented social process (Martin and Rose, 2008: 6). According to Martin and Rose (2008: 6), a genre is staged because it usually requires multiple steps to reach our goals, it is goal-oriented because we use genres to get things done and would feel frustrated if we don't accomplish the final steps, and it is a social process for the reasons that we participate in genres with other people and that writers shape their texts for readers of particular kinds.

There are three basic points about genre. Firstly, genres are recognizable due to their consistent patterns of meaning. As children, we learn to identify and differentiate the typical genres of our culture by observing these consistent patterns of meaning when we engage with others in different situations. As these patterns are relatively consistent for each genre, we can anticipate the likely progress of each situation and learn the appropriate ways to interact within it. This point can be illustrated by the game of "Hide and Seek".

To play "Hide and Seek" in real life, we"ll need no less than two players. Here are the steps commonly followed in America:

1. Designate one person as "it" through a random selection or by volunteering.
2. The person who is "it" must close their eyes or cover their eyes and start counting out loud to a predetermined number (e.g., 10, 20, or 30) while the other players find a hiding spot. The goal for the hiding players is to find a good hiding spot where they won"t be easily found.
3. After finishing the count, the person who is "it" will start searching for the other players.
4. If the person who is "it" finds a hiding player, they have to announce their discovery by calling out the player's name and the hiding player must come out of their spot and join "it" in searching for the remaining players.

5. The game continues until all the players are found, or a predetermined time limit expires.
6. The last player found becomes the new "it" for the next round, and the game starts again.

The steps listed above define what is "Hide and Seek". When we see a child covering his or her eyes with hands and counting out loud numbers or when we see a child enthusiastically calling out another child's name, we immediately recognize that they are playing "Hide and Seek" and can predict what will happen next. This is due to the consistent patterns of meaning associated with the game.

Such predictable patterns of meaning can vary from the relatively simple range of language resources we use to play games like "Hide and Seek", or to buy goods in a shop, to the more complex meanings we might find in scientific reports or political debates. But even such complex meanings fall into consistent patterns that make it possible for us to recognize and predict how each genre is likely to unfold, and so manage new information, and interact appropriately and strategically.

Secondly, the number of recognizably distinct genres in any culture may be quite large, but not unmanageably so. In contemporary western culture, there are several spoken genres that have predictable patterns of meaning, including "greetings cards", "service encounters", "casual conversations", "arguments", "telephone enquiries", "instructions", "lectures", "debates", "plays", "jokes", "games" and so on; and within each of these general types, many more specific genres can be identified.

Thirdly, genres relate to one another, and they form a taxonomy. For pedagogical purposes, Martin and Rose (2008: 138) illustratively build into a spiral the related genres that primary and high school students should master (see Figure 6.2).

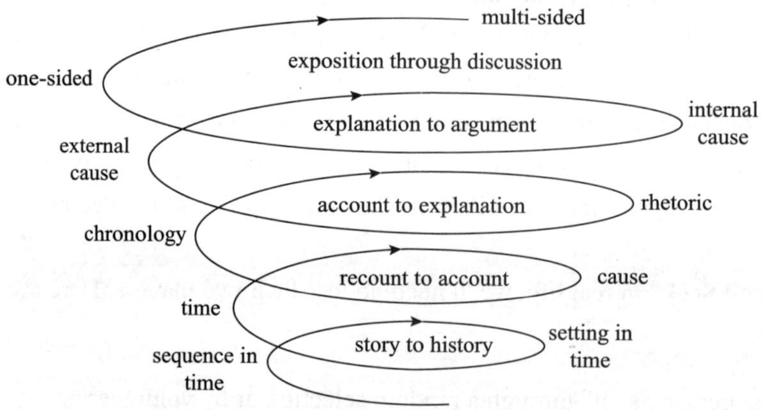

Figure 6.2 A spiral curriculum for history genres

This figure approximately outlines our encountering with primary genres from an ontogenetic perspective. We start with the genre of story, which comprises sub-genres like personal account (narrating what happened to us), (auto) biographical recount (narrating the story of our and others' lives), and historical recount (such as the so-called "grand narratives"). The story genre, on the whole, organizes its meaning along a temporal sequence. Then, we move on to historical account, which features causal connections and abstract participants. What comes next are factorial and consequential explanations. These genres explain the cause-and-effect relationships involved, either by depicting what leads to what or what follows from what. They highlight complex causal relations. The genres of explanation are followed by the genres of exposition and argument. The two genres present viewpoints and support them with arguments either for or against a particular position, and they involve either justifying or demolishing some problematic interpretations. It doesn't matter whether it is for or against, the arguments presented are typically one-sided. The one-sided argument and exposition are followed by the genre of discussion, where multiple interpretations are considered and analyzed. It allows for a more nuanced exploration of different viewpoints and encourages the exchange of ideas.

6.2.4 Discourse semantics

When we discussed the functional framework for discourse analysis (see Figure 2.3), we have introduced the three metafunctions of language recognized in functional linguistics. Incorporating metafunctions in his work on discourse, Martin (1992) developed Halliday and Hasan's (1976) seminal work on cohesion in English in terms of discourse semantics. In Martin and Rose (2007: 8), they identify six sets of resources for making meaning at the level of discourse semantics. These systems and their names are grouped along their metafunction in Table 6.2. The table also gives a brief gloss of the overall function of each system.

Table 6.2 Discourse systems and metafunctions

Discourse systems	Brief discription	Metafunction
Appraisal	"negotiating attitudes"	interpersonal
Ideation	"representing experience"	ideational
Conjunction	"connecting events"	ideational
Identification	"tracking people and things"	textual
Periodicity	"information flow"	textual
Negotiation	"enacting exchanges"	interpersonal

Martin and Rose (2007: 17) provide clear definitions of these discourse systems, which are briefly illustrated through the examples from *Lost and Found* (Appendix 6.1) and *From Little Things Big Things Grow* (Appendix 6.2). For more detailed explanations, please refer to Martin and Rose (2007: 17–21).

Appraisal is concerned with evaluation—the kinds of attitudes that are negotiated in a text, the strength of the feelings involved and the ways in which values are sourced and readers aligned. Appraisal resources are interpersonal in kind, which realize variations in the tenor of social interactions enacted in a text. The key meanings here have to do with evaluating things, judging people's characters and behaviors, and expressing their feelings, which are termed respectively as appreciation, judgement, and affect in Martin and White (2005).

All the three categories of resources can be found in *Lost and Found*. The use of the adjective *wonderful* in the last sentence illustrates appreciation, conveying a positive evaluation of *things*. A case of judgement is seen in the clause *he had made a big mistake*, indicating a negative judgement of the boy.

The story is rich in affect, starting with the penguin's sadness (*The penguin looked sad*) and the boy's disappointment (*That night, the boy couldn't sleep for disappointment*) when he initially failed to help the penguin. The disappointment shifts to delight (*The boy was delighted*) as he successfully helped the penguin return to the South Pole. However, the penguin's sadness persisted and intensified (*But it looked sadder than ever*) at the South Pole. Eventually, the boy realized that the penguin had been *lonely* rather than lost. They were happily reunited, as implied by the positive appreciation mentioned earlier, and went back home together.

Ideation focuses on the content of a discourse—what kinds of activities are undertaken, and how participants undertaking these activities are described and classified. These are ideational kinds of meaning, that realize the field of a text.

In the case of *Lost and Found*, the story primarily revolves around the activities of the boy and the lost penguin, which unfold sequentially (... *a boy who found a penguin in his door*, ... *it began to follow him everywhere, He checked in the Lost and Found Office*). According to the transitivity system discussed in Chapter 5, these activities are predominantly construed through material clauses. However, the story also incorporates other clause types. For instance, the opening clause *Once there was a boy* ... is an existential clause that introduces the main character.

The main characters in the story are the boy and the penguin. Other participants mentioned in the story include birds, the boy's toy duck, a big ship, the boy's rowboat, and the waves. As a fairy tale, these participants are often introduced without much detail, except for a few, such as the boy's rowboat.

Conjunction looks at inter-connections between activities—reformulating them, adding to them, sequencing them, explaining them and so on. These are also ideational types of meanings, but of the subtype 'logical'. Logical meanings are used to form temporal, causal and other kinds of connectivity.

> (1) Once there was a boy who found a penguin in his door. (2) The boy didn't know where it had come from, **but** it began to follow him everywhere. (3) The penguin looked sad **and** the boy thought it must be lost. (4) **So** the boy decided to help the penguin find its way home. (5) He checked in the Lost and Found Office. (6) **But** no one was missing a penguin.

In the second sentence, the conjunction *but* is used to move the story forward by narrating what happened after the boy found the penguin. The conjunction *and* in the third sentence indicates a weak causal relationship, justifying the boy's inference that the penguin was probably lost. The conjunction *so* at the beginning of Sentence 4 also indicates a cause-effect relationship, explaining the reason for the boy's decision to help the penguin find its way home. The conjunction *but* at the beginning of the sixth sentence connects the fifth and sixth sentences, showing that the effort to find the penguin's owner at the Lost and Found Office is unsuccessful.

Identification is concerned with tracking participants—with introducing people, places and things into a discourse and keeping track of them once there. These are textual resources, focusing on how discourse makes sense to the reader by keeping track of identities.

In the excerpt quoted above, the main character is introduced as *a boy*, and his identity is then kept track of using the definite article *the* and the pronouns *his* and *him*. The linguistic resources and their functions are summarized below (see Table 6.3).

Table 6.3 The linguistic resources of identification and their function in *Lost and Found*

Linguistic resources	Discourse functions	Wording
a boy	presenting a participant	indefinite reference
his	tracking a participant	pronoun
the boy	tracking a participant	definite reference
him	tracking a participant	pronoun
the boy	tracking a participant	definite reference
the boy	tracking a participant	definite reference
he	tracking a participant	pronoun

Periodicity considers the rhythm of discourse—the layers of prediction that flag for readers what's to come, and the layers of consolidation that accumulate through the meanings made. These are also textual kinds of meanings, concerned with organizing discourse as pulses of information.

In *From Little Things Big Things Grow*, the story doesn't immediately delve into the narrative of Vincent Lingiari leading Gurindji to fight for their land rights. Instead, the narrator provides an introduction that sets the stage and informs the readers that they will be presented with an eight-year-long story centered around power and pride. This establishes the genre (story) and theme from the very beginning, allowing readers to have a sense of what to expect. This kind of predictability is crucial for processing and understanding the information presented.

Gather round people I'll tell you a story
An eight year long story of power and pride

Furthermore, the narrator also indicates the conclusion of the story but then takes a significant leap back to the beginning by reiterating the story's theme. This serves as a way to wrap up the narrative and reinforce the central message:

That was the story of Vincent Lingiari
But this is the story of something much more
How power and privilege can not move a people
Who know where they stand and stand in the law

By restating the theme, the periodicity of the discourse is emphasized, bringing the story to a close while reinforcing its underlying message.

Negotiation is concerned with interaction as an exchange between speakers—how speakers adopt roles and assign them to each other in dialogue, and how moves are organized in relation to one another.

In the conversation rewritten from *From Little Things Big Things Grow,* the negotiation process is evident:

Vestey man: I'll double your wages
Eighteen quid a week you'll have in your hand
Vincent: Uhuh we're not talking about wages
We're sitting right here till we get our land

Here, the Vestey man initiated the exchange by making an offer to double the wages. However, Vincent responded with a denial, redirecting the focus of the conversation away from wages and emphasizing the collective goal of fighting for their land rights. This exchange exemplifies the negotiation dynamics in assigning roles and organizing moves in a conversation [see Martin (1992) for details].

6.3 Narrative stylistics

In Section 6.2.3, it states that there are numerous genres, making it impractical to cover all of them in a single chapter. Figure 6.2 visualizes the genre spiral, placing the genre of story at its inception. This section uses the genre of story as a prime illustration to explain the key elements of stylistic analysis at the discourse stratum. The genre of story encompasses novels and short stories in a broad sense.

Before delving into a detailed analysis, it is important to establish a fundamental distinction and provide clarifications on key terms to prevent confusion in the subsequent discussion. This distinction lies between "what happens" and the narration of those happenings. Different studies have referred to "what happens" as fabula, histoire, story, or plot (Simpson, 2014: 20; Black, 2006: 46; 申丹, 2019: 3–20), while the narration of happenings has been termed as sjužet, récit, text, or discourse (Simpson, 2014: 20; Black, 2006: 46; 申丹, 2019: 3–20).

In the literature of narrative stylistics, "what happens" is now widely referred to as story. But the term "story" is also unanimously used as the genre name to refer to a text type. To ensure clarity and to follow the tradition as well, the term "story" is reserved for the abstract storyline of a narrative, i.e., the sequence of elemental, chronologically ordered events; whereas, when cases of the genre of story are mentioned, they are referred to as novels or short stories. And "(narrative) text" or "narrative" is used to refer to a spoken or written text that presents a story. Finally, "discourse" is used to encompass both the act of narrating a story and the resulting narrative product.

6.3.1 Discourse structure of novels and short stories

The genre of story, as a form of discourse, exhibits notable distinctions from the genres of poetry and drama. In previous chapters, numerous poems have been introduced, and it is sufficient to describe them using a one-layered discourse structure, namely, the poet-reader relationship. On the other hand, the discourse structure of dramas is more intricate, requiring a two-layered model, as exemplified in Figure 6.3.

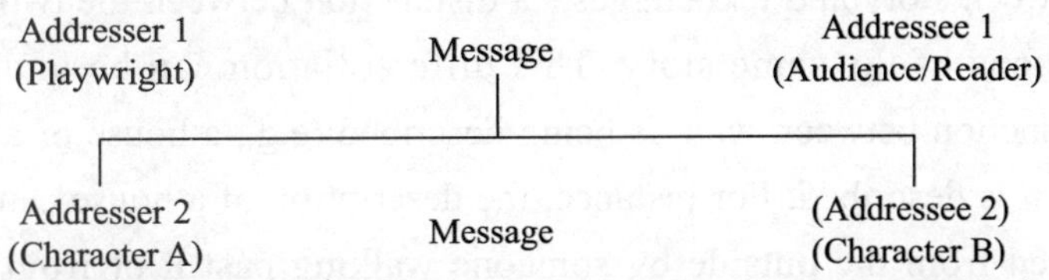

Figure 6.3 The discourse structure of drama (Short, 2013: 169)

Short (2013) contends that the discourse architecture of novels and short stories is much more complicated and that a narrator-narratee level is intervening between the author-reader level and the character-character level (see Figure 6.4).

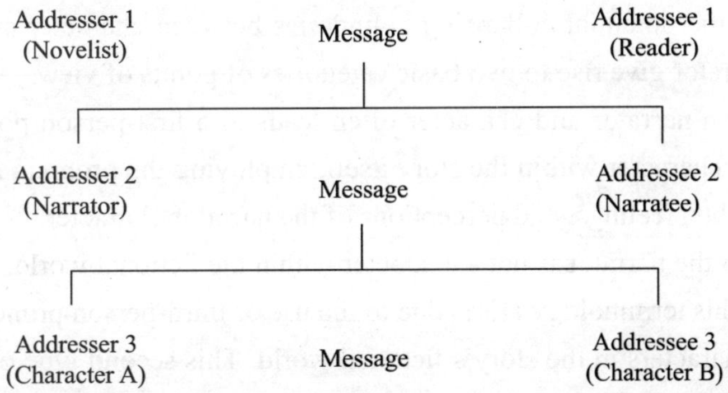

Figure 6.4 The discourse structure of narratives (Short, 2013: 257)

So the discourse structure in novels and short stories includes three main levels: the novelist-reader level, the character-character level, and the intervening narrator-narratee level. At the novelist-reader level, the addresser refers to the author or producer of the literary work. The addresser's social background and context provide valuable information for readers to understand the work. The character-character level represents the interactions between the characters in the story, similar to the way people engage in verbal communication in everyday life.

The intervening narrator-narratee level, however, requires further clarification. The narrator is the entity or voice responsible for presenting the narrative to the audience or reader. The narrator tells the story and provides a specific perspective through which events are conveyed. On the other hand, the narratee is the target recipient or audience of the narration.

This three-layered model helps explain how novels and short stories share stories in a general sense, with all three levels and all six participants playing their respective roles. However, it's essential to note that specific fictional works may neutralize some of the distinctions, multiply others, or do both at the same time as shown in the following sub-section.

6.3.2 Points of view

The distinction between story and text suggests a disjunction between the two, implying the existence of various textual versions of the same story. This differentiation can be understood by referencing Short's (2003: 256) distinction between what is being described (e.g., a house or a football match) and the perspective from which it is described. For instance, the description of a house can vary greatly depending on whether it is observed from the outside by someone walking past it or from the inside by someone residing in it. These different perspectives result in contrasting descriptions of the same house. Similarly, a football match can be described differently by a spectator, a player, or the referee, each providing their unique viewpoint.

Likewise, the potential multiple versions of a particular story results from different perspectives from which it is presented, which are commonly referred to as points of view. Concerning the framework presented in Figure 6.4, the potential collapsing boundaries between character and narrator and arguably between novelist and narrator give rise to two basic categories of points of view.

The collapse between narrator and character often leads to a first-person point of view. In this case, the story is narrated by a character within the story itself, employing the pronoun *I*. This perspective grants direct access to the thoughts, feelings, and perceptions of the narrator-character.

On the other hand, if the narrator is not a character within the fictional world, they are typically termed a third-person narrator. This terminology arises due to the use of third-person pronouns such as *he*, *she*, *it* or *they* when referring to characters in the story's fictional world. This second type of narrator is arguably the dominant form, as most narratives are written in the third-person perspective.

While the first-person narrator is relatively straightforward, the relationship between a third-person narrator and the author is more complex. Readers often assume that the narrator and the author are the same person, but this is not always the case. Authors may employ a third-person perspective to present attitudes they align with, but they are not obligated to do so. Additionally, an author's viewpoint can change over time, especially if they have written multiple works.

The lack of a direct identity between a third-person narrator and the author is matched on the "addressee" side of the above diagram by the fact that we often take on, during the reading of a fiction, a set of attitudes and assumptions which may be different, even markedly so, from those we normally hold. For example, when reading science fiction, readers assume that things can happen which patently cannot in the world we normally inhabit.

The complicated relationships between a third-person narrator and the author and between the normal assumptions of real readers and what they assume during the process of reading have led many critics (see Booth, 1961: 71–76, 137–139; Leech and Short, 1981: 259–62) to interpose another layer of discourse structure between the author-reader and narrator-narratee levels as mapped out in the above diagram. This extra layer involves an "implied Author" (that is, the author implied by our understanding of the text) and an "implied reader" (that is, the reader we have to "become" in order to read and react sensitively to the text).

In addition to the first-person and third-person points of view, there is also the second-person point of view, where the story is directly narrated to the reader using *you* as the pronoun. This perspective aims to engage the reader as an active participant in the narrative. However, when *you* refers to the addressee(s), it always assumes the presence of the addressor *I*. For example, in the lyric lines 划着船，过了河，你在水边看着我 (Rowing the boat, crossing the river, you watch me by the water), the addressee 你 (you) and the addressor 我 (I) are inseparable. Therefore, some argue that there is no true second-person point of view.

Nevertheless, even when both first-person and second-person pronouns are used in the same sentence, their roles differ depending on their structural positions. In Example 6.1a, 我 (I) is used as the subject, while 你 (you) is used as a modifier, thus giving 我 a more significant role. The opposite is true in Example 6.1b. Therefore, Example 6.1a is part of a narrative from a first-person point of view, while Example 6.1b is part of a narrative from a second-person point of view.

Example 6.1a

一年前，我路过，
你家屋前的那条路。

Example 6.1b

一年前，你走过，
我家屋前的那条路。

红山果

一朵花，一颗树；	绕过山，蹚过河，
一座房子一条路。	三天五天你装路过。
一座山，一条河；	你心里早有我，
一只小船一个我。	我要你现在就告诉我。
一颗心，一把火；	满（南）山野花开满坡，
一个木瓜一个你。	你东藏来我西躲。

划着船，过了河，	你要抓紧我的手，
你在水边看着我。	我们一起趟过河。
一年前，你走（我路）过，	你又摘来红山果，
我（你）家屋前的那条路。	一颗一颗送给我，
我悄悄地看着你，	日出日落都快乐，
你也偷偷地望着我。	一百年也要陪着我。

6.3.3 Narrative structure

The discourse structure of novels and short stories involves various layers of communication between the author and reader, narrator and narratee, and different characters. On the other hand, the narrative structure focuses on the message itself, i.e., the story itself.

Based on a collection of oral presentations of personal experiences, Labov and Waletzky (1967) propose that a narrative should comprise five components: orientation, complication, evaluation, resolution, and coda. Labov (1972: 359–363) further expands on this model and provides a visualization of the narrative structure, as shown in Figure 6.5.

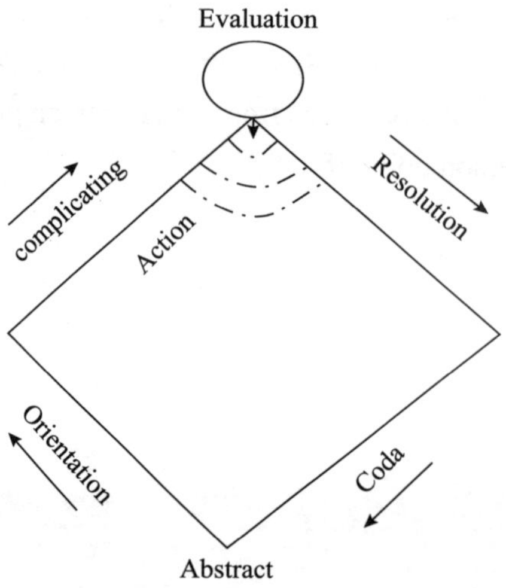

Figure 6.5 Narrative structure (cf. Labov, 1972: 369)

From Little Things Big Things Grow (see Appendix 6.2) is a very popular song that depicts the Aboriginal people's fight for their land rights. It provides an excellent illustration of Labov's (1972) model of narrative structure.

The "abstract" component of a narrative serves to provide a summary of the story, answering the question of what the story is essentially about. The opening lines of the song quoted below present the abstract of the story, informing the readers that it is a story featuring power and pride.

Gather round people I'll tell you a story

An eight year long story of power and pride

The "orientation" component of a narrative addresses the who, when, where, and what questions, providing information about the people involved, time, place, and situation. The ensuing lines following the first two serve as the orientation, introducing the protagonist and antagonist of the struggle and describing their contrasting circumstances.

British Lord Vestey and Vincent Lingiari
Were opposite men on opposite sides
Vestey was fat with money and muscle
Beef was his business, broad was his door
Vincent was lean and spoke very little
He had no bank balance, hard dirt was his floor

The "complication" component in a narrative describes the events or actions that unfold. The "evaluation" component, on the other hand, serves to show the significance or interest of these events. It gives purpose to the narrative and explains why it is being told. Typically, evaluation is interspersed within the complication component or even throughout the entire narrative.

In a story, the "complication" component, possibly together with sporadically distributed evaluation, forms the main body and presents a sequence of events. Often, a lengthy sequence of events can be broken down into multiple cycles of simple narratives, each containing its own complication sections. This is evident in *From Little Things Big Things Grow*, which consists of two rounds of complicating actions.

The first round primarily focuses on the Gurindji people's protest at Wattie Creek and their negotiation with Vestey. The evaluation in this round includes the anger of Vestey men and the persistence of the Gurindji people. The second round centers around the Gurindji's visit to Sydney and their return, with the ongoing evaluation highlighting their unwavering determination to reclaim their land rights.

The component of "resolution" or "result" goes with what finally happened. The final result of Gurindji's struggle is that they succeeded in achieving their goal.

The component of "coda" affords several possibilities. It can signal the end of the story, offer general observations or reflections, or bridge the gap between the narrative and the present moment. In the coda of *From Little Things Big Things Grow*, it signifies the conclusion of the story with the line *That was the story of Vincent Lingiari*. Additionally, it provides some general observations or interpretations of the story:

But this is the story of something much more
How power and privilege can not move a people
Who know where they stand and stand in the law

Not all stories include all six components. The abstract, orientation, and coda components are optional and may not be present in every narrative. Moreover, Martin and Rose (2008: 52) suggest that the structure proposed by Labov (1972) applies only to a specific type of story. They propose the existence of a family of story genres (see Table 6.4), each with different stages or structural components that distinguish them from one another.

Table 6.4 Family of story genres (Martin and Rose, 2008: 52)

Staging	Experience	Response	Experience	Attitude
recount	record	[prosodic]	–	variable
anecdote	remarkable event	reaction	–	affect
exemplum	incident	interpretation	–	judgement
observation	event description	comment	–	appreciation
narrative	complication	evaluation	resolution	variable

According to Martin and Rose (2008: 52), the obligatory components complication, evaluation and resolution define what they refer to as narrative. In addition to narrative, there are recount, anecdote, exemplum, and observation. Recounts "record a sequence of events without significant disruption" and the recorded events are "typically appraised prosodically as the recount unfolds"; anecdotes involve "some remarkable disruption to usuality, which is not resolved, but simply reacted to"; exemplums involve a disruption which is interpreted by judgement of people's character or behavior; observations provide "a description of a significant event, followed by a personal comment appreciating an aspect of it" (Martin and Rose, 2008: 52). Similar to narratives, the other story types could also begin with an orientation, where the "who, when, where, what" information is provided, and close with a coda.

The narrative type of story-telling has been exemplified in the analysis of *From Little Things Big Things Grow.* Among the other four, the first three are relatively easier to identify and comprehend. For example, the untitled poem by Wang Zhen chronicles the three stages of his revolutionary life in a sequential manner: the initial stage in Jingang Mountain, the maturing stage in Nanniwan, and the most recent stage in Xinjiang when the poem was composed. This poem effectively illustrates the process of recounting a personal journey:

生在井冈山，
长在南泥湾，
转战数万里，
屯垦在天山。

The fourth type of storytelling, observation, needs some explanations. The following is an example. In the beginning paragraph, a brief description of the event is provided: the personnel from Xinjiang Production and Construction Corps Reclamation Museum were shocked by old military uniforms they found in Wang Deming's house. The second paragraph acts as a transition, indicating that the following paragraphs will provide interpretations. The third and fourth paragraphs explain why soldiers like Wang Deming possessed such old clothes. The fifth paragraph gives a detailed description of the old military overcoat donated by Wang Deming and provides a highly positive evaluation of the overcoat. This positive evaluation is accompanied by admiration for the soldiers who lived an extremely frugal life and donated their savings to the development of industries in Xinjiang.

一件军大衣的故事①

20 年前，兵团军垦博物馆文物征集人员走进了八师一二一团一位普通军垦战士王德明老人的家中时，被眼前的一幕惊呆了：在老人家的杂物棚子里，架子上整整齐齐堆放着一摞摞旧衣服，有大衣、有衬衣、有手套、有袜子，甚至短裤。虽然这些衣服上布满了大大小小、花花绿绿、材质不一的补丁，但仍然依稀可以分辨出它们最初是一件件军装。

大家可能会有疑问，当时部队是供给制，军装全是配发的，怎么会穿得这么破旧呢?

为了发展生产，保障供应，开展对奸商的经济斗争，于 1949 年 12 月 10 日成立的新疆军区生产合作社，其主要任务是开办工厂。这个合作社当时没有任何资金，全靠指战员自力更生、白手起家去创办。王震司令员指示，军区直属部队每人每天节约口粮 250 克（为供给标准的 26%），菜金 9 分 6 厘（为供给标准的 60%），节约津贴费 50%。军服的双层衣领改为单层，四个口袋减为两个口袋，此后军衣都是单层衣领，只有两个口袋。一年节省一顶军帽，两套单衣减为一套单衣，每月 3 元津贴费拿出 2 元，平均每人每年节约 91.2 元支援国家建设。

铢积寸累，聚沙成塔，军垦战士把节约的资金投入合作社，作为工业建设投资资金。八一钢铁厂、七一棉纺织厂、乌拉泊水电站、六道湾煤矿等自治区最早的工业企业，都是这样建立起来的，没有向国家要过一分钱。军垦战士的奉献，终结了新疆没有现代化工业的历史。

王德明老人一辈子没舍得将这些破旧的衣物扔掉，这是他对当时峥嵘岁月的纪念。他把一件军大衣捐献给兵团博物馆，上面缝满了各种颜色的补丁 296 块！后来，这件军大衣被评为国家一级文物。军大衣上的片片补丁都述说着军垦人辉煌的故事，述说着军垦人不求索取、艰苦奋斗、无私奉献的精神，可以说一片片补丁就是一枚枚军功章！

6.3.4 Temporal ordering

The previous section focuses on the stylistic analysis of short stories and novels in terms of genre. This section will now focus on the ideational discourse semantics. Since stories are distinct in their temporal sequencing, the ideational analysis at the discourse semantics level primarily concerns the ordering of events and their presentation in novels and short stories.

① This version is from a street poster located close to the author's apartment in Shihezi. An online version of the story can be found at https://www.sizhengwang.cn/a/gmjsxlzl_btjs_gmjsxgs/220216/1030219.shtml.

At the beginning of Section 6.3, it has been made clear that a story tells a sequence of elemental, chronologically ordered events. However, it is rare for a story to be narrated strictly in chronological order (A-B-C). Certain re-orderings are often required by specific genres. For example, detective stories conventionally commence with the discovery of a corpse and then gradually reveal the sequence of events leading up to the murder (often in the order of C-B-A). For the sake of convenience, the chronological order of events (A-B-C) is referred to as the story time, while the narrating order (C-B-A) is referred to as the textual time (also known as discourse time, as mentioned in Black, 2006). According to Genette (1980, 1988), there are three aspects to consider when examining the temporal organization of novels and short stories:

1. Order: Addresses questions such as "What happened first, next, last?"
2. Duration: How long?
3. Frequency: How often?

6.3.4.1 Order

The category of order is the most obvious. Stylisticians are interested in whether the chronological order of the story remains preserved in the text. *From Little Things Big Things Grow* is a case where what happened first is also narrated first. When there is a mismatch between the story time and the textual time, it will lead to either flashback (analepsis) or flashforward (prolepsis).

Flashback is a narrative technique that disrupts the chronological order of events in a text. An example of this technique can be found in the Chinese lyrics《红山果》(see Section 6.3.2), where the time frame is initially set in the present but then jumps back in time to present events that occurred a year ago. Flashbacks are used to provide additional context, background information, or reveal crucial details that contribute to advancing the plot or developing the characters. In《红山果》, the flashback offers background information about the characters, indicating that they have known each other for a year and would meet every few days.

As previously mentioned, flashbacks are commonly employed in detective stories. In this genre, they serve to create tension, build suspense, and enhance the reader's understanding of the story. Flashbacks can be presented in various ways, such as through dialogue, memories, or dream sequences. In the case of《红山果》, although not explicitly indicated, the flashback is presented through the protagonist's memories. Here is another example where the use of flashback is indicated by the phrase *I remembered*:

> He sat looking at the sky for a long time. Then he took from his knapsack a bottle of wine, and drank some. *He remembered the night in the desert when he had sat with the alchemist, as they looked at the stars and drank wine together.* He thought of the many roads he had traveled, and of the strange way God had chosen to show him his treasure.
>
> (Coelho, 2015: 223–224)

Flashforward is a narrative technique that disrupts the chronological order of events by leaping forward in time to depict future events or scenarios. Unlike flashback, which looks into the past, flashforward offers a glimpse into what will happen later in the story. An example of flashforward can be observed in the film *Run Lola Run* (1998), where flashforwards are utilized to show the outcomes of the individuals Lola encounters as she races to save her boyfriend.

The use of flashforward serves to engage readers or viewers, building anticipation and curiosity by providing insights into the story's trajectory. It can create suspense, foreshadow future events, or reveal the consequences of the characters' actions. Flashforwards can be presented through various methods, including a character's vision, dreams, or a direct shift in the narrative timeline. Dreams are a commonly chosen approach, as shown in Coelho's (2015) *The Alchemist*, where the story commences with Santiago's dream of finding treasure in the pyramids of Egypt.

6.3.4.2 Duration

This is the most difficult and elusive of these categories, because it attempts to relate the time taken for the putative events to occur in the "real world", that is in "story time", to the time taken to narrate them. However, since it is impossible to measure the time it takes to narrate something, Genette (1980) suggests using the amount of space devoted to events in the narrative as a rough guideline.

There are four categories that describe the mismatch between story time and textual time. The first is summary, where the narrator compresses the narrative, resulting in shorter textual time than story time. For example: "So he went to Harvard and was extremely miserable for several months." (Lodge, 1978: 19)

The second category is ellipsis, which occurs when time passes and events happen without being mentioned in the text. Fictional narratives often skip less interesting parts of characters' lives, and it is also used in detective fiction to create mystery.

The third category is stretch, where events take longer to narrate than their actual occurrence would suggest. An example can be seen in Conrad's (1963) *The Secret Agent*, where the narrator describes the protagonist's perceptions and thoughts in detail before his death, creating a slowed-down narrative effect.

> He was lying on his back and staring upwards. He saw partly on the ceiling and partly on the wall the moving shadow of an arm with a clenched hand holding a carving knife. It flickered up and down. Its movements were leisurely. They were leisurely enough for Mr Verloc to recognize the limb and the weapon.
>
> They were leisurely enough for him to take in the full meaning of the portent, and to taste the flavour of death rising in his gorge. His wife had gone raving mad—murdering mad. They were leisurely enough for the first paralysing effect of this discovery to pass away before a resolute determination to come out victorious from the ghastly struggle with that armed lunatic. They were leisurely enough for Mr Verloc to elaborate a plan of defence, involving a dash behind the table, and the felling of the woman to the ground with a heavy wooden chair. But they were not leisurely enough to allow Mr

Verloc time to move either hand or foot. The knife was already planted in his breast.

(Conrad, 1963: 212)

The final category is pause, where story time is suspended but the discourse continues. This typically occurs in descriptive passages in the narrator's voice. An example of pause can be found in 《红山果》: "你心里早有我，我要你现在就告诉我". This sentence concludes the flashback and brings the narrative back to the present.

6.3.4.3 Frequency

The category of frequency is less problematic, and perhaps interpretively less interesting. It concerns about the frequency of an incident occurring in the story and how many times it is narrated in the text.

The possibilities are:

1. To tell once what happened once, or *n* times what happened *n* times (singulative).
2. To tell once what happened *n* times (iterative).
3. To tell *n* times what happened once (repetitive).

Singulative narratives are almost the norm. An example of this is *Lost and Found* (see Appendix 6.1), which narrates what happened to the boy and the lost penguin in a singulative way. Iterative narratives are also commonplace: they are characteristically marked by items such as *always*, *would* or *often*. 绕过山，蹚过河，三天五天你装路过 is an example in which the frequent passing by every 3–5 days is told only once. The following is an English example in which *always* is used to show the following events happen all the time:

> Always my father would locate the planet or the constellation first, then touch my shoulder and say: "Look now." And I would see, suspended in silence as if he had conjured it, the cosmic dust of a nebula unimaginably far, or a planet turning in silence like a gold coin ... he would say startling things: that beyond our own galaxy lay an estimated hundred thousand million more, some measuring hundreds of thousands of light years across ...

(Thubron, 1998: 39)

Repetitive narratives are not commonly found because they can lead to monotony. The following is an example in Chinese:

> 从前有座山，山上有座庙，庙里有个老和尚，老和尚在给小和尚讲故事。故事讲的是，从前有座山，山上有座庙，庙里有个老和尚，老和尚在给小和尚讲故事。……

Genette (1980: 115) classifies stories presented by different narrators into this category. If this is the case, Faulkner's (1930) *As I Lay Dying* should fall under this category.

6.4 A shift from authors' meaning-making to readers' comprehension

The examples mentioned earlier consist mainly of texts which contain all obligatory generic stages. However, there are also instances of one-sentence narratives, such as the famous short story often attributed to Ernest Hemingway: *For sale: baby shoes, never worn*. When analyzed with the concepts discussed previously, this short story only contains the element of resolution. Nevertheless, we still consider it a short story because readers are able to infer and mentally construct the complete series of events. This highlights a shift from emphasizing the author's intended meaning to prioritizing the reader's comprehension in interpreting a text.

The theory of text worlds is proposed to account for what is constructed in our mind. As a distinction between discourse and text is made at the beginning of this chapter, Werth (1999) and Gavins (2007) make a distinction between the "discourse world" and the "text world". The discourse world is the immediate situation in which communication takes place; the text world is a mental representation of the situation(s) evoked by the text (Semino, 2014).

The discourse world, in its most typical form, involves face-to-face communication between a speaker and a hearer who are physically present in the same space. Certain aspects of this shared physical environment can become topics of communication and therefore part of the text world, for example the size or temperature of the room. However, in written communication, the writer and readers are often located in separate discourse worlds that can be distant from each other in terms of space and time. In this case, the immediate physical contexts of the writer and reader are usually unimportant and inaccessible for criticism or linguistic analysis. Instead, the broader characteristics of these separate discourse worlds, such as the writer's identity, the reader's background and characteristics, and the broader historical and cultural contexts, become crucial in understanding the text and its reception. These aspects are of significant interest to reviewers, critics, linguists, and scholars studying reader response, among others.

In the case of the Six Word Stories (*For sale: baby shoes, never worn*), we have no information about the immediate discourse world in which it was written. Similarly, the immediate discourse worlds in which readers read the text are quite varied and different from the one of the writer. But if this short story is indeed written by Ernest Hemingway, the broader historical and cultural contexts do provide cues for our interpretation. Hemingway was known for his portrayal of war and its impact on individuals and his notable works include novels such as *The Sun Also Rises* and *A Farewell to Arms*. This background information helps us make the possible inference that the baby shoes were never worn due to a war-related incident.

Discourse worlds, whether retrievable or not, existed. But text worlds are mental representations that readers construct while reading or processing texts. They are in readers' minds, and allow readers to construct a mental image of the events, characters, and setting described, thus enhancing comprehension and engagement with the reading material. A text can introduce multiple text worlds that can be concurrent, divergent, or nested within each other. Readers constantly update and revise their understanding of these worlds as they encounter new information, conflicts, or shifts in perspective.

There are several theories that can explain how text worlds are constructed and constantly revised. The most influential one is the schema theory. Schemas, also known as frames, scripts, or scenarios, are long-term mental representations that contain our background knowledge of people, objects, actions, situations, and so on. They play a crucial role constructing text worlds: comprehension and the construction of relevant text worlds rely on possessing the background knowledge assumed by the text. Cognitive psychologists have shown how comprehension involves not only the availability of relevant schemas but also their activation while interpreting a text. The activation of relevant schemas is facilitated by linguistic items in the text, known as "headers", which refer to elements of a schema. There are four types of headers (Jeffries and McIntyre, 2010: 129):

1. Precondition headers refer to a necessary precondition for the application of the schema in question. For example, *Dan was feeling ill* may work as the precondition for the triggering of a doctor/patient interview schema.
2. Instrumental headers refer to actions that may lead to the invocation of a particular schema. *Dan entered the doctor's surgery* may be instrumental in triggering the doctor/patient interview script.
3. Locale headers are references to locations where the script in question is likely to be activated. *The doctor's surgery was a cold and forbidding place* provides a locale wherein we might expect the doctor/patient interview schema to be instantiated.
4. Internal conceptualization headers are references to actions or roles from the schema. *The doctor asked Dan how he was feeling* includes reference to both a role (*the doctor*) and an action (asking how the patient feels), both of which are likely to instantiate the schema in question.

Additionally, schemas exist at different levels and can form part-whole relationships. This means that specific schemas may subordinate to more general schemas and serve as components of larger schemas. For example, a doctor/patient interview schema can be embedded within a higher-level interview schema, which in turn may be part of a treatment schema.

Based on the concepts discussed earlier, we can provide a more systematic explanation of the six-word story *For sale: baby shoes, never worn.* Firstly, *for sale* functions as an internal conceptualization header, suggesting a general sale schema; *never worn*, also serves as an internal conceptualization header, indicating that the item being sold has not been used, possibly indicating a second-hand sale.

Secondly, the entire schema of a second-hand sale triggers a larger schema related to making a living during a war. A possible sequence of events can be imagined: a family purchased a pair of shoes for their baby, which was considered a luxury during the war. Unfortunately, the baby was either injured or passed away, resulting in the shoes remaining unworn. The heartbroken family then decided to sell the new shoes in order to acquire essential necessities like bread. This interpretation highlights the emotional impact and the hardships faced during times of war, illustrating a heartbreaking narrative within the constraints of a six-word story.

In Chapter 5, an excerpt from *The Inheritors* was analyzed at the stratum of lexico-grammar. Expressions like *A stick rose upright* were identified as having an unusual process, indicating underlexicalization on the part of the speaker.

The following excerpt from *The Name of the Rose* provides a similar example. The protagonist, Adso, describes an object used by Brother William. In terms of the schema theory, Adso lacks the schematic knowledge to refer to this object as "glasses" or "spectacles," so he resorts to describing its appearance and purpose in a lengthy manner.

> [*The Name of the Rose* is set in Italy in the Middle Ages. Adso, the narrator, is a novice monk and scribe to Brother William of Baskerville.]
>
> William slipped his hands inside his habit, at the point where it billowed over his chest to make a kind of sack, and he drew from it an object that I had already seen in his hands, and on his face in the course of our journey. It was a forked pin, so constructed that it could stay on a man's nose (or at least on his, so prominent and aquiline) as a rider remains astride his horse or as a bird clings to its perch. And, one on either side of the fork, before the eyes, there were two ovals of metal, which held two almonds of glass, thick as the bottom of a tumbler. William preferred to read with these before his eyes, and he said they made his vision better than what nature had endowed him with or than his advanced age, especially as the daylight failed, would permit. They did not serve him to see from a distance, for then his eyes were, on the contrary, quite sharp, but to see close up. With these lenses he could read manuscripts penned in very faint letters, which even I had some trouble deciphering. He explained to me that, when a man had passed the middle point of his life, even if his sight had always been excellent, the eye hardened and the pupil became recalcitrant, so that many learned men had virtually died, as far as reading and writing were concerned, after their fiftieth summer.
>
> (Eco, 1984: 48–49)

This suggests that Adso assumes his addressee lacks background knowledge of what he is describing, hence the need for the detailed explanation. This difference in schematic knowledge between Adso and the reader creates a sense of distance and adds to the riddle-like quality of the novel, which may contribute to its appeal. Overall, Adso's limited knowledge and the need for explicit descriptions can sometimes make it challenging for readers to fully construct the text world of the excerpt, but it also enhances the intrigue of the narrative.

Exercises:

1. What is the relationship between text and discourse? Why is it significant to distinguish the two in stylistics?

2. It is traditionally accepted that meaning is expressed by linguistic units of different sizes, including words, word groups/phrases, and clauses. What is the theoretical and practical significance in proposing a language level referred to as discourse semantics?

3. The following paragraph adopts a third-person point of view, please rewrite it from a first-person point of view.

   He rested his arms on the top of the wall and looked down the fifty feet or so to the tumbling white waters. Just upstream, the river Loran piled down from the forest in a compactly furious cataract. The spray was a taste. Beneath, the river surged round the piers of the viaduct that carried the railway on towards Lochgilpead and Gallanach.

   A grey shape flitted silently across the view, from falls to bridge, then zoomed, turned in the air and swept into the cutting on the far bank of the river, as though it was a soft fragment of the train's steam that had momentarily lost its way and was not hurrying to catch up. He waited a moment, and the owl hooted once, from inside the dark constituency of the forest. He smiled, took a deep breath that tasted of steam and the sweet sharpness of pine resin, and then turned away, and went back to pick up his bags.

   (Banks, 1993: 33)

4. The following is an imaginary poem, in which some items and phenomena familiar to us are presented in an unusual way. Try to figure out what are described in the poem.

   A Martian Sends a Postcard Home
   (Craig Raine)

   Caxtons are mechanical birds with many wings
   and some are treasured for their markings—

   they cause the eyes to melt
   or the body to shriek without pain.

   I have never seen one fly, but
   sometimes they perch on the hand.

   Mist is when the sky is tired of flight
   and rests its soft machine on ground:

then the world is dim and bookish
like engravings under tissue paper.

Rain is when the earth is television.
It has the property of making colours darker.

Model T is a room with the lock inside—
a key is turned to free the world

for movement, so quick there is a film
to watch for anything missed.

But time is tied to the wrist
or kept in a box, ticking with impatience.

In homes, a haunted apparatus sleeps,
that snores when you pick it up.

If the ghost cries, they carry it
to their lips and soothe it to sleep

with sounds. And yet, they wake it up
deliberately, by tickling with a finger.

Only the young are allowed to suffer
openly. Adults go to a punishment room

with water but nothing to eat.
They lock the door and suffer the noises

alone. No one is exempt
and everyone's pain has a different smell.

At night when all the colours die,
they hide in pairs

and read about themselves—

in colour, with their eyelids shut.

5. Choose one of your favorite short stories and analyze its narrative structure.

6. Many classic novels have been adapted for cinema or television. Please choose one of them and make a comparison of its verbal and multimodal versions by using the concepts explained in this chapter.

7. The following are three beginnings for a story. Please choose one of them and finish a well-structured story with at least four cycles of simple narratives.
   1) Once upon a time there lived a beautiful old lady in a small hamlet. When the sun set the old lady lighted a lamp. ...
   2) When I was six, I wanted a puppy so badly. My parents consulted many people and were convinced that an animal pet can make a good company. My parents decided to get me a puppy ...
   3) When my father told me the story of his high school, I was trying to solve a math problem. He was 16 and he was busy solving all kinds of study problems as well. One night, his father, my grandfather, came to his room, fetching him a bottle of milk ...

Chapter 7

Multimodality and Multimodal Stylistics

7.1 Modes and media

Functional grammar, as proposed by Halliday (2008), suggests examining linguistic units from a trinocular perspective: from above, from below, and from around. The examination of language as a semiotic system should be done likewise. In Chapter 6, the focus was on examining language from above, considering how discourse is shaped by genre and ideology. In this final chapter, the analysis extends to include examining language from below and from around, providing a complete understanding of the subject matter.

In Chapter 2, Table 2.3 shows that there is a particular level of substance within language, which can be further divided into phonic and graphic substances. This level of substance represents the medium through which language is "conveyed". Analyzing language "from below" requires in-depth exploration and analysis of both phonic and graphic substances.

In this book, the term "language" primarily refers to the natural language we use for communication. However, it is essential to note that the notion of "language" is also used in other contexts, such as body language, the language of music, and the language of architecture. These metaphorical uses of *language* indicate the meaning-making potential of these other semiotic systems. The study of language "from around" involves exploring these various meaning-making systems alongside our natural language.

Van Leeuwen (2022: 51–52) proposes a pair of terms to account for what needs to be taken into account when examining language from below and around: media and modes. According to him, a mode is a resource for functional design, which can be realized in different materialities. For example, language is a mode, and it can be realized by means of sounds (as speech) or by means of graphic traces (as writing). Likewise, the resources for visual communication also form a mode, and they can be realized materially in different ways—as drawings, photographs, paintings, and so on.

Van Leeuwen (2022: 52) identifies two kinds of media: production and distribution media. For our present purpose, we will only discuss production media in this chapter and refer to them as media for short. Media are the material resources that realize functional designs or the resources that materialize functional designs, and they also produce meaning.

The exploration of diverse modes for constructing meaning broadens the prospect of stylistic analysis. As shown in previous chapters, traditional stylistic approaches—with their concern with wording—for obvious reasons concentrate their analysis on verbal texts. This trend is closely related to the preference for monomodality within the Western cultures. For instance, highly valued written genres such as literary novels, academic papers, official documents and reports, are often materialized on dense, text-heavy pages free of illustrations. Likewise, works of art were commonly produced by using the same support (canvas) and the same medium (oils), irrespective of style or subject. However, a recent shift has signaled a decline in this monomodality dominance. Now, not only mass media outlets like magazines and comic books, but also documents produced by corporate entities, universities, and government departments are incorporating visual elements such as color illustrations, advanced layouts, and typography (Kress and van Leeuwen, 2001: 1).

The popularity of multimodality has made multimodal texts a new object of stylistic analysis. Multimodal texts, as defined in Baldry and Thibault (2006: 18), integrate selections from different semiotic resources into their principles of organization. These resources are not simply juxtaposed as separate modes of meaning-making but are combined and integrated to form a complex whole which cannot be reduced to or explained in terms of the mere sum of its separate parts.

Two prominent approaches dominate multimodal theorizing. One is Halliday's "social semiotics". Key works of social semiotic multimodal theory include Baldry and Thibault (2006), Bateman (2008), Kress and van Leeuwen (2001, 2006), O'Halloran (2004), O'Toole (1994) and van Leeuwen (2005, 2022). These works adapt the theoretical and methodological frameworks of Halliday's 'social semiotics' to investigate the extent to which multiple semiotic modes other than the verbal language may employ the principles of meaning-making captured by Halliday's language theory (refer to Section 2.5 of Chapter 2, Section 5.4 of Chapter 5, and Chapter 6). The other is informed by cognitive theory and is put forward by proponents such as Forceville (1996). One area in which a cognitive approach to multimodality has been particularly well developed is that of conceptual metaphor theory. Given that Halliday's theory of language has been sufficiently detailed in this book, the concluding chapter will provide a brief overview of the conceptual metaphor theory along with its application in multimodal analyses (see Section 7.5).

The introduction of media into stylistics also holds importance, as it allows the reach of multimodal stylistic analysis to be extended vertically to investigate the creation of meaning via the materialization of both monomodal and multimodal products. In terms of this vertical extension, this chapter will specifically concentrate on the multimodal analysis of speech sounds (more generally, sound quality) in Section 7.3 and delve into the multimodal analysis of written scripts as well as the general layout of printed materials in Section 7.4.

However, prior to moving on to the multimodal stylistic analyses of multimodal texts and their material realizations, Section 7.2 is dedicated to exploring different ways of meaning-making, which are common to different modes and media.

7.2 Different ways of making meaning

The basic unit of meaning making is a sign, which can be a word, symbol, gesture, image, or any other form that is used to represent or convey meaning. To examine the different ways of making meaning is to identify different categories of signs, which can be found in Peircean semiotics.

Peircean semiotics holds that a sign is connected to three things: interpretant, object, and ground. According to Peirce (2.228)①,

> A sign, or representamen, is something which stands to somebody for something in some respect or capacity. It addresses somebody, that is, creates in the mind of that person an equivalent sign, or perhaps a more developed sign. That sign which it creates I call the *interpretant* of the first sign. The sign stands for something, its *object*. It stands for that object, not in all aspects, but in reference to a sort of idea, which I have sometimes called the *ground* of the representamen.

The triadic relation described above may be diagrammed in Figure 7.1.

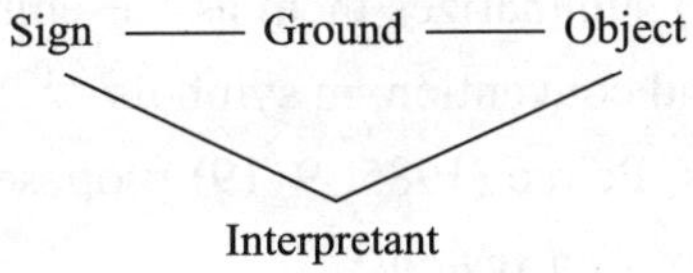

Figure 7.1 Peirce's semiotic triangle

Peirce (2.243) puts forward three criteria for classifying signs:

> Signs are divisible by three trichotomies; first, according as the sign in itself is a mere quality, is an actual existent, or is a general law; secondly, according as the relation of the sign to its object consists in the sign's having some character in itself, or in some existential relation to that object, or in its relation to an interpretant; thirdly, according as its Interpretant represents it as a sign of possibility or as a sign of fact or a sign of reason.

① Following the accepted practice, the book refers to Peirce's *Collected Papers* by volume and paragraph numbers, separated by a period.

Among them only the second one is relevant to the discussion here, and it is related to the ground of representation mentioned above. Innis (1985: 1–2) interprets the ground of representation as the "'standing for' relation" or "'semantic' relationships" between a sign and its object. For convenience of discussion, Innis' term 'standing for' will be adopted in the following discussion.

Following the definition given above, Peirce (2.229) argues that the "standing for" relation must be regarded as an indispensable relate of every sign because if a sign is related to an object, the relation must have some knowable basis.

> If a Sign is other than its Object, there must exist, either in thought or in expression, some explanation or argument or other context, showing how—upon what system or for what reason the Sign represents the Object or set of Objects that it does. (2.230)

As will be shown below, the knowable basis, either in thought or in expression, is just the criterion which Peirce employs for classifying signs.

Moreover, Peirce (1.551) argues that the process of searching for the "explanation or argument or other context" is a process of abstract comparison. According to him, in order to determine the respect in which two things are related, they must be compared, which presupposes a process of abstraction, because it requires that the qualities of the things be viewed apart from them ("we cannot comprehend an agreement of two things, except as an agreement in some *respect*, and this respect is … a pure abstraction …" (Peirce 1.551). The end result of this abstract comparison is the identification of the precise point of agreement between the two things in question, and when these two things are a sign and its object, the point of agreement is just the ground of the relation holding between them.

Peirce (1985: 7, 9–19) puts forward three respects, or grounds, in which a sign may be connected with its object. And Pharies (1985: 32) summarizes them as "resemblance, the ground of icons, existential connection or contiguity, in indexes, and convention, in symbols".①

According to these three grounds, Peirce (1985: 9–19) proposes his second trichotomy, according to which a sign is termed an *icon*, an *index*, or a *symbol*.

Peirce has defined the three types of signs differently on different occasions in order to stress different aspects of them. Epistemologically Peirce (1985: 10) defines an icon as "a Representamen whose Representative Quality is a Firstness of it as a First". That is, a quality that it possesses *qua* thing makes it fit to be a representamen. On other occasions, he made this abstract definition concrete and substantial:

> I call a sign which stands for something merely because it resembles it, an *icon*. (3.362)

> The Icon has no dynamical connection with the object it represents; it simply happens that its qualities resemble those of that object, and excite analogous sensations in the mind for which it is a likeness. (2.299)

① It should be noted that sometimes Peirce seems to attribute the relation as a feature of the sign itself.

These two definitions make clear the ground—resemblance—by which an icon is related to its object. But "resemblance" itself is still an elusive concept and open to many interpretations. Peirce made it clearer by classifying it further:

> But a sign may be iconic, that is, may represent its object mainly by its similarity, no matter what its mode of being. If a substantive be wanted, an iconic representamen may be termed a hypoicon. (2.276)
>
> Hypoicons may be roughly divided according to the mode of Firstness of which they partake. Those which partake of simple qualities, or First Firstnesses, are images; those which represent the relations, mainly dyadic, or so regarded, of the parts of one thing by analogous relations in their own parts, are diagrams; those which represent the representative character of a representamen by representing a parallelism in something else, are metaphors. (2.277)

The second member of the trichotomy is the index. Indexes differ from icons in that they have no significant resemblance to their objects, and differ from symbols in that they refer to individuals and direct the attention to their objects by blind compulsion. Peirce (1985: 12–13) emphasizes that an index refers to its object "because it is in dynamic (including spatial) connection both with the individual object, on the one hand, and with the senses of memory of the person for whom it serves as a sign, on the other hand". In terms of the ground of representation, Peirce (1985: 13) holds that the action of indexes, psychologically, depends upon association by contiguity, and not upon association by resemblance (as icons do) or upon intellectual operations (as symbols do). On another occasion, Peirce elaborated this point further:

> … the [indexical] sign signifies its object solely by virtue of being really connected with it. Of this nature are all natural signs and physical symptoms. (3.361)
>
> … the relation of the [indexical] sign to its objects consists … in some existential relation to that object … (2.243)
>
> An index is a sign which refers to the Object that it denotes by virtue of being really affected by that Object. (2.248)

The general interpretation of the above statements, especially the last one, is that the natural, cause-and-effect relationship is among the most obvious ways that connect an index to its object (Pharies, 1985: 39).

The final member of the trichotomy is the symbol. Peirce (1985: 16) defines it as "a Representamen whose Representative character consists precisely in its being a rule that will determine its interpretant". Following this definition closely, he points out that all words, sentences, books, and other conventional signs are symbols, which he exemplified as follows:

> We speak of writing or pronouncing the word "man"; but it is only a replica, or embodiment of the

word, that is pronounced or written. The word itself has no existence although it has a real being, *consisting in* the fact that existents *will* conform to it. It is a general mode of succession of three sounds or representatmens of sounds, which becomes a sign only in the fact that a habit, or acquired law, will cause replicas of it to be interpreted as meaning a man or men.

This definition and its elaboration stress the nature of the symbol itself, that is, a symbol is a law. However, he also intends to interpret the ground of representation that connects a symbol to its object as a law:

A *Symbol* is a sign which refers to the Object that it denotes by virtue of a law, usually an association of general ideas, which operates to cause the Symbol to be interpreted as referring to that Object. (2.249)

This theory of sign typology helps explain different ways of making meaning. Van Leeuwen (2022: 42–51) presents three principles in arriving at social semiotic interpretation: experiential meaning potential, provenance, and contextuality. The first one is grounded in common experience; provenance, grounded in visually and verbally documented cultural history; contextuality, grounded in ethnographic and documentary evidence. These principles for interpretation essentially lean on the underlying mechanism of metaphorical and indexical logic as explained above.

7.3 Parametric systems for sound quality and speech sounds

Sounds are omnipresent and produced in many different ways. In communication, we mainly make use of sounds produced with our vocal apparatus, and with our hands as we pluck, stroke, tap, beat and bang material objects. Even the sounds we produce with our feet whilst walking can occasionally bear significance. The speech sounds explored in Chapter 3 are a part of the sounds produced with our vocal apparatus.

7.3.1 Parametric system for sound quality

Van Leeuwen (1999, 2022) pioneers the study of the material basis of sounds produced with our vocal apparatus, hands, feet, and various instruments. According to him, these sounds share several parameters, which are all at play simultaneously. Each parameter is defined by a gradable distinctive feature. He has identified seven such parameters and outlined the systematization in Figure 7.2.

The features grouped into the seven parameters are semiotically loaded mostly following the metaphorical and indexical logic. That is, their significations are derived from what we do when we produce the sounds, either vocally or with our hands and/or feet. Van Leeuwen (1999) has explained and illustrated the parametric systems in detail. The following summary provides a list of the main points.

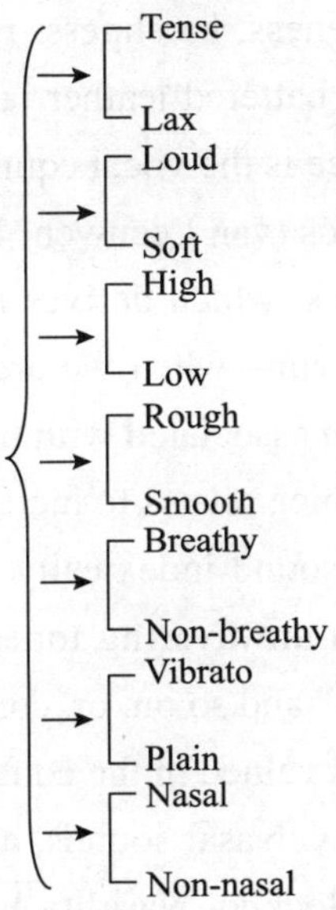

Figure 7.2 Parametric system for sound quality (van Leeuwen, 1999: 151)

The first parameter can be referred to as the parameter of tension, which summarizes the graded feature ranging from maximally tense to maximally lax. The tense sounds are produced when we tense the muscles of our throat. In the tensed state, the walls of the throat cavity squeeze the airstream to produce higher, sharper, brighter, and, above all, more tense voice. When the muscles relax, the voice becomes more relaxed and mellow. Resulting from tensing, the tense sound indexically means "tense" and leads to tension. In different contexts, the tense sounds possibly indicate "aggression", "repression", "excitement" and other meanings which can be said to include the idea of "tension". (van Leeuwen, 1999: 130–131)

The second is the parameter of loudness, along which sounds can range from maximally loud to maximally soft. It relates to the need to cover distance. The longer the distance, the louder the sound. The spatial or physical distance metaphorically mirrors social distance. Therefore, the loud voice carries furthest and claims most territory; the soft voice, on the other hand, excludes all but a few others, and can thus become associated with intimacy and confidentiality (van Leeuwen, 1999: 133).

The third is the parameter of pitch register. This parameter is firstly indexically associated with size based on the fact that small things make high noises while large things low noises. Secondly, it also has metaphorical signification. The louder voice also tends to rise in pitch, so that "high" can have many metaphoric extensions related to power and status. Power and status are then considered "high", and "rising" is associated with increased power or status. Thirdly, it relates to gender because men's voices are on average lower than those of women and children (van Leeuwen, 1999: 134, 140–141).

The fourth is the parameter of roughness, concerning a graded feature ranging from maximally rough to maximally smooth, and it can be metaphorically extended to other sense modalities and other experiences of friction and irregularity. In a rough voice we can hear other things besides the tone of the voice itself, such as friction sounds, hoarseness, harshness, rasp, which metaphorically remind us of the roughly plastered wall, the faded jeans, the battered leather jacket. In contrast, the smooth sound is clean, "well-oiled", and noiseless. The smooth voice is the vocal equivalence of unblemished young skin, polished surfaces, designer plastic, immaculate tuxedos (van Leeuwen, 1999: 132).

The fifth is the parameter of breathiness, which derives its meaning indexically from our knowledge of the kinds of situation in which it can occur—when we are out of breath, or unable to control "heavy breathing" due to excitement. It is most often associated with intimacy (van Leeuwen, 1999: 140).

The sixth is the parameter of vibrato, which relates to increased emotionality or loss of control (inability to keep the voice "steady"). The vibrating sound indexically relates to what makes us tremble: emotions (van Leeuwen, 1999: 134). Whereas, plain unwavering tones can come to signify anything that can be interpreted as "steady", "unwavering", "firm" and so on, or, conversely, as "dull", "bland", "expressionless" and so on, depending on how emotionality is valued in the context (van Leeuwen, 1999: 141).

The seventh is the parameter of nasality. Nasal sounds, as discussed in Chapter 3, are produced with the soft palate lowered and the mouth unblocked. Nasality here basically means the effect produced by holding the nose closed. This nasal blocking is accompanied by the tension of voice. And nasality will disappear when the overall muscle tension is reduced. Thus, nasality is closely related to tension, which explains why pinched and nasal tones pervade many of the sounds of pain, deprivation and sorrow, and why we perceive nasality in moaning, wailing and screaming (van Leeuwen, 1999: 135–136).

7.3.2 Multimodal interpretation of speech sounds

The features summarized in Figure 7.2 apply to all sounds, which can be alternatively referred to as voices. Speech sounds are more articulate and definable. Short (2013) summarizes three parameters that apply to all English sounds, van Leeuwen (1999) more elaborately discusses features innate to finer categories of vowels and of consonants, and Short (2013) and Jeffries and McIntrye (2010) also point out that some phonemes and consonant clusters have meaning.

7.3.2.1 General phonetic features and their interpretations

Short (2013: 116–121) identifies three features shared by all English sounds. The first feature is length. Both vowels and consonants require a certain amount of time to pronounce, and this duration reflects some aspects of the non-linguistic reality. Traditionally, vowels have been classified as either long or short, such as /iː/ and /i/. Similarly, consonants also vary in length. Stop consonants, the liquid sounds (/l/ and /r/) and the semi-vowels (/w/ and /j/) are shorter in duration compared to fricatives (e.g. /f/, /v/, /s/, /z/, /θ/, /ð/), nasals (/m/, /n/, and /ŋ/) and affricatives (/tʃ/ and /dʒ/).

The iconic interpretation of sounds of different lengths is illustrated by the following two examples in Short (2013: 116–117):

Example 7.1

Only the stuttering rifles' rapid rattle (Wilfred Owen, *Anthem for Doomed Youth*)

Example 7.2

Watching the last oozings hours by hours (Keats, *To Autumn*)

In Example 7.1, the high density of short vowels (/ɪ/, /ə/, /ʌ/) and consonants (/l/, /t/, /r/, /p/, /d/), together with the subject matter being described, enacts the firing guns. Whereas, in Example 7.2, the high incidence of (af)fricatives (/z/, /ð/, /tʃ/) and long vowels (/ɑː/, /uː/) and diphthongs (/aʊ/, /aɪ/) enact the slowness of the process.

The second is the pitch level at which sounds are produced, which has been discussed as the third parameter in Figure 7.2. According to Short (2013: 118), certain phonemes are produced at higher or lower pitches within our normal vocal range. This distinction can be attributed to the differences in the shape of the oral cavity involved. For instance, vowels produced towards the front and higher positions in the mouth tend to have a higher pitch than vowels produced towards the back or lower positions in the mouth.

Example 7.3

A child sitting under the piano, in the boom of the tingling strings. (D. H. Lawrence, *Piano*)

In Example 7.3, the vowel /ɪ/ and the syllable in which it occupies the nucleus position (that is, /'tɪŋglɪŋ/) are higher pitched than the vowel /uː/ and the syllable /buːm/. This contrasting feature functions to represent two alternative viewpoints on the same event. The adult narrator assumes a position away from the piano, and the notes of the piano sound relatively highly pitched and distinct; whereas, the child narrator, sitting under the piano, is closer to the strings while someone else plays, and the sounds appear louder but less distinct. Thus, the phrase *the boom of the tingling strings* fuses the adult and child viewpoints (Short, 2013: 118).

The third feature is indistinctness. Crisp and sharp consonants such as /t/ and /p/ are typically perceived as distinct sounds. However, certain categories of sounds tend to be less distinct, including longer voiced consonants, nasals, and vowels produced towards the back of the mouth.

Example 7.4

Clunk Click Every Trip

The slogan in Example 7.4 capitalizes on the two sound categories, effectively serving to convince people to fasten their seatbelts as they enter their cars. The indistinct nature of the /ʌ/ vowel and the nasal /ŋ/ in the word *clunk* is fitting for the muffled sound of a car door shutting, a result of rubber separating two metal surfaces. Conversely, *click*, composed of clear sounds, is suitable for the metal-on-metal sound of the seatbelt being secured. The sequence *clunk click* aligns with the usual order of actions: shutting the car door followed by fastening the seat belt. Furthermore, the assonance and loose alliteration between *trip* and *click* help forge a strong associative link between the catchy *clunk click* phrase and the idea of habitually wearing a seatbelt when driving a car (Short, 2013: 119).

7.3.2.2 General features of vowels and consonants and their interpretations

Upon narrowing our focus, we can identify even more refined attributes. As stated in Chapter 3, English vowels primarily differ based on tongue position and lip roundness. Van Leeuwen (1999: 146–147) has outlined three features linked to these two factors, offering some interpretations from a multimodal perspective.

The first one is frontality, which is the dimension of front vs back (for example, /ɪ/ vs /ɑː/). This feature can give rise to metaphorical extensions related to the idea of distance. For example, the /ɪə/ of "near" is frontal and the /ɑː/ of "far" is pronounced far back in the mouth.

The second is height, which is the dimension of high vs low. This feature can give rise to sound symbolism and metaphorical extension in the same way as frontality. For example, the /ʌ/ of "up" is high and the /aʊ/ of "down" is low.

The third is aperture, which concerns the difference between vowels pronounced with the mouth comparatively closed and with the mouth comparatively open. This difference can give rise to metaphorical extensions related to size. For example, the /ɑː/, /ʊ/, and /ɔː/ (*large*, *book*, *paw*) are open vowels, and the /iː/ and /e/ (*bead*, *bed*) are closed vowels.

Consonants are produced in ways different from vowels. Table 3.1 in Chapter 3 summarizes two ways to classify consonants. One is the manner of articulation, and the other is the place of articulation. Between the two, the manners of articulation are semiotically more significant.

Voicing is the feature resulting from the vibration of vocal folds when the air from the lungs passes between them. Voiced sounds are produced when vocal folds vibrate, and voiceless sounds are produced with no vibration. Van Leeuwen (1999: 147) observes that words for "silence" and "stillness" (and for all manner of silent and still people, places, and things) start with the unvoiced /s/ or /ʃ/ in many languages.

Plosives are consonants produced with the releasing of blocked airstream. As shown in Table 3.1, they include the voiced /b/, /d/ and /g/ and the unvoiced /p/, /t/ and /k/. Plosives are apt for iconically expressing things that are sudden, unexpected, explosive and so on, which can be illustrated by *boom*, *bomb*, *bang*, *burst*, etc.

Fricatives involves constricting the airstream, making a very narrow passage for it, and thereby creating the turbulence we hear. The typical fricatives include the voiced /v/, /ð/, /z/ and /ʒ/ and the unvoiced /f/, /θ/, /s/ and /ʃ/. They are particularly good at iconically expressing anything to do with friction, for example the fluent flow of air, the *swelling* and *swirling* of water, the *scraping* and *scratching* of surface, and human actions like *huffing* and *puffing*, *sniffing* and *snuffing* (van Leeuwen, 1999: 148).

Nasals (/m/, /n/, and /ŋ/) are produced with the air flowing through the nose but blocked in the oral cavity. This means that the sound is not actually uttered and "kept inside". It remains a *hum*, a *murmur*, a *mumble. Mmmm* can be the most non-committal of reactions, neither "yes" nor "no", the act of explicitly keeping your thoughts inside (van Leeuwen, 1999: 149).

7.3.2.3 Phonaesthemes

Besides the features shared among voices and specific sound categories, some sound sequences possess semiotic potential. Chapter 3 explains that phonemes are speech sounds lacking inherent meaning; they serve as language's building blocks. In contrast, Chapter 4 describes morphemes as the smallest linguistic units that convey meaning. In English, certain phoneme sequences seem to fall between phonemic and morphemic statuses; these are typically called phonaesthemes (Short, 2013: 119). For instance, the word-initial cluster "gl-" is not a morpheme, yet it is associated with light and sight-related concepts, as evidenced by *gleam*, *glimmer*, *glisten*, *glare*, *glint*, and *glance*. In *The Rime of the Ancient Mariner*, Coleridge employed the word *glittering* to depict the fearsome light in the eye of the ancient mariner.

Example 7.5

It is an ancient Mariner
And he stoppeth one of three.
"By thy long grey beard and **glittering** eye,
Now wherefore stopp'st thou me?"

7.3.2.4 Onomatopoeia

Even larger than phonaesthemes are onomatopoeic words, which, despite their limited number in all languages, are also used for rhetorical purposes. Onomatopoeia involves constructing a word in such a way that its sounds mimic the referential sounds; for instance, *miaow*, *bow-wow*, and *crack*. The excerpt of *The Inheritors* analyzed in Chapter 5 provides an illustration, where *clop* is used to mimic the sound produced by the arrow when hitting the dead tree by Lok.

7.4 Graphology and typography

Graphology was first proposed to refer to the study of the physical characteristics and patterns of handwriting, purporting to be able to identify the writer, indicating the psychological state at the time of writing, or evaluating personality characteristics. And it is primarily used in fields like psychology and forensic science. Typography is mainly concerned with the appearance of printed matter, involving the art and technique of arranging type in order to make the printed text clearer and more appealing to recognition and learning. In traditional stylistics which focuses on written texts, graphology is widely used to refer to the study of the substance of the language in visual forms, dealing with both shapes of written scripts and arrangements of written texts (Jeffries and McIntyre, 2010: 44; Simpson, 2014: 5–6). In multimodal stylistics concerning multimodal texts, however, typography is used to refer to the study of visual shapes of all types and their layout. For our purpose here, there is no need to distinguish one from the other, and they are used interchangeably. Publishers and writers often manipulate the written texts or their basic components, that is, written scripts, to make meanings. Our discussion in this section comprises two parts: textual layout or arrangement, and typography of written scripts.

7.4.1 Textual layout or arrangement

Icons, detailed in Section 7.2, are classified into three categories: images, diagrams, and metaphors. It's common for written texts to be arranged in a way that visually mirrors their content, forming an image or creating a structure that has a diagrammatic connection to the information they hold.

The poem by Nicholson, introduced in Section 2.4, arranges its words into the shape of a mushroom, echoing the subject matter of the dreadful effect of nuclear weapons. *Easter Wings* by George Herbert provides another illustration.

Lord, who createdst man in wealth and store,
Though foolishly he lost the same,
Decaying more and more,
Till he became
Most poore:
With thee
O let me rise
As larks, harmoniously,
And sing this day thy victories:
Then shall the fall further the flight in me.

My tender age in sorrow did beginne:
And still with sicknesses and shame
Thou didst so punish sinne,
That I became
Most thinne.
With thee
Let me combine
And feel this day thy victorie:

For, if I imp my wing on thine,
Affliction shall advance the flight in me.

Easter Wings is a religious sonnet, and it presents a plea to Christ for help in achieving heavenly joy. The layout of lines in each stanza creates the shape of wings, showcasing the spiritual flight the poem discusses.

The poem *40-Love* by Roger McGough provides an example of structural similarity between the shape of the poem and its topic.

40-LOVE	
middle	aged
couple	playing
ten	nis
when	the
game	ends
and	they
go	home
the	net
will	still
be	be
tween	them

The poem is broken up into two columns, which structurally represent the two halves of the tennis court. This textual layout forces the reading of the poem into a to-and-fro movement, which, in turn, metaphorically describes the play of the game. The to-and-fro movement, furthermore, implies the conflict between the couple.

This graphical meaning making was adopted in a double-page magazine ad for Philips color TV. The ad displays its copy over a TV picture of a professional tennis match, as follows:

you	haven't
seen	tennis
on	television
until	you've
seen	it
on	a
Philips 41"	screen

This arrangement makes the ad's reader move his or her eyes from side to side, as though at a tennis match.

7.4.2 Typography of written scripts

Written scripts can be either letter-based, pictograph-based, or a mixture of the two. Van Leeuwen (2006) proposes a system network of the distinctive features of letter forms. These features have largely been technologically enhanced. For instance, software such as Microsoft Word offers users a broad array of typefaces that embody the distinct features outlined by van Leeuwen (2006). Among these features are weight, expansion, and slope.

Weight refers to both the difference between **bold typefaces** and regular typefaces and that between different versions of a certain typeface as shown by **Arial Black** and Arial. Increased weight can help to achieve visual salience. The visual salience sometimes triggers metaphorical interpretation. For example, bold can be used to mean "daring", "assertive", or "solid" and "substantial", while its opposite can be used to mean "timid" or "insubstantial" (van Leeuwen 2006: 148).

Expansion refers to the difference between the condensation and expansion of a typeface, as shown here by Bahnschrift Condensed and Bahnschrift. Maximally condensed typefaces make maximal use of limited space, and thus metaphorically suggest precision and economy. By contrast, wide typefaces extend themselves around, using space as if it is in unlimited supply (van Leeuwen, 2006: 148).

Slope refers to the difference between cursive, sloping, and "script"-like typefaces and upright typefaces, as shown here by the difference between *Segoe Script* and Segoe UI. The meaning potential of this contrast is generally based on the meanings and values we associate with handwriting and printing. Depending on the context, it might indexically signify a contrast between the "organic" and the "mechanical", the "personal" and the "impersonal", the "formal" and the "informal", the "mass-produced" and the "handcrafted", the "new" and the "old" and so on (van Leeuwen, 2006: 148).

For analytical purposes, these features can be individually discussed. But in practice, all of them can be combined and their interpretations are conditioned by their contexts. *The Curious Incident of the Dog in the Night-Time* by Mark Haddon is a murder mystery novel. The cover of the novel published by Vintage Books[①] designs the title by making use of all the three features and even more. Firstly, some letters in the title are designed to have a 3D effect and thus gain weight, such as the letter *T* in the first word *The*. Secondly, the spaces between letters and between some of the words are clearly expanded. Thirdly, the letters in the title are cursive and sloping. Furthermore, the first three words of the title are in white, while the others are in black; most words in the title contain a mixture of upper-case and lower-case letters; and

① The cover can be accessed by clicking the following links: https://www.ibs.it/curious-incident-of-dog-in-libro-inglese-mark-haddon/e/9780099470434.
https://www.exlibris.ch/de/buecher-buch/english-books/mark-haddon/the-curious-incident-of-the-dog-in-the-night-time/id/9780099470434/.

the letters *d* and *n* in the words *dog* and *night* are designed as forks. With all these features, the title forms a big contrast with the wording "WINNER OF THE WHITBREAD BOOK OF THE YEAR", which adopts a default typeface.

Van Leeuwen (2006: 150) has proposed regularity as an independent feature in his system network. Perhaps it can also be used as a cover term to refer to an overall effect resulting from the interplay of several features as illustrated above. The irregular layout of the title is quite meaningful. The foremost is that the novel is most likely written for children as the title seems to be written by a schoolboy. Secondly, it does arouse readers' curiosity because the title is designed like a mysterious code that contains both uppercase and lowercase letters with various shapes. Thirdly, the novel is imaginative because there are wider spaces between lines, words, and letters.

7.5 Multimodal texts and multimodal stylistics

The book cover discussed in the last section provides an excellent illustration of multimodal texts, where different modes are employed to make meaning. In addition to the verbal text, the cover also makes use of visual images: a blue background, two clouds, a moon, six stars, a dog, and a garden fork. The blue background, the moon, and the stars indexically construct the circumstantial information of "night", which is thus represented visually as well as linguistically. The visually presented dog and garden fork work to extend the meaning of a "curious incident", illustrating the dog having been killed by somebody planting a garden fork in its chest. Both in the verbal title and in the visual images, the one who killed the dog is absent, contributing to the construction of "mystery".

An important topic in analyzing a multimodal text is text-image relation. The analysis offered above suggests at least two types of text-image relation found in the multimodal text featured in the book cover. Firstly, the verbally and visually "transmitted" messages exhibit some overlap, as seen in both visual and verbal representations of "dog" and "night". Secondly, the visual elements offer an elaboration of the verbal message: the verbalized "incident" presented in the title is visually clarified through an image of the violent event—the killing of a dog using a garden fork. This is conveyed both directly via an image of a garden fork and indirectly implied through the shape of the letters *d* and *n* in the words *dog* and *night*. These letters mimic the shape of forks, suggesting additional layers of symbolism.

Besides the overlap and elaboration found in text-image relationships, Liu and Song (2017) recognize various other relationships between distinct modes. One such relationship is metaphoric relationship, which is frequently employed due to its rhetorically powerful nature. Among the numerous theoretical perspectives on metaphor, the conceptual metaphor theory developed by Lakoff and his colleagues (Lakoff and Johnson, 1980; Lakoff, 1993; Kövecses, 2002) is often favored for its robust explanatory power.

Central to this theory is the idea that the core of a metaphor involves understanding or perceiving one thing in terms of another. In other words, a metaphor comprises two "things": a "literal" primary subject and a "figurative" secondary subject. In the framework of conceptual metaphor theory, these subjects are referred to as the source domain and the target domain. Functionally, a metaphor operates by mapping concepts from the source domain to their corresponding concepts in the target domain (Lakoff, 1993: 229).

A metaphor can be realized solely verbally or multimodally. A multimodal metaphor refers to a metaphor whose source and target domains are realized in different modes. Forceville (1996) found that multimodal metaphor is prevalent in advertisements. Liu and Song (2017) found that multimodal metaphor is equally popular in illustrated literary works. The following is an example from《世说新语》.

殷仲堪不失节俭本色

殷仲堪既为荆州，值水俭，食常五碗盘，外无余肴，饭粒脱落盘席间，辄拾以啖之。虽欲率物，亦缘其性真素。每语子弟云："勿以我受任方州，云我豁平昔时意，今吾处之不易。贫者，士之常，焉得登枝而捐其本？尔曹其存之。"

晋青瓷羊

In this multimodal text, there is no mention of the Celadon sheep of the Jin Dynasty in the verbal component. The most likely interpretation of the interplay of the verbal component and the image is that there is a metaphorical relationship between the two. The Celadon sheep of the Jin Dynasty realizes the source domain. As a priceless antique, it has the attributes of beauty, elegance, antiquity, rarity, and so forth. These attributes are mapped into the target domain which features Yin Zhongkan. That is, Yin Zhongkan's conduct, just like the Celadon sheep, is beautiful, elegant, and full of ancient virtue.

The brief analysis of the two multimodal texts demonstrates that different modes, when combined within the same text, construct meaning that is more comprehensive than when each mode is considered independently. Multimodal stylistics, a relatively new branch of stylistics, has been established to systematically analyze and interpret the increasingly popular multimodal texts. This approach aims to expand the range of modes and media to which stylistic analyses can be applied.

According to Nørgaard, Montoro and Busse (2010: 30–34), the extended multimodal stylistic toolkit, besides being useful for analyzing printed verbal texts, helps reveal how other semiotic modes, such as typography, color, layout, and visual images, also contribute to meaning construction (see, for example, Gibbons, 2010). In fact, multimodal stylistics views all communication and texts as inherently multimodal—even conventional literary narratives without special visual effects, since written language always involves wording, typography (or graphology), and spatial realization in terms of layout.

Nørgaard, Montoro and Busse (2010: 30–34) also point out that multimodal stylisticians expand the concept of, for instance, a novel to include not only the narrative's wording, visual images, typography, and layout, but also elements like the book cover, paper quality, and other aspects of the book's material realization. Additionally, by focusing on meaning-making as a multi-semiotic phenomenon, multimodal stylistics allows for more comprehensive stylistic analyses of drama and film (see Simpson and Montgomery, 1995; McIntyre, 2008).

Due to the limitation of space, the course book has to come to an end at this point. But this ending must be taken as a launch pad for your thrilling journey into the world of stylistics. An example of this, as modelled in this chapter, is multimodal stylistics, which aims to create systematic descriptive "grammars" for all semiotic modes, comparable to those already developed for language (i.e., the lexical and grammatical aspects of language). Hence, there is much more to explore and achieve.

Exercises:

1. What are the differences between modes and media?

2. It is said that different modes share the same ways of making meaning. Please illustrate this point by using some verbal and visual examples.

3. This chapter has discussed some multimodal interpretations of English sounds. Does the same principle apply to Chinese sounds?

4. In Chapter 6, a comparison is asked to be made between the verbal and visual versions of a classic novel at the discourse and genre levels. Please choose some interesting visual shots and compare them with their verbal narrations to see whether one mode can always be re-semioticized by another.

5. Chinese calligraphy is a form of artistic expression (e.g., Figure 3.1). Try to devise a system to account for a particular style of Chinese calligraphy with reference to the concepts introduced in Section 7.4.

Appendix 2.1

An excerpt from *The Old Man and the Sea*

He knelt down and found the tuna under the stern with the gaff and drew it toward him keeping it clear of the coiled lines. Holding the line with his left shoulder again, and bracing on his left hand and arm, he took the tuna off the gaff hook and put the gaff back in place. He put one knee on the fish and cut strips of dark red meat longitudinally from the back of the head to the tail. They were wedge-shaped strips and he cut them from next to the back bone down to the edge of the belly. When he had cut six strips he spread them out on the wood of the bow, wiped his knife on his trousers, and lifted the carcass of the bonito by the tail and dropped it overboard.

"I don't think I can eat an entire one," he said and drew his knife across one of the strips. He could feel the steady hard pull of the line and his left hand was cramped. It drew up tight on the heavy cord and he looked at it in disgust.

"What kind of a hand is that," he said. "Cramp then if you want. Make yourself into a claw. It will do you no good."

Come on, he thought and looked down into the dark water at the slant of the line. Eat it now and it will strengthen the hand. It is not the hand's fault and you have been many hours with the fish. But you can stay with him for ever. Eat the bonito now.

He picked up a piece and put it in his mouth and chewed it slowly. It was not unpleasant.

Chew it well, he thought, and get all the juices. It would not be bad to eat with a little lime or with lemon or with salt.

"How do you feel, hand?" he asked the cramped hand that was almost as still as rigor mortis. "I'll eat some more for you."

He ate the other part of the piece that he had cut in two. He chewed it carefully and then spat out the skin.

"How does it go, hand? Or is it too early to know?"

He took another full piece and chewed it.

"It is a strong full-blooded fish," he thought. "I was lucky to get him instead of dolphin. Dolphin is too sweet. This is hardly sweet at all and all the strength is still in it."

There is no sense in being anything but practical though, he thought. I wish I had some salt. And I do not know whether the sun will rot or dry what is left, so I had better eat it all although I am not hungry. The fish is calm and steady. I will eat it all and then I will be ready.

"Be patient, hand," he said. "I do this for you."

I wish I could feed the fish, he thought. He is my brother. But I must kill him and keep strong to do it. Slowly and conscientiously he ate all of the wedge-shaped strips of fish.

He straightened up, wiping his hand on his trousers.

(Hemingway, 1952: 63–66)

Appendix 5.1

Extracts from *The Inheritors*

The bushes twitched again. Lok steadied by the tree and gazed. A head and a chest faced him, half-hidden. There were white bone things behind the leaves and hair. The man had white bone things above his eyes and under the mouth so that his face was longer than a face should be. The man turned sideways in the bushes and looked at Lok along his shoulder. A stick rose upright and there was a lump of bone in the middle. Lok peered at the stick and the lump of bone and the small eyes in the bone things over the face. Suddenly Lok understood that the man was holding the stick out to him but neither he nor Lok could reach across the river. He would have laughed if it were not for the echo of the screaming in his head. The stick began to grow shorter at both ends. Then it shot out to full length again.

The dead tree by Lok's ear acquired a voice.

"Clop!"

His ears twitched and he turned to the tree. By his face there had grown a twig: a twig that smelt of other, and of goose, and of the bitter berries that Lok's stomach told him he must not eat. This twig had a white bone at the end. There were hooks in the bone and sticky brown stuff hung in the crooks. His nose examined this stuff and did not like it. He smelled along the shaft of the twig. The leaves on the twig were red feathers and reminded him of goose. He was lost in a generalized astonishment and excitement. He shouted at the green drifts across the glittering water and heard Liku crying out in answer but could not catch the words. They were cut off suddenly as though someone had clapped a hand over her mouth. He rushed to the edge of the water and then rushed back. On either side of the open bank the bushes grew thickly in the flood; they waded out until at their farthest some of the leaves were opening under water; and these bushes leaned over.

The echo of Liku's voice in his head sent him trembling at this perilous way of bushes towards the island. He dashed at them where normally they would have been rooted on dry land and his feet splashed. He threw himself forward and grabbed at the branches with hands and feet. He shouted:

"I am coming!"

(Golding, 1961: 106–107)

Appendix 6.1

Lost and Found

Once there was a boy who found a penguin in his door. The boy didn't know where it had come from, but it began to follow him everywhere. The penguin looked sad and the boy thought it must be lost. So the boy decided to help the penguin find its way home. He checked in the Lost and Found Office. But no one was missing a penguin. He asked some birds if they knew where the penguin came from. But they ignored him. Some birds are like that. The boy asked his duck. But the duck floated away. He didn't know either. That night, the boy couldn't sleep for disappointment. He wanted to help the penguin but he wasn't sure how. The next morning he discovered that penguins come from the South Pole. But how could he get there?

He ran down to the harbor and asked a big ship to take them to the South Pole. But his voice was much too small to be heard over the ship's horn.

Together, the boy decided, he and the penguin would row to the South Pole. So the boy took his rowboat out and tested it for size and strength. He told stories to the penguin to help pass the time. Then packed everything they would need and pushed the rowboat out to sea. They rowed south for many days and many nights. There was lots of time for stories, and the penguin listened to every one, so the boy would always tell another. They floated through good weather and bad when the waves were as big as mountains. Until, finally, they came to the South Pole. The boy was delighted, but the penguin said nothing. Suddenly it looked sad again as the boy helped it out of the boat. Then the boy said good-bye and floated away. When he looked back, the penguin was still there. But it looked sadder than ever.

It felt strange for the boy to be on his own. There was no point telling stories now because there was no one to listen except the wind and the waves. Instead, he just thought. And the more he thought, the more he realized he had made a big mistake. The penguin hadn't been lost. It had just been lonely. Quickly he turned the boat around and rowed back to the South Pole as fast as he could. At last he reached the Pole again. But where was the penguin? The boy searched and searched, but he was nowhere to be found. Sadly, the boy set off for home.

But then the boy saw something in the water ahead of him. Closer and closer he got, until he could see the penguin! And so the boy and his friend went home together, talking of wonderful things all the way.

Appendix 6.2

From Little Things Big Things Grow

Gather round people I'll tell you a story
An eight year long story of power and pride
British Lord Vestey and Vincent Lingiari
Were opposite men on opposite sides

Vestey was fat with money and muscle
Beef was his business, broad was his door
Vincent was lean and spoke very little
He had no bank balance, hard dirt was his floor

From little things big things grow
From little things big things grow

Gurindji were working for nothing but rations
Where once they had gathered the wealth of the land
Daily the pressure got tighter and tighter
Gurindji decided they must make a stand

They picked up their swags and started off walking
At Wattie Creek they sat themselves down
Now it don't sound like much but it sure got tongues talking
Back at the homestead and then in the town

From little things big things grow
From little things big things grow

Vestey man said I'll double your wages
Eighteen quid a week you'll have in your hand
Vincent said uhuh we're not talking about wages
We're sitting right here till we get our land
Vestey man roared and Vestey man thundered
You don't stand the chance of a cinder in snow
Vince said if we fall others are rising

From little things big things grow
From little things big things grow

Then Vincent Lingiari boarded an aeroplane
Landed in Sydney, big city of lights
And daily he went round softly speaking his story
To all kinds of men from all walks of life

And Vincent sat down with big politicians
This affair they told him is a matter of state
Let us sort it out, your people are hungry
Vincent said no thanks, we know how to wait

From little things big things grow
From little things big things grow

Then Vincent Lingiari returned in an aeroplane
Back to his country once more to sit down
And he told his people let the stars keep on turning
We have friends in the south, in the cities and towns

Eight years went by, eight long years of waiting
Till one day a tall stranger appeared in the land
And he came with lawyers and he came with great ceremony
And through Vincent's fingers poured a handful of sand

From little things big things grow
From little things big things grow

That was the story of Vincent Lingiari
But this is the story of something much more
How power and privilege can not move a people
Who know where they stand and stand in the law

From little things big things grow
From little things big things grow
From little things big things grow
From little things big things grow

Primary sources for stylistic analyses

Banks, Iain. 1993. *The Crow Road*. London: Abacus.
Coelho, Paulo. 2015. *The Alchemist*. London: Thorsons.
Conrad, Joseph. 1963. *The Secret Agent*. London: Penguin Books.
Eco, Umberto. 1984. *The Name of the Rose*. New York: Warner Books.
Faulkner, William. 1930. *As I Lay Dying*. New York: Jonathan Cape and Harrison Smith.
Golding, William. 1961. *The Inheritors*. London: Faber and Faber Ltd.
Hemingway, Ernest. 1952. *The Old Man and the Sea*. New York: Charles Scribner's Sons.
Lodge, David. 1978. *Changing Places: A tale of two places*. Harmondsworth: Penguin Books Ltd.
O'Brien, Sean. (ed.) 1998. *The Firebox*. London: Picador.
Thubron, Colin. 1998. *Distance*. London: Penguin Books.

References

布龙菲尔德 [Bloomfield]，1980，《语言论》，袁家骅、赵世开、甘世福译，北京：商务印书馆。

冯友兰 [Feng, Youlan]，2015，《中国哲学简史》，赵复三译，北京：外语教学与研究出版社。

韩礼德 [Halliday, Michael A. K.]，2010，《功能语法导论（第二版）》，彭宣维、赵秀凤、张征等译，北京：外语教学与研究出版社。

胡壮麟 [Hu, Zhuanglin]，朱永生，张德禄，李战子，2017，《系统功能语言学概论》，北京：北京大学出版社。

刘勰 [Liu, Xie]，2012，《文心雕龙》，王志彬译注，北京：中华书局。

申丹 [Shen, Dan]，2019，《叙述学与小说文体学研究（第四版）》，北京：北京大学出版社。

沈家煊 [Shen, Jiaxuan]，2011，《语法六讲》，北京：商务印书馆。

张德禄 [Zhang, Delu]，张国 [Zhang, Guo]，张淑杰 [Zhang, Shujie]，胡永近 [Hu, Yongjin]，2016，《英语文体学教程（第二版）》，北京：高等教育出版社。

Baldry, Anthony, and Paul J. Thibault. 2006. *Multimodal Transcription and Text Analysis: A multimedia toolkit and coursebook*. London: Equinox.

Bateman, John A. 2008. *Multimodality and Genre: A foundation for the systematic analysis of multimodal documents*. Hampshire: Palgrave MacMillan.

Bernstein, Basil. 1971. *Class, Codes and Control, Volume I: Theoretical studies towards a sociology of language*. London: Routledge & Kegan Paul.

Black, Elizabeth. 2006. *Pragmatic Stylistics*. Edinburgh: Edinburgh University Press Ltd.

Booth, Wayne C. 1961. *The Rhetoric of Fiction*. Chicago: Chicago University Press.

Brooks, Cleanth, and Robert P. Warren. 2004. *Understanding Poetry*. Beijing: Foreign Language Teaching and Research Press.

Brown, Gillian, and George Yule. 1983. *Discourse Analysis*. Cambridge: Cambridge University Press.

Burke, Michael. 2010. Why Care about Pedagogical Stylistics? *Language and Literature* 19(1): 7–11. doi: 10.1177/0963947009356805.

Bussmann, Hadumod. 2000. *Routledge Dictionary of Language and Linguistics*, translated and edited by Gregory P. Trauth and Kerstin Kazzazi. Beijing: Foreign Language Teaching and Research Press.

Carroll, Lewis. 1902. *Through the Looking-Glass*. New York and London: Harper & Brothers.

Chomsky, Noam. 1965. *Aspects of the Theory of Syntax*. Cambridge, MA: MIT Press.

Chomsky, Noam. 1966. *Topics in the Theory of Generative Grammar*. The Hague: Mouton.

Cruse, Alan. 2014. *Meaning in Language: An introduction to semantics and pragmatics*. Beijing: Foreign Language Teaching and Research Press.

Crystal, David. 1995. *The Cambridge Encyclopedia of the English Language*. Cambridge: Cambridge University Press.

Douthwaite, John. 2020. Conveying Alterity and Racism. In *Communicating English in Specialized Domains: A Festschrift for Maurizio Gotti*, edited by Stefania Maci, Michele Sala, and Cinzia Spinzi. Newcastle upon Tyne: Cambridge Scholars Publishing. 347–368.

Forceville, Charles. 1996. *Pictorial Metaphor in Advertising*. London and New York: Routledge.

Gavins, Joanna. 2007. *Text World Theory: An introduction*. Edinburgh: Edinburgh University Press.

Gee, James P. 2005. *An Introduction to Discourse Analysis: Theory and method*. London: Routledge.

Genette, Gérard. 1980. *Narrative Discourse*, translated by Jane E. Lewin. Oxford: Blackwell.

Genette, Gérard. 1988. *Narrative Discourse Revisited*, translated by Jane E. Lewin. Ithaca: Cornell University Press.

Gibbons, Alison. 2010. "I contain multitudes": Narrative multimodality and the book that bleeds. In *New Perspective on Narrative and Multimodality*, edited by Ruth Page. London: Routledge. 99–114.

Halliday, Michael A. K., and Ruqaiya Hasan. 1976. *Cohesion in English*. London: Longman.

Halliday, Michael A. K., Angus McIntosh, and Peter Strevens. 1964. *The Linguistic Sciences and Language Teaching*. Bloomington: Indiana University Press.

Halliday, Michael A. K. 1971. Linguistic Function and Literary Style: An inquiry into the language of William Golding's *The Inheritors*. In *Literary Style: A symposium*, edited by Seymour Chatman. Oxford: Oxford University Press. 330–368.

Halliday, Michael A. K. 2008. *An Introduction to Functional Grammar* (3rd edn.), revised by Christian M. I. M. Matthiessen. Beijing: Foreign Language Teaching and Research Press.

Halliday, Michael A. K. 2013. Meaning as Choice. In *Systemic Functional Linguistics: Exploring choice*, edited by Lise Fontaine, Tom Bartlett, and Gerard O'Grady. Cambridge: Cambridge University Press. 15–36.

Hasan, Ruqaiya. 1989. *Linguistics, Language, and Verbal Art* (2nd edn.). Oxford: Oxford University Press.

Hayes, Bruce. 2008. *Introductory Phonology*. Oxford: Wiley-Blackwell.

Innis, Robert E. (ed.). 1985. *Semiotics: An introductory anthology*. Bloomington: Indiana University Press.

Jakobson, Roman. 1960. Closing Statement: Linguistics and poetics. In *Style in Language*, edited by Thomas A. Sebeok. Cambridge: The MIT Press. 350–377.

Jeffries, Lesley, and Dan McIntyre. 2010. *Stylistics*. Cambridge: Cambridge University Press.

Jeffries, Lesley. 2014. *Opposition in Discourse: The construction of oppositional meaning*. London: Bloomsbury.

Jones, Daniel. 1999. *English Pronouncing Dictionary*, edited by Peter Roach and James Hartman. Shanghai: Shanghai Foreign Language Education Press.

Kress, Gunther, and Theo van Leeuwen. 2001. *Multimodal Discourse: The modes and media of contemporary communication*. London: Arnold.

Kress, Gunther, and Theo van Leeuwen. 2006. *Reading Images: The grammar of visual design* (2nd edn). London and New York: Routledge.

Kövecses, Zoltán. 2002. *Metaphor: A practical introduction*. Oxford: Oxford University Press.

Labov, William, and Joshua Waletzky. 1967. Narrative Analysis: Oral versions of personal experience. In *Essays on the Verbal and Visual Arts*, edited by June Helm. Seattle: University of Washington Press. 12–44.

Labov, William. 1972. *Language in the Inner City: Studies in the black English vernacular*. Philadelphia: University of Pennsylvania Press.

Ladefoged, Peter. 1993. *A Course in Phonetics* (3rd edn.). Fort Worth, T.X.: Harcourt Brace.

Lakoff, George, and Mark Johnson. 1980. *Metaphors We Live By*. Chicago: Chicago University Press.

Lakoff, George. 1993. The Contemporary Theory of Metaphor. In *Metaphor and Thought* (2nd edn.), edited by Andrew Ortony. Cambridge: Cambridge University Press. 202–251.

Leech, Geoffrey N., and Michael N. Short. 1981. *Style in Fiction*. Harlow: Longman.

Leech, Geoffrey N. 1974. *Semantics*. Middlesex: Penguin Books.

Leech, Geoffrey N. 2013. *Language in Literature: Style and foregrounding*. London: Routledge.

Lemke, Jay L. 1995. *Textual Politics: Discourse and social dynamics*. London: Taylor & Francis Ltd.

Lewis, Michael. 1993. *The Lexical Approach: The state of ELT and a way forward*. Hove: Language Teaching Publications.

Liu, Shisheng, and Chengfang Song. 2017. Ways of Illustrating and Ways of Explicating: Multimodal symbolic articulation in illustrated Shì Shuō Xīn Yǔ. In *Applying Systemic Functional Linguistics: The state of art in China today*, edited by Jonathan J. Webster and Xuanwei Peng. London: Bloomsbury. 267–281.

Martin, James R., and David Rose. 2007. *Working with Discourse: Meaning beyond the clause* (2nd edn.). London: Continuum.

Martin, James R., and David Rose. 2008. *Genre Relations: Mapping culture*. London: Equinox.

Martin, James R., and Peter R. R. White. 2005. *The Language of Evaluation: Appraisal in English*. Basingstoke: Palgrave Macmillan.

Martin, James R. 1992. *English Text: System and structure*. Philadelphia/Amsterdam: John Benjamins Publishing Company.

Maton, Karl. 2014. *Knowledge and Knowers: Towards a realist sociology of education*. London: Routledge.

McArthur, Tom. (ed.). 1998. *Concise Oxford Companion to the English Language*. Oxford: Oxford University Press.

McIntyre, Dan. 2008. Integrating Multimodal Analysis and the Stylistics of Drama: A multimodal perspective on Ian McKellen's Richard Ⅲ. *Language and Literature* 17(4): 309–334. doi: 10.1177/0963947008095961.

McIntyre, Dan. 2011. The Place of Stylistics in the English Curriculum. In *Teaching stylistics*, edited by Lesley Jeffries and Dan McIntyre. New York: Palgrave Macmillan. 9–29.

Nørgaard, Nina, Rocio Montoro, and Beatrix Busse. 2010. *Key Terms in Stylistics*. London and New York: Continuum.

O'Halloran, Kay L. (ed.). 2004. *Multimodal Discourse Analysis: Systemic functional perspectives*. London and New York: Continuum.

O'Toole, Michael. 1994. *The Language of Displayed Art*. London: Leicester University Press.

Peirce, Charles S. 1931–1935, 1958. *The Collected Papers of Charles Sanders Peirce*, Vols. Ⅰ–Ⅵ, edited by Charles Hartshorne and Paul Weiss, Vols. Ⅶ–Ⅷ, edited by Arthur W. Burks. Cambridge, M.A.: Harvard University Press.

Peirce, Charles S. 1985. Logic as Semiotic: The theory of signs. In *Semiotics: An introductory anthology*, edited by Robert E. Innis. London: Hutchinson. 4–23.

Pharies, David A. 1985. *Charles S. Peirce and the Linguistic Sign*. Amsterdam/Philadelphia: John Benjamins Publishing Company.

Quirk, Randolph, Sidney Greenbaum, Geoffrey Leech, and Jan Svartvik. 1985. *A Comprehensive Grammar of the English Language*, indexed by David Crystal. London: Longman.

Rogers, Henry. 2013. *The Sounds of Language: An introduction to phonetics*. London and New York: Routledge.

Semino, Elena. 2014. Text Worlds in Poetry. In *Language and Style*, edited by Dan McIntyre and Beatrix Busse. Beijing: Peking University Press. 116–132.

Short, Mick, and Michael Breen. 1988. Innovations in the Teaching of Literature (1): Putting stylistics in its place. *Critical quarterly* 30(2): 3–10.

Short, Mick. 2011. A Teaching Career in Three Chapters and Three Examples: Why I teach stylistics, how I teach it, and why I enjoy it. In *Teaching stylistics*, edited by Lesley Jeffries and Dan McIntyre. New York: Palgrave Macmillan. 30–50.

Short, Mick. 2013. *Exploring the Language of Poems, Plays and Prose*. London: Routledge.

Simpson, Paul, and Martin Montgomery. 1995. Language, Literature and Film: The stylistics of Bernard MacLaverty's Cal. In *Twentieth-century Fiction: From text to context*, edited by Peter Verdonk and Jean J. Weber. London: Routledge.

Simpson, Paul. 2004. *Stylistics: A resource book for students*. London: Routledge.

Simpson, Paul. 2014. *Stylistics: A resource book for students* (2nd edn.). London: Routledge.

Sinclair, John. 2004. *Trust the Text: Language, corpus and discourse*, edited by Ronald Carter. London: Routledge.

Thornborrow, Joanna, and Shân Wareing. 2000. *Patterns in Language: Stylistics for students of language and literature*. Beijing: Foreign Language Teaching and Research Press.

Tomlin, Russell S. 1994. Functional Grammars, Pedagogical Grammars. In *Perspectives on Pedagogical Grammar*, edited by Terence Odlin. Cambridge: Cambridge University Press. 140–178.

Turner, Jonathan H. 2007. *Human Emotions: A sociological theory*. London: Routledge.

Van Leeuwen, Theo. 1999. *Speech, Music, Sound.* London: Macmillan.

Van Leeuwen, Theo. 2005. *Introducing Social Semiotics*. London: Routledge.

Van Leeuwen, Theo. 2006. Towards a Semiotics of Typography. *Information Design Journal* 14(2): 139–155. doi: 10.1075/idj.14.2.06lee.

Van Leeuwen, Theo. 2022. *Multimodality and Identity*. London: Routledge.

Wales, Katie. 2001. *A Dictionary of Stylistics* (2nd edn.). Harlow, England: Pearson Education Limited.

Werth, Paul. 1999. *Text Worlds: Representing conceptual space in discourse*. London: Longman.

Wilkins, David A. 1972. *Linguistics in Language Teaching*. Cambridge, M.A.: The MIT Press.

Yule, George. 2020. *The Study of Language* (7th edn.). Cambridge: Cambridge University Press.

中国人民大学出版社读者信息反馈表

尊敬的读者：

感谢您购买和使用中国人民大学出版社的____________________一书，我们希望通过这张小小的反馈表来获得您更多的建议和意见，以改进我们的工作，加强我们双方的沟通和联系。我们期待着能为更多的读者提供更多的好书。

请您填妥下表后，寄回或传真回复我们，对您的支持我们不胜感激！

1. 您是从何种途径得知本书的：
   □书店　□网上　□报纸杂志　□朋友推荐
2. 您为什么决定购买本书：
   □工作需要　□学习参考　□对本书主题感兴趣　□随便翻翻
3. 您对本书内容的评价是：
   □很好　□好　□一般　□差　□很差
4. 您在阅读本书的过程中有没有发现明显的专业及编校错误，如果有，它们是：

____

____

____

5. 您对哪些专业的图书信息比较感兴趣：

____

____

____

6. 如果方便，请提供您的个人信息，以便于我们和您联系（您的个人资料我们将严格保密）：

您供职的单位：______________________________

您教授的课程（教师填写）：________________________

您的通信地址：______________________________

您的电子邮箱：______________________________

请联系我们：黄婷　程子殊　王新文　王琼

电话：010-62512737，62513265，62515580，62515573

传真：010-62514961

E-mail：huangt@crup.com.cn　chengzsh@crup.com.cn　wangxw@crup.com.cn
crup_wy@163.com

通信地址：北京市海淀区中关村大街甲59号文化大厦15层　邮编：100872

中国人民大学出版社